The CHARACTER
of CHRISTIAN SCRIPTURE

STUDIES *in* THEOLOGICAL INTERPRETATION

THE CHARACTER
OF CHRISTIAN SCRIPTURE

The Significance *of a* Two-Testament Bible

CHRISTOPHER R. SEITZ

Baker Academic

a division of Baker Publishing Group
Grand Rapids, Michigan

© 2011 by Christopher R. Seitz

Published by Baker Academic
a division of Baker Publishing Group
P.O. Box 6287, Grand Rapids, MI 49516-6287
www.bakeracademic.com

Printed in the United States of America

Library of Congress Cataloging-in-Publication Data
Seitz, Christopher R.
    The character of Christian Scripture : the significance of a two-Testament Bible / Christopher R. Seitz.
       p.   cm.
    Includes bibliographical references and indexes.
    ISBN 978-0-8010-3948-5 (pbk. : alk. paper)
    1. Bible. N.T.—Relation to the Old Testament. 2. Bible—Theology. I. Title.
BS2387.S38 2011
230′.041—dc23   2011025005

11 12 13 14 15 16 17   7 6 5 4 3 2 1

For the students in the Scripture and Theology seminar
at the University of St. Andrews, 1998–2007

CONTENTS

Series Preface

As a discipline, formal biblical studies is in a period of reassessment and upheaval. Concern with historical origins and the development of the biblical materials has in many places been replaced by an emphasis on the reader and the meanings supplied by present contexts and communities. The Studies in Theological Interpretation series seeks to appreciate the constructive theological contribution made by Scripture when it is read in its canonical richness. Of necessity, this includes historical evaluation while remaining open to renewed inquiry into what is meant by history and historical study in relation to Christian Scripture. This also means that the history of the reception of biblical texts—a discipline frequently neglected or rejected altogether—will receive fresh attention and respect. In sum, the series is dedicated to the pursuit of constructive theological interpretation of the church's inheritance of prophets and apostles in a manner that is open to reconnection with the long history of theological reading in the church. The primary emphasis is on the constructive theological contribution of the biblical texts themselves.

New commentary series have sprung up to address these and similar concerns. It is important to complement this development with brief, focused, and closely argued studies that evaluate the hermeneutical, historical, and theological dimensions of scriptural reading and interpretation for our times. In the light of shifting and often divergent methodologies, the series encourages studies in theological interpretation that model clear and consistent methods in the pursuit of theologically engaging readings.

An earlier day saw the publication of a series of short monographs and compact treatments in the area of biblical theology that went by the name Studies in Biblical Theology. The length and focus of the contributions were salutary features and worthy of emulation. Today, however, we find no consensus regarding the nature of biblical theology, and this is a good reason to explore anew what competent theological reflection on Christian Scripture might look like in our day. To this end, the present series, Studies in Theological Interpretation, is dedicated.

PREFACE

I began what is the second part of this project while on leave at the Center of Theological Inquiry, and it has taken some time to get my own thinking clarified on the topic being addressed: How does the Old Testament (OT) extend its horizon beyond and in conjunction with the New Testament (NT), as Christian Scripture and not as background literature for the NT or as a resourceful document to be cited for a discrete subject? I had previously worked on a long essay on the canonical approach associated with Brevard Childs of Yale and had at the time a view to expanding it, such as it presently appears in this book. The death of Professor Childs and the appearance of his final work, on the Pauline Letter collection, urged me to work through the older essay and amplify and sharpen certain points made there. The result is the present work, which I have titled *The Character of Christian Scripture*. I have endeavored to think through the implications of a two-testament Bible, which is neither a single long story, nor a two-part play, but a genre with its own unique character. Because there is at present much interest on the part of NT specialists in bringing precision to the hermeneutical implications of the use of the OT by NT authors, it seems timely to ask what effect such studies have on the OT as Christian Scripture *per se*.

I have also been made aware, through teaching on the early church's use of the OT, that the kind of theological use of the OT these early interpreters undertook had a genuine freshness that was more than replication of the NT authors' own practices, much less a studied account of how such practices might be explained and imitated. The centrality of Proverbs 8:22–31 is a case in point; it is probably the most important text for early trinitarian reflection and one of the most worked-over texts in early Christian exegesis, and yet its centrality cannot be explained, nor is warranted, by its use in the NT. It takes on a life of its own, in the light of Christ, and it is but one example of many.

I want to thank the Center of Theological Inquiry for the opportunity to think through the project and begin the writing phase. In the course of the past years I have moved from the University of St. Andrews to the University of Toronto, where I am Research Professor of Biblical Interpretation at Wycliffe College. I was also asked to give public lectures at Golden Gate Baptist Seminary, Acadia Divinity School, Concordia Seminary in St. Louis, and Concordia Seminary in Ft. Wayne. These lectures forced me to deal with the helpful reactions and responses of students and faculty and to think through the implications of several of the chapters. I also completed a small monograph on the canon that was scheduled ahead of this project. So the present book has taken more time to complete than I first planned.

At St. Andrews I was very fortunate to be able to conduct a seminar on theological exegesis and the history of biblical interpretation, which ran for several years. Of incomparable value was the presence of Dr. Mark Elliott, who helped organize the seminars in the latter years. He is a church historian, biblical theologian, and careful reader of texts, and the seminars were very helpful especially in the use of the Bible in the early church. I am thankful to have had Mark's companionship intellectually and personally and have learned much from him. I have also been researching a volume on Theodore of Mopsuestia and Antiochene exegesis and have benefitted enormously from a close reading of this "school," especially in Psalms and the Minor Prophets.

It is not possible to name all those who have read through the chapters and responded, but I would like to mention Russell Reno, Markus Bockmuehl, Kavin Rowe, Ephraim Radner, Gary Anderson, Mark Elliott, Nathan MacDonald, Joel Green, and Walter Moberly. I am particularly indebted to former students Mark Gignilliat and especially Don Collett for their feedback. Jim Kinney at Baker Academic has been a patient, wise, and kind editor, as is his custom. Robert Kashow assisted with the preparation of the typescript, and I mention his work with gratitude. Finally, a version of chapter 1 first appeared in Craig Bartholomew et al., eds., *Canon and Biblical Interpretation*, Scripture and Hermeneutics Series 7 (Grand Rapids: Zondervan, 2006), 58–110.

The Bible has a character. I was struck by this point when rereading the long essay by Hans Frei on the genre of the Gospels (which appeared in print as *The Identity of Jesus Christ*) and teaching through the book with students at St. Andrews. Frei struggled to describe the achievement of the Gospel form, chiefly through attention to general hermeneutics and literary theory. It was an experimental book, in my view.

In this book I have endeavored to wrestle with the form of the two-testament Bible and to understand its unique character. There is nothing else like it. One usually speaks in this way about its subject matter—God in Christ Jesus—and rightly so. But one can also speak this way about its formal character as a two-testament account. Indeed, it is that form that enables its subject to come to us, confront us, change our horizons forever, and show us a life hidden in him and awakened as we read and reread the Scriptures that tell of his divine character in Israel and in the church, the One Lord God: the Father, the Son, and the Holy Spirit.

A canonical approach to the Bible seeks to attend to and defer to those formal and associative aspects of Scripture that allow it most fully to speak. That the NT uses the Old presents a special kind of challenge, for potentially it means coming to terms with God's providential ordering of time in Christ. But to see this as a matter of individual witnesses in the NT making this or that "use" of the OT also potentially threatens the NT as itself a canonical totality and stops short of hearing the discrete witnesses of Old and New as they both speak of Christ in their own registers. My hope is that this book will be read in conjunction with the newer specialist studies as a way of thinking through the hermeneutical issues and of attaching the topic to the long history of interpretation in which the OT is so central.

Christopher Seitz
Toronto

ABBREVIATIONS

ABD	Anchor Bible Dictionary
ANF	*Ante-Nicene Fathers*
EvT	*Evangelische Theologie*
ExAud	*Ex Auditu*
HBT	*Horizons in Biblical Theology*
HTR	*Harvard Theological Review*
IJST	*International Journal of Systematic Theology*
JECS	*Journal of Early Christian Studies*
JSNT	*Journal for the Study of the New Testament*
JSOT	*Journal for the Study of the Old Testament*
JSOTSup	Journal for the Study of the Old Testament: Supplement Series
JTS	*Journal of Theological Studies*
JR	*Journal of Religion*
LXX	Septuagint
ModTh	*Modern Theology*
MT	Masoretic Text
NovT	*Novum Testamentum*
NT	New Testament
OT	Old Testament

ProEccl	*Pro Ecclesia*
RBén	*Revue Bénédictine*
RBL	*Review of Biblical Literature*
SBET	*Scottish Bulletin of Evangelical Theology*
SJT	*Scottish Journal of Theology*
ThTo	*Theology Today*
TynBul	*Tyndale Bulletin*
ZAW	*Zeitschrift fur die alttestamentliche Wissenschaft*

INTRODUCTION

Starting Points

"And on three Sabbath days he reasoned with them from the Scriptures, explaining and proving that the Christ had to suffer and rise from the dead." (Acts 17:2–3)

The Christian church at its origin received the Scriptures of Israel as the sole authoritative witness (the "Law and the Prophets"; "the oracles of God entrusted to the Jews"; "it is written"). These Scriptures taught the church what to believe about God: who God was; how to understand God's relationship to creation, Israel, and the nations; how to worship God; and what manner of life was enjoined in grace and in judgment. The church understood her character and purpose to be shown under a type in Israel and so read the Scriptures as speaking to her through the idiom of this "Old Testament," as it would come to be called. When a second witness would in time emerge and take form, the first witness would be retained in its own form, and a dual scriptural canon would constitute the Christian Scriptures. The "New Testament" scriptural authority was given its logic and its material form with reference to the Scriptures as first received by the church. "Old" then referred not merely to something temporally precedent, but rather provided the signal point of reference by which to understand a second witness to the work of God in Christ.

It is here that the logic of the rule of faith operative in the ante-Nicene period must be properly grasped. What the received Scriptures said of God was everywhere held to be true of God and his essential character—as against rival claims, including those of the Marcionites and Valentinians, among others. Because this only true God sent his only true Son, the received Scriptures revealed the trinitarian God of Christian faith. The Logos was active in the life of Israel, from creation to election to law-giving to cult to prayer and praise to prophetic word to final promise, because the only Son was of one being with the Father.[1] The exegetical implications of the rule of faith were enormous in respect to the received scriptural witness, not least because as the sole Scripture of the early church, it served to preach Christ and show that his earthly life was in accordance with the purposes of God from all time, manifested in the literal and extended senses of what would come to be called the "Old Testament." So the received Scriptures spoke of God as God was and is, and in so doing spoke of the Triune God, under figures and occupying that space prepared for such an extended understanding by virtue of the dynamic life of a personal God with his people.

The NT is of course not simply a later scriptural witness whose point is to show culminating events that temporally follow after those of the first Scripture, focusing on Jesus Christ as the Son of God by virtue of his earthly life, crucified under Pontius Pilate and raised on the third day. The NT cannot speak of these events—final as they are—without constant reference to the received Scriptures. It is not possible to speak of Christ without speaking of him "in accordance with the Scriptures." That is, the confession of Christ as Lord can only follow when Lordship is stipulated as that life of God in the Scriptures that reveal him, the "One with whom we have to do." To be given the name that is above every name (Phil. 2:9) requires that we know what that name is, what that name means, and what it declares about God's forbearing and desisting mercy and judgment. Jesus Christ crucified and risen is that name bearing witness to God's self and final purpose. And this Jesus Christ is at

---

1. St. Irenaeus of Lyons, *On the Apostolic Preaching*, trans. John Behr (Crestwood, NY: St. Vladimir's Seminary Press, 1997).

the same time the one through whom all things were made in the beginning with God.

Given that the first witness appears repeatedly and in manifold ways in the second, the present two-testament canon presents a challenge. The First Testament was not glossed with mature Christian confession ("My God why hast thou forsaken me, he cried from the tree"). Neither was its end opened up and a continuous final set of chapters appended, which put the first chapters in their place as scene setting or crucial preliminary plot staging. Something ended, a material form was stabilized and received as such, and a Second Testament slowly over time emerged and took up its place alongside the venerable and undoubted authority of the first. Naturally, given the way the rule of faith cooperated to bring extended senses forth from the received Scriptures for the purpose of preaching Christ in the early church, collaterally and at the same time the apostolic writings were also manifesting this same process of accordance and fulfillment. That is, the material witness of the NT everywhere shows use of the Scriptures in order to speak of Christ. They do this with a very wide range of exegetical and hermeneutical reflections. Christ says "before Abraham was, I am" (John 8:58 NRSV). Christ is promised both prophetically ("a shoot will come up," Isa. 11:1) and figurally (the suffering David of Psalms). Israel is a type of the church, in mercy and in judgment, the twelve tribes and twelve prophets serving as types of the twelve apostles. The Scriptures' declarations of election and ingathering are assumed and said to be on the point of fulfillment. The Law is good and holy, but also tutor to Christ, and—as it is so often in the OT—exposer of sin. The prayers of Israel are the prayers of Christ, who knew no sin, but whom God made to be sin (see the history of interpretation of Ps. 22—Israel and Calvary, David and Christ—the different interpretations enriching our understanding of them both). The list can be extended further to include salvation history, type and antitype, moral continuity and deepening. The point is that the rule of faith opened the Scriptures to a reading of extended senses, which were argued to be embedded in the literal sense of the OT in its given form and in its historical life, in order to clarify the most basic theological and trinitarian confession in the church's lived life. The NT offers a sample of this kind of reflection, but within the larger framework of describing the earthly life of Jesus Christ and its culminating significance for Israel, creation, and the whole world.

At present in NT scholarship, for a wide variety of reasons that need not detain us here, the use of the OT in the NT has moved to the forefront of scholarly exegetical and more theologically reflective attention. Great precision is being sought in how properly to understand this dimension: *Vetus Testamentum in Novo receptum*. Less clear is the point of the exercise, on theological grounds. One concern is that the character of Christian Scripture will become obscured, that is, as a two-testament canonical presentation in which a first witness is retained in its given form, and a second comes alongside it and makes use of it in its proclamation of the work of God in Christ. What does it mean to speak of the OT primarily through the lens of the NT's use of it and not as its own witness, through all its parts, to the work of God in Christ, in its own specific idiom, as an older and foundational witness? The term "character" is here being used because Christian Scripture exists in a specific material form, and appreciation of that is crucial to understanding the respective Testaments in their integrity as well as their dialectical relationship. The formal aspect of the Bible—viewed through the final form of two respective Testaments, and in the conjunction of Old and New—is a dimension that must be taken seriously, precisely because it opens onto a further dimension. The way Augustine phrased this is hard to improve on: Jesus Christ latent in the Old and patent in the New. Here he makes a claim about the Scriptures' theological character, based upon respect for its canonical form.

The point of this book is that what is latent of Jesus Christ in the Old has a character commensurate with this witness in its present form. Stated negatively, the theological dimension of the OT is not chiefly to be grasped by a historical reconstruction of what may or may not be going on when the second witness uses the first. It may well be very interesting, theologically and exegetically, to probe this dimension, and it is certainly true that once the engine is released to this purpose, better and worse forms of reconstruction can be found, and so, understandably, a sophisticated discussion ensues. Is Israel's exile of critical significance in reading the NT? Do we better grasp the NT's message when we are aware of intertextual echoes and such like, and how can we organize this dimension in a meaningful way? Does the discussion by Paul of law and justification make sense as exegetically pressured in some way by the final form of the Pentateuch or the Minor Prophets? These questions are all very important ones, but at issue is the question of proportion, and of the character of the witness of Christian Scripture and the implications—stated or unstated—for proper appreciation of this character. Is the OT chiefly what the New makes of it, and if not, just what does highlighting this dimension entail for appreciation of the OT as Christian Scripture? Stated differently, how does an inquiry into use of the OT in the NT relate to biblical theology?

It has been held by some that there is only a *Vetus Testamentum in Novo receptum*, and if this is not so, what do studies of use of the OT in the NT mean to say about where this discipline fits, theologically, in respect of the OT and its interpretation by the church?

Concern with the character of Christian Scripture, against this present NT interest in use of the OT in the NT, is concern that the OT retains its theological voice as a witness to the Triune God. This theological voice may well map out against what one sees here and there in the canonical presentation of the NT, but the character of the first witness unto itself is not identical with the second; thus the classic tradition used great caution in interpreting the theological sense of the OT through the lens of the NT. And of course it would know nothing of historical reconstructions of the intentions of NT authors or the rules of exegesis said to exist at the time of the NT's formation and crucial for an interpretation of it in a generic or in a particularized, uniquely "Christian" form.

To be sure, this "unto itself" of the OT (*Vetus Testamentum per se*) has for several centuries been held captive to history-of-religion accounts of the OT's message, and these can end up for theological purposes being either semi-tragic (Bultmann) or semi-heroic (von Rad). "Unto itself" in the context of concern for the character of Christian Scripture is a theological category in the first instance, based upon the historical witness of the OT as canon. The OT has a salvation-historical dimension, but that dimension is by no means the chief way to understand the Scriptures of Israel as a Christian witness. That it has emerged in this way has to do with intellectual trends of the eighteenth and nineteenth centuries, and however salutary they may have been in focusing fresh creative attention on the literal sense of the OT (and the NT), theological and hermeneutical sophistication did not follow in like measure. If one incautiously combines historical accounts of the use of the OT in the NT with a salvation-historical framework for assessing a two-testament Bible, the result is deep confusion about how the early church might have used a rule of faith, and how the character of Christian Scripture might otherwise be grasped, when it comes to reading the OT as a witness that both precedes, accords with, and follows the NT. Stated differently, the character of Christian Scripture, Old and New, involves thinking of their temporal relationship in terms other than salvation-historical only. It entails thinking about the OT figurally as well as predictively. It entails coming to terms with achievements of association often better set forth in older lectionary pairings. The dimension of use of the OT in the NT would enormously cramp and foreshorten the capacity of the OT both to speak of God in Christ and to be heard in relationship to the NT in ways the NT need not have contemplated or set forth in its own material form.

Behind many of the newer studies lies a sincere concern to show how fundamental the role of the OT is in the formation of the NT and in the way it makes its christological, theological, and ecclesiological points. What requires clarification is how such concern is actually related to the reading of the OT as such. Does the NT apprehension of the function of law or of justification by faith need to line up with the way the witness of the First Testament sets this out, or is the relationship of necessity more dialectical? Is "exile" a major index of the OT in its canonical form, or does this prioritizing come from a particular construal based upon salvation-historical reconstructions (in which Zion's glorification or the ingathering of the nations—arguably far more prominent in the canonical presentation of Isaiah—emerge as derivative themes because less concretely "historical")? Can a NT emphasis on such or such a theme become so totalizing that the canonical witness of the OT is actually subsumed?

But crucial in all this is just what it means to focus on the use of the OT in the NT and how this affects in turn our handling of the Scriptures of Israel as an abiding witness in their own right. It is fair comment to note that the fact of a two-testament canon often leads to a disparagement of the first on the grounds that the second allegedly presses us to this conclusion: "Jesus brought a different religion." It is less clear if the way to confront this challenge is by showing that the NT uses the OT appreciatively and that perhaps so should we.[2] At ground is a basic theological question: Does the OT speak of God in constructive trinitarian ways—to be sure in its own idiom—such that pitting the Testaments against each other can only result in an attack on them both (as Marcion ably demonstrated)? At issue are the theological deliverances of the OT as such, the status of the OT as Christian Scripture, and finally the character of Christian Scripture as a two-testament canonical authority. Showing that the OT is used appreciatively by the New, and that the NT sheds light on matters in the OT is likely an important exercise. But it does not address the fundamental question of how the OT is itself a witness to the Triune God, which is the real matter lurking in most questioning of the "religion of the Hebrews" as against the "religion of Jesus."[3]

It is clear that interpreters should not be criticized for not doing what others wish they had done. But the problem is more subtle, and that is the reason for our concern. The danger of a maximal account of the OT that focuses on its use in the NT is that, rather than providing good reasons for proper interpretation of the OT, it can only speak of the importance of the OT in reference to its resourcefulness, historical centrality, and literary and material application as the NT bears witness to these. To speak of the OT as Christian Scripture requires a genuine interpretation of its literal sense according to its canonical form and character. This need never line up with this or that material use of the OT in the NT in the precise form that the NT demonstrates, much less in a form we are able to reconstruct and then imitate. The witness of the OT is far more manifold, far more

2. Richard B. Hays, "Can the Gospels Teach Us How to Read the Old Testament?" *ProEccl* 11 (2002): 402–18. Brevard S. Childs offers a brief critique in his new work on Paul (*The Church's Guide for Reading Paul: The Canonical Shaping of the Pauline Corpus* [Grand Rapids: Eerdmans, 2008], 32–42). Hays is seeking to redress a misunderstanding of the OT as Scripture (he gives a particularly unflattering modern example).

3. See recent essays by Kavin Rowe, Kendall Soulen, Nathan MacDonald, and Christine Helmer, cited below. I have also written an entry on "The Trinity in the Old Testament" for Oxford University Press (forthcoming).

theologically ambitious, far more temporally challenging than can be comprehended by recourse to *Vetus Testamentum in Novo receptum*. At most the NT points toward a rich potential, yet untapped, and in that sense its material use of the OT is always a threshold and not the hearth. The danger in focusing on the use of the OT in the NT is that this reality falls from view. This is so precisely at the point where commendation of the OT finds its warrant in how the NT makes use of it, and not in how in its present canonical form it functions alongside the NT to speak of God in Christ.

In the chapters that follow we begin first with a summary introduction to the canonical approach of Brevard Childs. This helps set the stage for the main argument, found in chapters 2 through 7. I have chosen the word "character" because the proper assessment of the OT as Christian Scripture is not a two-dimensional matter. The very fact that the material can be appropriated as a foundation for modern Jewish religious life—read through the lens of secondary Jewish interpretation—or for religious purposes of a different kind, as background to Christian religion or as part of the welter of ancient Near Eastern religion, is testimony that the canon of the OT or Tanak requires some marriage between what it says and is, and what is held to be true about it in a more final sense, consistent with its literal sense. When the Christian claim is that the Scripture of Israel is a First Testament whose sense is properly disclosed by a second, it states this in terms of accordance—accordance and conformity with the claims the first makes in its own literal sense. "Old" is not a temporal term only, but a term pointing to a character understood only in relationship with a second witness. The second witness only gains its character as Scripture by its insistence that it is built upon the first and so its newness is not novelty or progress/development, but a drawing out of the intention of the first by a proper grasp of its own literal sense. This happens in such a way that the first is not subsumed or bid adieu, but the historicality of the second witness both in speaking of what God truly has done and who he truly is, is in relationship to final intentions consistent with his character and purpose revealed in the first. The economic (historical, narrative) reality of the First Testament is always also an ontological reality, because the subject of the Scriptures is God himself: "the LORD, compassionate and merciful, slow to anger" making himself and his will known through time, yet consistent with his eternal character and self. To speak of the "character of Christian Scripture" is therefore to keep the character of its subject matter at the center and so to seek to honor the economic priority of the first witness by allowing its literal sense to connect with what the first witness strains to say more fully about the character of the One God, confessed as revealed in the subject matter of the second: God in Christ Jesus. That Jews and historians of religion will hear that finality differently (within their own ranks as well as against classical Christian claims) gets precisely at the necessity for entertaining as legitimate an inquiry into what we are calling the character of the OT and the character of Christian Scripture itself.

1

THE CANONICAL
APPROACH AND
THEOLOGICAL
INTERPRETATION

In previous publications I have written extensively, and appreciatively, about the canonical approach associated with Brevard Childs, and have adopted a similar approach in commentaries on Isaiah and in other writings. Much of what I say here will not be new to those familiar with my publications.

Nevertheless, this book on the character of Christian Scripture provides an excellent opportunity to review reactions to the canonical approach and to organize a fresh assessment of its strengths and of the horizons of this movement in theological interpretation. I hope that a basic examination of the canonical approach will serve as a proper introduction to the chapters that follow, where the use of the OT in the NT, the relationship between Old and New Testaments in one Christian Scripture, and the rule of faith are discussed in more detail.

One can also note, in the present period, a raft of new publications promoting an avenue of approach broadly termed "the theological interpretation of Scripture. " It will be useful therefore to locate the canonical approach within this broader movement by giving attention to its parameters and ongoing concerns, as well as to the limits it believes are properly placed on theological reflection in light of the witness of Old and New Testaments in one canon of Christian Scripture.

Introduction

Uncontroversial is the observation that "canon" and "theological interpretation" are terms with wide usage at present. Their meaning is less clear. Where once historical-critical or form- or tradition-critical were the adjectives of special coinage and currency amongst interpreters, now we can observe the limitation, recalibration, or rejection of these objective approaches, or at least a sense that something more must be done. Here the term "hermeneutics" has pushed its way to the front.

But a lack of precision may mar what the terms "canon" or "theological interpretation" convey. Is a canonical approach "canon criticism" and if not, what is intended by the term and to what degree does a canonical approach build upon the prior phase of critical interpretation in which historical approaches dominated, in their own diverse and sometimes confusing ways?

This chapter will provide an overview of the canonical approach as it has been associated with the work of Brevard Childs. It is a working thesis of this chapter that already in 1970 the basic defining features of the approach had been laid out.[1] These have been modified only subtly, or in extending efforts as he proceeded to publish a series of magisterial works on the Old and New Testaments, the book of Exodus, OT and biblical theology, and the history of interpretation, including significant work in the book of Isaiah.[2] It is true that "canon criticism" was an approach associated in the 1980s

---

1. Brevard S. Childs, *Biblical Theology in Crisis* (Philadelphia: Westminster, 1970).

2. Brevard S. Childs, *Introduction to the Old Testament as Scripture* (Philadelphia: Fortress, 1979); Childs, *The New Testament as Canon: An Introduction* (Philadelphia: Fortress, 1984); Childs, *Old Testament Theology in a Canonical Context* (Philadelphia: Fortress, 1985); Childs, *Biblical Theology of the Old and New Testaments* (Minneapolis: Fortress, 1994); Childs, *Isaiah*, Old Testament Library (Louisville: Westminster, 2001); Childs, *The Struggle to Understand Isaiah as Christian Scripture* (Grand Rapids: Eerdmans, 2004).

with James Sanders,[3] but that project took the form of hermeneutical suggestions, based upon text-critical and tradition-historical instincts, and it never developed into a full-blown approach with subsequent publications or anything like the breadth of Childs's *oeuvre*. Indeed, it would be unfair to compare the two models or evaluate the merits of the two terms, as though they were valid competitors in a market yet to make up its mind.[4]

Already in Childs's 1970 work, *Biblical Theology in Crisis*, now over forty years old, one can see at least five features emerging that have proved durable and of sustained interest for a canonical approach:

1. a critiqued and recalibrated use of the historical-critical method;
2. a unique handling of the final form of the text that, as we shall see, eschews harmonization and the peril of "the disappearing redactor" on one side, but also judges the partial observations of historical criticism to be much less compelling than the whole represented by the final stabilization of the diverse sources and traditions in a coherent literary form;
3. passing yet pregnant observations on the status of the Hebrew and Greek text traditions;
4. sensitivity to the so-called premodern history of interpretation and even to what has been pejoratively called dogmatic reading, but with a critical evaluation of this history based upon insights from our own historical-critical season of reading and analyzing texts; and
5. biblical-theological handling of the two Testaments, in which the Old retains its voice as Christian Scripture and biblical theology is more than a sensitive appreciation of how the New

3. James A. Sanders, *Torah and Canon* (Philadelphia: Fortress, 1982); Sanders, *Canon and Community* (Philadelphia: Fortress, 1984); Sanders, *From Sacred Story to Sacred Text* (Philadelphia: Fortress, 1987).

4. See, however, the analysis of Childs and Sanders (for whom the term "canonical criticism" is deemed appropriate) by Robert W. Wall, "Reading the New Testament in Canonical Context," in *Hearing the New Testament*, ed. Joel B. Green (Grand Rapids: Eerdmans, 1995), 370–93. See also Frank A. Spina, "Canonical Criticism: Childs Versus Sanders," in *Interpreting God's Word for Today*, ed. Wayne McCown and James E. Massey (Anderson, IN: Warner, 1982), 165–94.

handles the Old—a dimension that Childs otherwise handles with aplomb in a series of fresh exegetical illustrations in the final section of *Biblical Theology in Crisis.*

The last of these concerns requires lengthier examination due to the present popularity of treatments of the use of the OT in the New, undertaken by NT scholars concerned to bring precision to the way Paul or the Gospels work with the Scriptures of Israel.[5] Subsequent chapters will stay with this topic in more detail.

What one sees in the 1970 publication is that a canonical approach is fully a child of its own age (I mean this in the best possible sense; see Neil MacDonald's work on Barth in which a similar point is made[6]). The canonical approach belongs to an age in which the questions of historicity and ostensive reference are foreground ones[7] and must be taken seriously for their own face value as well as evaluated theologically (much in the way that concerns with creation *ex nihilo* occupied the earliest generations of Christian biblical interpretation; or the Reformation period refocused the question of literal sense). That may be clearer now than at the time, when the critical analysis of the then regnant historical-critical approach threatened (so it was held, in our view wrongly) to highlight the discontinuity of the approach with what preceded. In our view, what was radical in the approach was not so much discontinuity, but what was being attempted: nothing less than the reconstruction, in a new form to be sure, of the length and breadth of aspects of critical reading that

5. Mention should also be made of the work of OT scholar Peter Enns (*Inspiration and Incarnation: Evangelicals and the Problem of the Old Testament* [Grand Rapids: Baker Academic, 2005]). Enns sees the exegesis of the OT in the NT as a species of Second Temple interpretation whose significance is registered by attending precisely to the peculiarities of reading strategies characteristic of the period. The ability of the OT to exert a specific kind of theological pressure due to the canonical authority of the Scriptures of Israel, over against rival modes of reading, forms no significant control in his evaluation. The NT's distinction between "traditions of elders" and the letter of the text ("it is written") is not a factor in his analysis. See also Enns, "Fuller Meaning, Single Goal," in *Three Views on the New Testament's Use of the Old Testament,* ed. Kenneth Berding (Grand Rapids: Zondervan, 2008).

6. Neil B. MacDonald, *Karl Barth and the Strange New World within the Bible: Barth, Wittgenstein, and the Metadilemmas of the Enlightenment* (Carlisle: Paternoster, 2000).

7. Hans Frei, *The Eclipse of Biblical Narrative* (New Haven: Yale University Press, 1972).

had devolved into various subspecialties, such that an organic and integrated presentation of the biblical witness might be had once again. History, literary analysis, text criticism, Old and New Testaments, the earlier history of interpretation—all these facets were brought back onto a single field of play by a figure whose competence was only slightly, if at all, outmatched by the ambition needed for such an undertaking. And history bore out the truth of that, for the next forty years would show Childs making good on detailed and painstaking analysis of each of these several disciplines in a series of major publications, culminating in a study of the implications of the canon for reading Paul.[8]

The "canonical approach" is a modern, historical approach, and it operates in this mode in a self-conscious sense. It does not seek to repristinate past approaches, even as it judges our capacity to learn from them at times obscured by thick historicist lenses or a failure to see the sophistication of appraisals of the literal sense in a period before that sense was identified with historical reference.[9] It does not deny the historical dimension as crucial to what makes biblical texts something other than modern literature, nor the text's inherent relationship to time and space and what has been called "ostensive reference,"[10] even as it has a view of history that is far more than this.[11] It does not ignore dimen-

8. Brevard S. Childs, *The Church's Guide for Reading Paul* (Grand Rapids: Eerdmans, 2008).

9. Christopher R. Seitz, *Figured Out: Typology and Providence in Christian Scripture* (Louisville: Westminster John Knox, 2001); Brevard S. Childs, "Sensus Literalis of Scripture: An Ancient and Modern Problem," in *Beiträge zur alttestamentlichen Theologie: Festschrift für Walther Zimmerli zum 70 Geburtstag*, ed. Herbert Donner, Robert Hanhart, and Rudolf Smend (Göttingen: Vandenhoeck & Ruprecht, 1977): 80–93.

10. Frei, *Eclipse*, 75–104.

11. On the difficulty of disentangling types of senses (literal, figural, allegorical) and then relating these to history, as this had meaning in a different period, see Frances Young, *Biblical Exegesis and the Formation of Christian Culture* (Cambridge: Cambridge University Press, 1997); or David Dawson, *Christian Figural Reading and the Fashioning of Identity* (Berkeley: University of California Press, 2002). See also Christopher R. Seitz, "What Lesson Will History Teach? The Book of the Twelve as History," in *"Behind" the Text: History and Biblical Interpretation*, Scripture and Hermeneutics Series 4, ed. Craig Bartholomew et al. (Grand Rapids: Zondervan, 2003), 443–69; "History, Figural History, and Providence in the Dual Witness of Prophet and Apostle," in *Go Figure! Figuration in Biblical Interpretation*, Princeton Theological Monograph Series 81, ed. Stanley D. Walters (Eugene, OR: Pickwick, 2008), 1–6.

sions of the text that can only be explained by recourse to "sources" or "authors," which account for divergences and tensions in the final form, but it judges the task far from complete when attention to these features fails to ask what effect has been achieved by bringing them together in one historical-theological portrayal in the final form of the text.[12]

One difficulty attending the task of presenting the "canonical approach" is the degree to which it is tied to one individual. Almost any defense or criticism can easily become personalized, as, sadly, has been the tendency in some quarters.[13] An account that only took its lead from criticisms would be incomplete or disproportionate. Yet because the project has ranged so widely, and has maintained a centrality for such a long period of time, it is inevitable that in its wake, specific and sometimes trenchant criticisms have been leveled. It would be artificial to proceed as if these were not a useful, if limited, way to organize a positive assessment. Fortunately, there is a small cottage industry in evaluating the contribution of Brevard Childs and the project of the "canonical approach" associated with him,[14] and several of these evaluations have sought helpfully to referee aspects of critical engagement with him. So that need not be my chief task. It is simply an inevitable aspect of the ambition of the project of Brevard Childs that it would succeed in stirring up such a wide-scale and engaging debate. Childs has never himself majored in spotting deficiencies as a project unto itself, even as he has been a tireless evaluator of the field of biblical and theological studies.

One sadness I experience when reading Childs, especially in his later works,[15] involves the awareness that Childs is one of the last persons

---

12. Christopher R. Seitz, "The Changing Face of Old Testament Studies," in *Word without End: The Old Testament as Abiding Theological Witness* (Grand Rapids: Eerdmans, 1998), 75–82; C. Kavin Rowe, "Biblical Pressure and Trinitarian Hermeneutics," *ProEccl* 11, no. 3 (2002): 295–312.

13. James Barr, *The Concept of Biblical Theology: An Old Testament Perspective* (London: SCM, 1999), 401–38.

14. Mark G. Brett, *Biblical Criticism in Crisis? The Impact of the Canonical Approach on Old Testament Studies* (Cambridge: Cambridge University Press, 1991); Paul R. Noble, *The Canonical Approach: A Critical Reconstruction of the Hermeneutics of Brevard S. Childs* (Leiden: Brill, 1995); Daniel R. Driver, *Brevard Childs, Biblical Theologian: For the Church's One Bible*, Forschungen Zum Alten Testament 2 (Tübigen: Mohr Siebeck, 2010).

15. Childs, "The Canon in Recent Biblical Studies: Reflections on an Era," *ProEccl* 14 (2005): 26–45.

actually able to critique the discipline, and, more importantly, *to catalog it and identify it as a discipline in the very first place*.[16] Postmodern attacks on objectivist approaches not only challenge historical-critical readings; they also obscure the actual historical character of the discipline of reading itself, both in its premodern and now in its modern form. Historical-critical approaches to reading once upon a time declared themselves a kind of unique mode of interpretation, superior to what preceded in the premodern period because capable of laying hold of a dimension of "historicality" unknown to previous periods. This threatened to cut away one aspect of history (reception history in its premodern form) in the name of another (the "real history" of Israel and Jesus to which the biblical texts erratically and imperfectly gave us recourse). Early practitioners could have little anticipated that the same fate would lie in store for them, as in time the need to account for the field as a coherent movement would fall to the side, now in the name of the reader in front of the text, with a tyrannical resistance to seeing him- or herself as historically limited and invariably in need of correction from a long history of reading—including the more recent phases of historical-critical analysis. But perhaps the real culprit here was the overreaching claims of the historical-critical method, which birthed endless subdisciplines and specialties, whose number and relationship became evermore difficult to taxonomize. Childs not only gave us a fresh approach. He is one of the last figures to comprehend the discipline he was critiquing and to control it at its maximal length and breadth, even as it was becoming unwieldy in the wake of its own limiting claims, on the verge of crumbling because it was simply too vast an empire. To be vast is not necessarily to be durable, coherent, compelling, or true.[17]

It has been argued since its inception that the canonical approach has this or that Achilles' heel or minor weakness; is limited or defi-

---

16. That Childs actually sought to present himself as a serious NT scholar was by no means undercut by his command of the field, which most conceded was impressive. The same control of secondary literature—especially, e.g., recent studies of the Pastorals—marks *Church's Guide*.

17. David C. Steinmetz, "The Superiority of Pre-Critical Exegesis," *ThTo* 37 (1980): 27–38; repr. in *ExAud* 1 (1985): 74–82; and in *A Guide to Contemporary Hermeneutics: Major Trends in Biblical Interpretation*, ed. Donald K. McKim (Grand Rapids: Eerdmans, 1986), 65–77.

cient in certain key areas; or is ill-conceived and disqualified as an approach. Rarely is it said that it seeks to do too much and is disqualified by virtue of its ambition. As noted above, it is this *desire for comprehensiveness* that I shall argue is the hallmark of the canonical approach and its legacy for our day, and so the fact that this is not singled out as a fault is worth keeping in mind as we consider the various weaknesses that are said to mar the approach. As we shall see, these "weaknesses" are often deemed to be such by those holding diametrically opposing views.

Among the several faults detected in the canonical approach, we can list:

1. insufficient attention to "the facts of history" as constitutive of any serious theological approach;
2. lack of attention to these same facts as crucial for nontheological reasons;
3. the importation of a dogmatic lens that overreaches and is prejudicial to an "unbiased" account of things;
4. overemphasis on the text as exercising a pressure or coercion on the reader, as an objective material witness;[18]
5. confusion about what is meant by special attention to the final form of the text, in light of its acknowledged literary prehistory (the "disappearing redactor" and other problems);
6. wrongful privileging of the text's final form over against earlier phases of its development, and so giving a kind of moral authority to later institutionalizing instincts instead of the "genius of the original inspiration";
7. the same criticism made on the grounds of a theory of original inspiration and inerrancy threatened by too many later hands at work (several Isaiahs, etc.);[19]

---

18. Walter Brueggemann is not keen on this. He characterizes Childs's appeal to "canonical restraints" as "apodictic"; such "restraints" are personal and not text-immanent. See "Against the Stream: Brevard Childs's Biblical Theology," *ThTo* 50 (1993): 279–84.

19. Christopher R. Seitz, "Isaiah and the Search for a New Paradigm," in *Word without End*, 113–29.

8. wrongful attention to the "discrete voice of the Old Testament" as a theological witness, independent of the New;[20]

9. failure to let the God of the OT be a God without reference to the New.[21]

The list could be lengthened indefinitely, but one thing that should be manifest is: many of the criticisms of the canonical approach come from opposite standpoints and point to disagreements that plague the discipline *in any event*. The canonical approach, given its range and ambition, illustrates the deep and abiding disagreements that afflict the field of biblical studies in its modern and postmodern guises. This does not mean that the criticisms simply cancel one another out, but it does mean that the canonical approach requires careful study and attention to nuance. It has been around long enough now to engender discussion on various sides of the theological spectrum, at a time when the methods of biblical study are in disagreement about key issues, including: the objectivity of the text, what is meant by history, authorial intentionality, inspiration, the pressure of historical-critical findings on interpretation, the relationship between the Testaments, and the character and desirability of biblical theology as such. The point of listing challenges to the canonical approach at this juncture, before turning to a brief assessment of several of them, is to underscore that adjusting the approach to meet the demands of one kind of challenge will of necessity reinforce whatever criticism was aimed from the opposing direction. One conclusion to be drawn from this is that the canonical approach cannot be inherently flawed, for if it were, critiques on either side would be left to devour one another or pass like ships in the night.

The canonical approach, then, occupies a meaningful location in our late-modern environment, where anxiety over truth and meaning is high. The fact that opponents aim their objections from

20. Francis Watson, *Text and Truth: Redefining Biblical Theology* (Edinburgh: T&T Clark, 1997), 209–19; Christopher R. Seitz, "Christological Interpretation of Texts and Trinitarian Claims to Truth," *SJT* 52 (1999): 209–26.

21. One could associate the names of Brueggemann, Rendtorff, and Goldingay with concerns of this kind, and their publications are generally well known.

opposing directions could well confirm that the canonical approach offers the most compelling, comprehensive account of biblical interpretation and theology presently on offer. That is the verdict of the present chapter.

Canonical Approach: Features and Challenges

Historical Reference

Some have argued that a canonical approach does not pay sufficient attention to history. Here is a classic place where criticisms are leveled for different reasons from different sides of the theological spectrum. What might it mean to pay better attention to history, one might ask?

It might mean trying to show that the Bible's literal sense fairly directly and unimpeachably reports matters of ostensive reference, and that for theological reasons it is invested in this kind of referentiality and a commitment to it above other things, *evenhandedly across its length and breadth*. This being the case, the interpreter is to show that the Bible straightforwardly lodges historical claims (Isaiah wrote the book of Isaiah; Jonah went into the alimentary canal of a great fish; hills of foreskins could be excavated and shown to line up with accounts about them; the sea parted and dry ground existed on the terms given by the words used to say this; the letters attributed to Paul were all written personally by him in the same basic way we think of individual authorship today) and that interpretation ought to move from text to reference at this level of concern, or a defense of it against competing claims, in a sustained way.

Of course, an opposite challenge would be to say that a canonical approach, insofar as it sees historical reference as taken up into a fresh account of what history in fact is, lodged at the level of the literary presentation of the final form, introduces a kind of history at odds with the concerns of modernity and its definition of history. Here both challenges meet as strange and probably unexpected bedfellows.

It has also been said that a canonical method subsumes history into intratextuality, or "the text's own world." Childs has himself worried about this aspect of reading more generally attributed to "the Yale

School."[22] The "strange new world of the Bible" to which Barth referred was not simply a story or community-creating narrative, however much it may have functioned this way in subsequent use. Indeed, it is the fact that the Bible *refers realistically to the world* that has kept the canonical approach insistent that a difference must be registered between midrash and the way traditional Christian approaches have thought about the Bible's truth-engendering literary development.[23]

What the canonical approach has done is to use the findings of historical-critical methods and then ask historical questions about what has in fact been discovered in light of the text's final presentation. An example from Childs's treatment of Exodus 33–34 will suffice. A problem exists in the presentation of the tent of meeting in Exodus 33 when one reads the larger accounts. The canonical approach accepts that a genuine problem is being encountered and that the best explanation for this is that different sources lie behind the final form of the text, with a certain roughness resulting.[24] There is no attempt to argue that Moses had two different tents, as a matter of ostensive reference; or that at the level of "story" some deeper significance is to be seen in the tension, independent of the fact that a tent did indeed get pitched and used at some point in time and space in the life of Moses and Israel, and that the text refers ostensively to this. Still, it is not the primary task of the interpreter to take the historical-critical observation for the purpose of reasonable literary explanation and then go about leaving the literary world and reconstructing the tent and the history of tent-sanctuaries in the ancient Near East as a piece of elaborated ostensive reference. This would be wrongly to proportionalize one dimension of the exegetical discipline and art. The canonical approach returns to the text and now asks why an aspect of historical reference that causes friction has been allowed to

22. See appendix A in Childs's *New Testament as Canon.*

23. B. S. Childs, "Critique of Recent Intertextual Canonical Interpretations," *ZAW* 115 (2003): 173–84. Compare the concerns of M. Sternberg, *The Poetics of Biblical Narrative: Ideological Literature and the Drama of Reading* (Bloomington: Indiana University Press, 1985).

24. "I fully agree with the literary-critical assessment of the passage as reflecting an old tradition of the tent of meeting which parallels the later Priestly account" (B. S. Childs, *The Book of Exodus: A Critical, Theological Commentary,* Old Testament Library [Louisville: Westminster, 1974], 591).

stand, in light of some other theological issue that is the true concern of the final form of the text. As it happens in this case, that concern has to do with the theological significance of Moses as intercessor.[25] History of the ostensive reference variety is not unimportant, but the biblical narrative uses this realm of reference to write history of its own kind. Moreover, the development of the text into its final form is also a historical fact, worthy of investigation.[26]

The preoccupation with historical reference (for reasons of apologetic defense of "facticity" and literal sense; in order to focus on original sources and their divergent accounts of the world of ostensive reference, as prolegomena to telling us what really happened; or as failing to deal with the text's final presentation as a fact worthy of historical attention of its own kind, that is, in the text's own historical emergence

25. Childs: "In its present position, without being specifically altered, the section witnesses to the obedient and worshipful behavior over an extended period of time, thereby providing Moses with a warrant to intercede in vv. 12ff" (ibid., 592).

26. Timothy Ward, *Word and Supplement: Speech Acts, Biblical Texts, and the Sufficiency of Scripture* (Oxford: Oxford University Press, 2002), 248–50. Compare also the subtle critique by Childs of Francis Watson's reading of the Exod. 34 account of Moses's veil, which he judges to be limited in part because he reads the OT without sufficiently serious attention to the diachronic features that now make evaluation of the veil more complicated (*Church's Guide*, 128–31). Second Corinthians 3 takes certain advantages of this uneven dimension of the literal sense in order to speak of life in the Spirit (enabling unveiled access as Moses had experienced). Failure to attend to this diachronic reality could lead to such a simplification as the following: Paul laid hold of the genuine intention of Exodus and its referentiality (Moses was seeking to hide the fact of a fading glory from the Israelites), rather than seeing the exegesis as creative theological reading governed by other factors about which Paul is concerned (the life of the Spirit). Compare the reading of Rowe, "Pressure," 202. A lengthy quote from Childs demonstrates the enduring role that proper assessment of the historical dimension plays in theological reading:

> Some of the anomalies of Exodus 34 derive from compositional growth from diverse oral traditions and literary sources. . . . Although I do not suggest for a moment that a historical critical reconstruction replace the final canonical context when reading the biblical text, this historical dimension cannot be disregarded as done by Watson. The hermeneutical significance of my argument is that not every gap in the biblical narrative belongs a priori to its canonical shaping involving a theological intentionality. Attention to the historical critical dimension serves as a check against exegetical overinterpretation of 2 Corinthians 3. The canonical function of the mask as a hiding of the fading glory remains a Christian understanding of the text. Whether this reading derives from Paul's exploitation of a tension within the biblical text, or stems from a prior Christian theological understanding, is not crucial and is often hard to determine. (130–31)

More on the problem of the normative character of use of the OT in the NT below.

as what it is in the form in which we find it) has had a double fallout from the perspective of a canonical approach. Such an approach does not minimize the historical dimension; neither does it seek to do away with approaches that take it seriously enough to spot problems and tensions in the literary presentation. What is at issue is proper proportion and care to return to the final form of the text as its own piece of historical reality and witness to God's ordering of the world.

Harmonization and "The Disappearing Redactor": The Final Form of the Text

It has been argued by John Barton that the canonical approach doubles back on itself when it seeks both to honor the historical dimension (the depth of sources and traditions behind the final form) and at the same time believes the sum (final form) is greater than the parts. If the final redactor is so clever at merging the disparate sources into a tidy portrayal, why was he ever there to begin with?[27]

This kind of criticism would appear to merge nicely with another concern of Barton's, namely, that the canonical approach has a tendency to harmonize or smooth over disagreement when it handles the biblical material. But in fact, the criticisms are distinct, if inconsistent.

Childs is quite prepared to indicate where the tension remains in the final form of the text, and indeed he has been critical of those who have sought to eliminate this element.[28] He does not in fact seek

---

27. John Barton, *Reading the Old Testament: Method in Biblical Study*, 2nd ed. (London: Darton, Longman & Todd, 1996), 56–58. According to Barton, Childs's analysis of Gen. 1–2 illustrates the close affiliation between the canonical approach and "redaction criticism proper" (49). Redaction critical analyses of Gen. 1–2, however, fall prey to the following dilemma: "If, say, Genesis 2 follows on so naturally from Genesis 1, then this is indeed evidence for the skill of the redactor *if we know that Genesis 1 and 2 were originally distinct*; but the only ground we have for thinking that they were is the observation that Genesis 2 does *not* follow on naturally from Genesis 1. Thus, if redaction criticism plays its hand too confidently, we end up with a piece of writing so coherent that no division into sources is warranted any longer; and the sources and the redactor vanish together in a puff of smoke, leaving a single, freely composed narrative with, no doubt, a single author" (57). Similar concerns with Childs's use of redaction criticism are registered in Timothy Ward's survey in *Word and Supplement*, 250–51.

28. See Childs's remarks on Calvin in his treatment of the tent traditions (more on this below). R. W. L. Moberly, *At the Mountain of God: Story and Theology in Exodus 32–34*, JSOTSup 22 (Sheffield: JSOT Press, 1983), may also be open to this same criticism.

to be so clever in showing the work of the redactor that he pulls the ground out from under the threshold acknowledgment that sources or different authors in fact exist. A brief look at any of the places where Childs calls attention to the genius of the final form's handling of its prior literary history will demonstrate this. There are two different tent traditions. They cannot be harmonized; there is a problem with the first tent appearing when it has not yet been constructed and standing outside the camp rather than inside it. Or, there are two "creation accounts." The fact that a redactional notice seeks to link the two in the way Childs and others have noted does not eliminate the source-critical finding, nor does it amount to disappearance of the redactor. And in the classic area of harmony, the fourfold Gospel record, no one could find in Childs any interest in the typical harmonization. Indeed, he is a rather traditional deployer of the Markan priority theory and does very little in the way of minimizing the challenge of hearing the one gospel through four discrete witnesses.[29]

What Barton's analysis fails to grasp is the organic character of what Childs has referred to, probably imperfectly, as "canonical consciousness." For Barton, canon is an external force that seeks to set limits or arrange things after the fact of their literary stabilization. For Barton, signs of efforts to relate things in the process of a text's coming to be can only be a literary move, and one cannot attribute to it any serious theological intentionality, much less use the term "canonical consciousness" to distinguish it from a bare literary move.[30]

Yet what Childs is seeking to highlight need not be obscured because of the difficulty of terms used to describe it. When Jeremias shows how the messages of Amos and Hosea are related, he does not

---

Childs's particular indebtedness to diachronic (historical-critical) findings as crucial for apprehending "the canonical shape" has also been reaffirmed recently by Jon D. Levenson in his very insightful essay, "Is Brueggemann Really a Pluralist?" *HTR* 93 (2000): 265–94. See also the evaluation by Childs of Watson in n26 above.

29. B. S. Childs, "The One Gospel in Four Witnesses," in *The Rule of Faith: Scripture, Canon, and Creed in a Critical Age*, ed. E. Radner and G. Sumner (Harrisburg, PA: Morehouse, 1998).

30. See my remarks about the "achievement of association," building on the work of J. Jeremias, R. Van Leeuwen, Rendtorff, and others in *The Goodly Fellowship of the Prophets: The Achievement of Association in Canon Formation* (Grand Rapids: Baker Academic, 2009). The achievement is intrinsic and emerges from a theological concern for hearing the Word of God pressing forward through time.

describe a move at the level of what Barton would call "canon" (an external decision somehow to relate the two; something, by the way, Barton would probably question as having occurred even at the level of canon in the case of Amos and Hosea—the books are separated by Joel[31]). Jeremias sees the pupils of the two prophets seeking to edit the developing traditions in such a way that the two prophets are then viewed as a comprehensive and related witness.[32] There is no disappearing redactor. One can see easily enough, in Jeremias's analysis, where the older tradition ends and the newer editing begins; there is no confusion as to what the distinctive features of each respective prophet are; these features remain. But at the earliest level of their text's circulation, long before the books receive final literary stabilization (including deuteronomistic superscriptions), an effort is being manifested, and Jeremias shows this clearly, to bring the message of the two into coordination. This is not for reasons of literary or aesthetic tidiness. It has to do with theological convictions regarding God's one word spoken through two discrete prophets.

A further example of the subtlety of Childs at this point can be seen in Bauckham's work on the Gospel collection, to return to the example above.[33] Bauckham argues that John knows Mark and seeks

31. Incidentally, this is precisely why Joel has become the source of such attention and renewed interest in recent work on the Minor Prophets. In the development of the Book of the Twelve, Joel's placement points to "canonical shaping" at the level of theology and hermeneutics. This "canonical shaping" is literary and theological, and does not sit easy to distinctions Barton would like to draw. Among a great many others, see Raymond C. Van Leeuwen, "Scribal Wisdom and Theodicy in the Book of the Twelve," in *In Search of Wisdom: Essays in Memory of John G. Gammie*, ed. Leo G. Perdue, Bernard B. Scott, and William J. Wiseman (Louisville: Westminster John Knox, 1993), 31–49; and on Joel as "literary anchor" see James D. Nogalski, "Joel as 'Literary Anchor' for the Book of the Twelve," in *Reading and Hearing the Book of the Twelve*, ed. James D. Nogalski and Marvin A. Sweeney (Atlanta: SBL, 2000), 91–109. I have produced my own account of canonical shaping in the Twelve in *Prophecy and Hermeneutics: Towards a New Introduction to the Prophets*, Studies in Theological Interpretation (Grand Rapids: Baker Academic, 2007).

32. Jörg Jeremias, "The Interrelationship between Amos and Hosea," in *Forming Prophetic Literature: Essays on Isaiah and the Twelve in Honor of John D. W. Watts*, JSOTSup 235, ed. James W. Watts and Paul R. House (Sheffield: Sheffield Academic Press, 1996), 171–86.

33. Richard Bauckham, "John for Readers of Mark," in *The Gospels for All Christians: Rethinking the Gospel Audiences*, ed. Richard Bauckham (Grand Rapids: Eerdmans, 1998), 147–71.

to relate his Gospel to that witness. The Gospel takes form with attention to both itself and something outside it. The contours of Mark are not thereby blurred; it remains a discrete witness. So too, John can be read by itself. If Trobisch or others seek to show that a redactor has closed John with a notice that relates his message to the others in a final fourfold collection, this does not happen in such a way that the redactor need disappear, nor John and the other three merge into one.[34]

Below we will return to the question of "the final form" and the degree to which it can be said to comprehend earlier traditions but also make its own special statement. What is at issue is the way in which what the canonical approach calls "the final form" requires the diachronic dimension as the lens to grasp its force and specificity as a theological witness. Related to this is the way in which "the final form" relates to, but also transcends the delineated prehistory. At stake here are complex understandings of "intentionality" and also "coercion" or the pressure exerted by the text. For now, the crucial thing to note is that "the final form of the text" requires attention to the text's diachronic prehistory (with the proviso that this history will always be difficult to sketch, in specific literary terms, and so is always a kind of heurism). Ironically, perhaps, here it is that Childs commits himself clearly to a form of referentiality, in the realm of history. This is not "ostensive reference" in the form of "brute facts" requiring specification (how many Hittites were there? when did Amos write the parts of his book we believe he wrote? etc.), even as this dimension is the arena in which God's Word, promised and then enacted, begins its journey on the road called "revelation."[35] The referentiality exhibited by diachronic method entails various levels of authorial intentionality

34. David Trobisch, *The First Edition of the New Testament* (Oxford: Oxford University Press, 2000); Trobisch, *Paul's Letter Collection: Tracing the Origins* (Minneapolis: Fortress, 1994). See also Stanley E. Porter, ed., *The Pauline Canon* (Leiden: Brill, 2004). I also have a brief discussion of this issue in "Booked Up: Ending John and Ending Jesus," in *Figured Out*, 91–102.

35. Long ago Barr did rightly note, "A God who acted in history would be a mysterious and supra-personal fate if the action was not linked with this verbal conversation. . . . In his speech with man, however, God really meets man on his own level and directly" (*Old and New in Interpretation: A Study of the Two Testaments* [New York: Harper & Row, 1966], 78).

as realities in history. The "final form of the text" is the way in which God has so commandeered that history as to speak a word through the vehicle of the text's final form, as a canonical approach seeks to comprehend and appreciate that. In so doing, the prior history is not done away with, nor do editors appear and disappear, even as the prior history is taken up into a stable expression of how God is ordering the world and continuing to speak through the "final form" of the biblical text.

"Final form" will also require reattachment to "literal sense" as classically understood. Such a concern, however, moves us into the area of typology and how one text and another are related according to the "literal sense." This is not the place to address such a significant issue, but it does remain the task of a canonical approach to show why its concerns have a much higher likelihood of linkage with the prior history of interpretation than historical-critical approaches.[36]

Prejudicial "Dogmatic" Predisposition

This charge[37] is best suited to an environment in which "objectivist" reading was running on all cylinders. As we shall see, Childs has his own concern for the "objectivity" of the text and is criticized in other quarters for daring to use the noun "coercion" to describe it.

So this is one of those areas where the deep disagreements—with fault-lines people struggle to comprehend by recourse to terms like "modern" and "postmodern"—pollute the environment in which any reasonable discussion can be entertained in the first instance. How can Childs be characterized as "subjectively predisposed" toward this or that dogmatic stance, when he himself believes that a canonical approach must assume something like stable and objective meaning, or the quest for that as morally obligatory and theologically demanded?[38]

36. See my final comments in "What Lesson Will History Teach?" in *"Behind" the Text*, 466.

37. From James Barr: "As we shall see, in many respects this book [*Biblical Theology of the Old and New Testaments*] is neither a work of biblical theology nor one of canonical theology; it is more like a personal dogmatic statement provided with biblical proofs" (*Concept*, 401).

38. He quotes Sternberg to this effect in *Biblical Theology of the Old and New Testaments*, 20.

The answer of course is that Barr believes there is some kind of objective dimension to the Bible that Childs has encroached upon with his appeal to "canonical reading," and the culprit must be a force outside the text, in this case, "Calvinism" or "Barthianism" or "Lutheranism"—all parts of a Reformation heritage Childs honors and which Barr feels Childs has not understood. This makes for an odd indebtedness and misrepresentation rolled into one.

Recently Barr has revealed that the extent of his concern at this level also reaches rather urgently to the newer reader-response methods, on the one hand (these do not believe in "objective" intentions and such like in texts; meaning resides in those doing the reading), and newer historical approaches, on the other (which eliminate any early depth in texts, as a historical fact, arguing instead that Israel's account of history and itself is a very late importation).[39] So Barr appears consistent in his urgency, though the target is a moving one so far as he is concerned.

It would of course be very useful indeed to know just what kind of objectivity Barr believes Childs is encroaching upon, since by its own statement, a canonical approach seeks to pay attention to the literal sense of the text, and there is nothing if not a certain objectivist concern lurking about that sentiment. For Barr, the "literal sense" cannot do the objective work Childs seeks to make it do; when Childs does attempt this in each of his publications, he demonstrates thereby that a canonical approach is simply the expression of personal theological proclivities (or prejudices), and one can use whatever label one wants to attach to them ("Barthianism," "Calvinism," "Reformed dogma," whatever).[40] That is, Barr has never sought to show that these various

---

39. James Barr, "The History of Israel," in *History and Ideology in the Old Testament* (Oxford: Oxford University Press, 2000), 58–101. This appears to be his effort to improve on criticisms leveled by Iain Provan against the excesses of Lemche, Whitelam, and P. Davies, among others.

40. Barr:

No one who knows modern theology will doubt that this entire work is a manifestation of one particular offshoot of Barthian theology. There are indeed three heroes of the work: Luther, Calvin and Barth, in ascending order. The opinion that most of modern scholarship is in a poor state, which might have some truth in it, is coupled with the converse notion that the Reformation had the right answers all along, a pious delusion which even Childs does not seek to demonstrate. Anyway, the three heroes are pretty well always in the right, or would be, except when they differ amongst themselves. Then there

labels point to distinctive features, which surely they must, and then that these can be seen point by point in the canonical approach. "Calvinism" is less a coherent system than a kind of insistence by Barr that when Childs puts his finger on an objectivity in the text, and it is not the one Barr himself likes, then it cannot qualify as objective and so must come from somewhere else—call it whatever you will.

It would be far more reasonable if Barr simply left himself to the observation that he believes the Bible does a certain kind of objective work (in the history-of-religion) and not in the area of "literal sense," without then adding to his problems by associating Childs with a species of reading he has not bothered to describe or justify as applicable in Childs's particular case. Instead what we find is a kind of disparate rant, void of objective analysis—described by one reviewer as "academic terrorism."[41] If Barr wants to say, "Karl Barth has these five tendencies in his small print exegesis (see Job) and Childs does the same thing," fine. But the question would be no further answered: is this a genuinely disqualifying matter, and if so, why? And not satisfied with this kind of tirade against Childs, he will then turn the tables and say that Barth or Calvin or Luther believed X or Y and Childs does not believe that anyway. Part of the

---

is a definite pecking order. When Luther differs from Calvin, it is Calvin who is right. Sometimes Calvin is superior to Barth. Barth's exegesis can be poor in comparison with Calvin's . . . which would make it look as if Calvin was the top hero. (*Concept*, 401)

On it goes. This simply cannot be credited as objective analysis, but instead is a kind of prejudicial mockery of Childs. As we shall see, Childs has a canonical approach with certain objective contours, and it is on this basis that he renders judgments about the success of the exegesis of Calvin, Luther, or Barth. But from Barr's analysis, it sounds as though this is just a personality disorder in Childs, whom he claims gives no reasons for his judgments. This is one of the more embarrassing chapters in modern biblical studies for its devolution into highly personal, *ad hominem* evaluation.

41. A very judicious and fair review can be found in Walter Brueggemann, "James Barr on Old Testament Theology: A Review of *The Concept of Biblical Theology: An Old Testament Perspective*," HBT 22 (2000): 58–74. This is a sensitive and careful analysis, which also registers deep concern at the tone adopted by Barr and the substance of his account of Childs. He characterizes Barr's treatment as "polemic," "an embarrassing *ad hominem* attack," "dismissive and contemptuous of all those who differ," "emotionalism that contributes nothing to the discussion" (68), and then at the close tries even to provide a kind of psychological explanation for the invective "sense of wound from authoritarianism" (72). When the emotion runs as high as it does in Barr's account, it is difficult to refrain from psychological speculation in an effort to reestablish a kind of equilibrium.

confusion is that Barth or Calvin or Luther do not appear in careful treatments, dealing with them as exegetes or theologians, but only in impressionistic and idiosyncratic ways.

Of course, Childs is fully on record about the kinds of limitations he spots in "dogmatic" reading (to choose one of Barr's labels). To return to the example of Exodus 33, Childs shows how Calvin "was certainly on the right track"[42] but was nevertheless hedged in by a specific view of the text's relationship to reality, which forced him to adopt a midrashic instinct whereby Moses moved the tent outside the camp "because the people had just proved themselves unfit for God to dwell in their midst." Childs is sympathetic with Calvin's move and sees it as an improvement over other options, but it remains the case that Childs is operating with an entirely different range of options when it comes to his assessment of the issue. The Exodus commentary is replete with examples where Childs assesses the "objective" solutions (for that is what they claim to be, at a different period of interpretation) offered in premodern reading, and points out the difference between his approach and these earlier efforts—sometimes with sympathy when he spots a "family resemblance" (his term from the 2004 *Struggle to Understand Isaiah as Christian Scripture*) he can appreciate, and at other times, critically.[43] Childs refuses to countenance moves that ask that evidence be provided from something other than the plain sense of what the witness delivers, and his concern in our age with history-of-religion is precisely at the same level: that is, it has reproportionalized what the text literally delivers and so produces evidence and explanations that, however interesting or compelling in their own realms of concern, are to the side, literally. What Barr likely sees as "objective" in history-of-religion, Childs sees as objective but external to the proper task of exegesis.

It is also possible to turn to sections of the early Childs for essential objections to "dogmatic reading" as obscuring what the canonical approach is about. Indeed, Childs likens the obscuring potential of modern systematic theological reflection to the use by biblical scholars of theories of history (Barr's history-of-religion would be

---

42. Childs, *Exodus*, 592.

43. Childs: "All these theories remain unsupported from any evidence within the biblical text itself" (ibid., 590).

an example).[44] Both lead us away from the plain sense. Dogmatic readings in the premodern period do this less by recourse to philosophical categories and more by direct utilization of doctrinal claims. Childs views Luther's use of Psalm 8 to describe the two natures of Christ as obliterating the voice of the OT, on the false understanding that what makes the Old a Christian voice must be the hearing of it through the categories of the New.[45] More on this below, as it gets at the crucial issue of what is at stake in hearing the OT's own voice, but as Christian Scripture.

Calvin's approach is different because he does try to hear the voice of the OT through recourse to a kind of doctrinal symmetry across the Testaments, due to their shared commitment to the theological world of covenant. Calvin therefore tries to hear the psalm as speaking of an ideal state in the garden of Eden, from which humanity has fallen.

This honors the OT's capacity to speak theologically, yet it imports a dubious context from the OT's own doctrinal storehouse that is extraneous to the psalm in order to secure this reading. Childs sees Calvin as useful in his emphasis on the OT as a witness to the One God and his Christ, in its own idiom. But when an external dogmatic overlay secures that voice, it substitutes for the displacing voice of the New the displacing voice of doctrine and destroys the context (canonical shape) of the witness being interpreted. Childs seeks instead to hear the doctrinal voice emerging from the plain sense of Psalm 8, as a distinctive voice, in reciprocity with the New. At the end this will amount

44. Childs: "For systematic theologians the overarching categories are frequently philosophical. The same is often the case for biblical scholars even when cloaked under the guise of a theory of history" (*Biblical Theology in Crisis*, 158).

45. Luther does not always have this kind of instinct, and that should be duly noted (see Christine Helmer, "Luther's Trinitarian Hermeneutic and the Old Testament," *ModTh* 18 [2002]: 49–73). As is well known, Luther changes direction rather famously, in part because of his prolific style (this is particularly true in his many works on the Psalms), and because he is trying to conflate a literal sense reading with a christological referent (rejecting the fourfold sense and seeking to make a letter/spirit distinction work without recourse to allegory), and this requires numerous passes at the issue. In his latter years he looks at Hebrew as a purveyor of trinitarian semantics, as the Holy Spirit speaks through David and reveals the inner trinitarian life of the Father and the Son. At issue would be how far this kind of evaluation might extend, beyond select psalms. More on this below. The classic treatment remains James Samuel Preus, *From Shadow to Promise: Old Testament Interpretation from Augustine to the Young Luther* (Cambridge, MA: Harvard University Press, 1969).

to a return to Psalm 8 and its strong doctrine of creation as the OT's Christian and doctrinal corrective of (a potential mishearing by) the Letter to the Hebrews, drawing upon the OT's own plain sense. Here we get a clear sense of how Childs regards the OT in relationship with the New, which allows both voices to register, and not with the second voice being the way to assure that the first has a Christian word to say at all.[46] In this, he allows the concerns of early doctrinal readings to demonstrate possible options, but in the end he rejects them both as an insufficient interpretation measured against a canonical approach.

In sum, it is more accurate to say that Childs has sympathy for the doctrinal instincts of the earlier history of reading, to a degree that sets him apart from the vast array of modern biblical scholars. But it is equally true that Childs feels inadequacies can be spotted and he does this by careful attention to the concerns of the canonical approach as a distinctive mode of theological interpretation.[47] Childs is no more a "Calvinist" or "Lutheran" or "Catholic" reader than he is a canonical reader, and frequently there is sympathetic overlap. At times, we can see in the earlier history of interpretation aspects of a broader two-testament concern for interpretation that resonate and show us interpretative moves that modern reading has shut off, to its detriment. But the analysis is not a one-way street, and a canonical approach is not inoculated from registering criticisms of the past, anymore than it is inoculated from self-criticism or the kinds of limitations that are bound to afflict any, even comprehensive, approach. We shall see this below, where we look briefly at the adjustments the canonical approach has made within its own brief life span in order to take account of limitations spotted by others or by Childs himself.[48]

---

46. See Richard Hays's essay "Can the Gospels Teach Us How to Read the Old Testament?" or, by sharp contrast, Brueggemann's emphasis on the Old as a non-Christian yet theological voice in his *Theology of the Old Testament: Testimony, Dispute, Advocacy* (Minneapolis: Fortress, 1997). I deal in greater detail with the example of Ps. 8 in Hebrews in chapter 3 below.

47. See Childs, *The Struggle to Understand Isaiah as a Christian Scripture* (Grand Rapids: Eerdmans, 2004).

48. It is an incidental reference and so will not be pursued in detail, but an example of mishearing Childs when he adjusts an earlier view can be seen in Andrew Lincoln's essay "Hebrews and Biblical Theology," in *Out of Egypt: Biblical Theology and Biblical Interpretation*, Scripture and Hermeneutics Series 5, ed. C. Bartholomew et al. (Grand Rapids: Zondervan, 2004), 316n10. In 1970 Childs wanted to be sure the New's use of the Old was taken seriously as a theological achievement and not dismissed as exotic exegesis. So he focused on the biblical

The "Superiority" of the Final Form: In What Does This Consist?

This topic is allied to the one discussed above, but it situates itself more narrowly on what kind of claim it is to attend to the final form of the text, over against earlier levels of tradition. In this sense, it is a topic that deals with the relationship between modern reconstructions of "tradition-history" and the fact of there being an end point in that history, in the more or less stable (given text-critical realities) final literary form, arrangement, and presentation.

In a recent textbook account,[49] John Collins writes of the relationship between "original or earliest prophetic speech" and the later shaping and presentation of that into a corpus or canon. He is quoted at length as a fair and representative voice, in that his own work has clearly taken issue with Childs and the canonical approach.

> Much of the history of scholarship over the last two hundred years has been concerned primarily with the original words of the prophets. In recent years the pendulum has swung toward a focus on the final form of the prophetic books, in their canonical context. Both interests are clearly legitimate, and even necessary, but it is important to recognize the tension between them. The historical prophets whose oracles are preserved in these books were often highly critical of the political and religious establishments of their day. The scribes who edited their books, however, were part of the establishment of later generations. Consequently, they often try to place older oracles in the context of an authoritative tradition. In some cases, this has a moderating effect on oracles that may seem extreme outside (or even in) their historical context. In other cases, the editorial process may seem to take the edge off powerful prophetic oracles and dull their effect. The preference of an interpreter for the original prophets or for the canonical editors often reflects his or her trust or distrust of political and religious institutions in general.[50]

---

theological insights to be gained from such an analysis. When later he realized the danger latent in this—perhaps he has observed it in NT scholarship in the meantime—he pointed out the limitations of using the New as a lens on the Old for the purpose of biblical theology. Lincoln not only wrongly speculates on the reasons for this; he also pushes forward to argue that the great freedom of the New in respect of the Old (a new version of the "exotic") ought to be a license for our treating the New in precisely the same way. See the discussion in chapter 3 below.

49. John J. Collins, *Introduction to the Hebrew Bible* (Minneapolis: Fortress, 2004).

50. Ibid., 286.

Probably four things are being said here that demand fuller explication. Is the final psychological hunch a good guide to anything, except perhaps to Collins's own instincts or personal worries? What does the term "establishment" actually mean in the history-of-religion? Did these scribes, if they existed, think they were linking something to an "authoritative tradition"? Does the movement from early to later track according to Collins's hunches? All these are questions that could be pursued in the history-of-religion of Israel or the modern sociology-of-religion (M. Weber et al.). But it is a fair observation that a pendulum has swung, to use Collins's language, and he is to be commended for acknowledging that.

From the standpoint not of the sociology of religion, but of canonical method, is Collins's brief account the only way to describe what it means to give attention to the final form? Collins's points can nevertheless be used to tease out what might be meant by attention to the final form, in relationship to earlier levels of tradition (however we, in fact, lay our hands on "the original words of the prophets").

Is there really a "tension" between original prophet and later editorial shaping in the narrow sense implied by this quote? Another way to view the process of development in prophetic books is to withhold judgment until one actually tracks what is happening, which may also look different from book to book. Not every prophet is highly critical of religious institutions; some have mixed attitudes (Hosea); some focus on the nations (Obadiah); some require belief in a remnant or a superior plan of God for the king and people (Isaiah); some preach forgiveness and undeserved grace (Deutero-Isaiah). So the starting point may not be the same at all.

Second, Jeremias and others have shown the complex ways in which prophetic books acquire additions. In Hosea, the southern kingdom may be contrasted with the fate of Israel. But Judah can also be editorially supplemented into the same book in order to emphasize that she falls under the same word of judgment as her northern neighbor.[51] Frequently we see a movement from local to global that heightens and does not relax the sharpness of the original word. This is particularly

---

51. Childs focused on this dimension in his *Introduction* account on Hosea, and Jeremias pursues a similar interest in his work on Hosea and Amos (see n32 above).

true in the case of the Day of the Lord, for example, in the Book of the Twelve. Where Hosea may be shifted to first position to emphasize the grace of God in dealing with a wayward people (thus shifting what we mean by "original" in the strict historical—chronological—sense; cf. Amos), the latest canonical book actually raises the stakes in what one might believe to be the remnant of God as the Day of the Lord approaches. The canonical shaping reconstrues the beginning points as well as the later ones, and the presentations do not follow simple, straightforward patterns.

In sum, it may well be that notions such as those entertained by Collins are actually the result of historical-critical investigatory instinct and not the neutral findings of that method when it has done its allegedly objective developmental work. The canonical arrangement of the Twelve is but one place where, far from moving from sharp word to domesticated institutionalization, we find the Word of God gathering a kind of steam that resists any such characterization at all.[52]

It is also possible to take issue with valorizing the final form of the text not on the grounds of obvious sociological or theological bias, but simply because it is selective. Is there some good reason why later levels of traditions ought to be given priority over earlier ones, regardless of how one characterizes the movement itself?

Frequently it sounds like this is a matter of examining a series of integers, all laid out in a row, and choosing the last ones over the first ones.[53]

---

52. Indeed, in many diachronic treatments we end up with a grid of development in which the sharpness of an Amos gives way to the ambiguities of a Jonah, as in, e.g., Blenkinsopp's textbook account (see my analysis in *Prophecy*, 22–23, 142–46). What prevents a diachronic reading from some form of philosophical predisposition is as old a problem as Wellhausen's *Prolegomena* or genuinely Hegelian approaches in the previous century. See my discussion, "Prophecy in Nineteenth Century Reception," in *The Hebrew Bible/Old Testament III*, ed. M. Saebo (Göttingen: Vandenhoeck & Ruprecht, forthcoming).

53. See Childs's discussion of this issue in *Struggle*, 320–21. He mentions his disagreement with Nicholson over the characterization of his work—a confusion he sees as traceable to Barr (*Holy Scripture: Canon, Authority, Criticism* [Philadelphia: Westminster, 1983]), picked up by Barton (*Reading the Old Testament*, 1st ed. [Philadelphia: Westminster, 1984]), and now continuing in the work of Trebolle Barrera (*The Jewish Bible and the Christian Bible: An Introduction to the History of the Bible*, trans. Wilfred G. E. Watson [Grand Rapids: Eerdmans, 1998]) and others. Nicholson quotes with favor the work of von Rad in Genesis on levels in the text (*The Pentateuch in the Twentieth Century: The Legacy of Julius Wellhausen* [Oxford: Oxford University Press, 1998]). I have discussed this same appeal by von Rad and conclude that he is a far more likely candidate for seeing the genius of

But a canonical approach disagrees precisely with this understanding of the growth of tradition, and at this juncture it offers an alternative understanding of tradition-history. The book of Isaiah is not what the purported last levels of tradition say about it. Later levels of tradition seek to gain a hearing alongside and not above what precedes. If "Trito-Isaiah" says nothing about David, that cannot say anything decisive about what the book of Isaiah, in its final form, says on this matter.[54] A canonical approach does not value the later over the earlier because the final form of the text does not follow this kind of developmental logic: earlier levels of tradition may even be highlighted by secondary and tertiary accumulations of tradition. Joel may well bring into sharper focus the call for repentance issued at the end of Hosea, as it provides a concrete liturgical enactment of this call as its central burden.[55]

Later intrusions of penitential voices in Jeremiah's opening chapters do not lessen the prophetic denunciations in Jeremiah's day; rather, they call attention to these and underscore how imperative it was to heed them, the failure to do so leading to such an awesome and dark tragedy of judgment. Later editors feel the need to say "let us lie down in our shame" and not "glad that did not happen to me, here in my institutional redoubt."[56]

In the context of a different discussion of this issue, Ward has also issued a challenge that might catch the allegedly "historical" purveyors of interpretation off guard. A canonical method, he suggests, does not value the later hands because of some moral superiority—or lack of it, in Collins's view—they possess. Rather, the later hands have a greater historical perspective, due to the sheer range of their awareness of the

---

the final form of the text than is traditionally held (see "Prophecy and Tradition-History: The Achievement of Gerhard von Rad and Beyond," in *Prophetie in Israel: Beiträge des Symposiums "Das Alte Testament und die Kultur der Moderne" anlässlich des 100. Geburtstags Gerhard von Rads (1901–1971) Heidelberg, 18–21. Oktober 2001*, ed. I. Fischer, K. Schmid, H. G. M. Williamson [Münster: Lit-Verlag, 2003], 30–51).

54. Christopher R. Seitz, "Royal Promises in the Canonical Books of Isaiah and the Psalms," in *Word without End*, 150–67.

55. Christopher R. Seitz, "On Letting a Text 'Act Like a Man'—The Book of the Twelve: New Horizons for Canonical Reading, with Hermeneutical Reflections," *SBET* 22 (2004): 151–72.

56. Christopher R. Seitz, "The Place of the Reader in Jeremiah," in *Reading the Book of Jeremiah: A Search for Coherence*, ed. Martin Kessler (Winona Lake, IN: Eisenbrauns, 2004), 67–75.

past, which is still unfolding at the time of early tradition-levels.[57] History lies out in front of "the original words of the prophets" because of what God is doing with them, under his providential guidance. It is a legacy of romantic theories of "inspiration" and "origins" that has set much historical-critical work off on the wrong foot, and it cannot be emphasized enough that this wrong footing has tripped up both conservative interpreters and their putative opposites.[58] This results in maximalist or minimalist accounts of what can be secured for the "original, inspired author/prophet/source/tradition," starting from the same quest for an authoritative base independent of the canon's own final-form presentation.

The final editors do not have any moral superiority, and it is not for this reason that a canonical approach values the final form of the text. The final form of the text is a canonical-historical portrayal, and the final editors have never ceased hearing the Word of God as a word spoken through history. Their very nonappearance, moreover, is testimony to the degree to which they have sought to let the past have its own say and in the case of Isaiah, have deferred to God's inspired Word as it presses ahead in all its accomplishing work. No morally superior, or balefully institutional, second or third Isaiahs get the final word. That would be far too thin an understanding of what a canonical approach has sought to comprehend when hearing the present sixty-six-chapter book in its final form.

Biblical Theology and a Canonical Approach: Vetus Testamentum in Novo Receptum?

The state of biblical theology as a coherent movement, method, or discipline is under discussion at present, with James Barr providing a sustained and argumentative account in his 1999 publication (based apparently upon lectures originally delivered in 1968).[59] His book is subtitled *An Old Testament Perspective*. While there may be a decline in biblical theology—and the reasons for this are the subject of a good deal of profitable reflection—one development has not been chronicled, so

57. Ward, *Word and Supplement*, 249.
58. See the discussion in Seitz, "On Letting a Text."
59. Barr, *Concept*.

far as I am aware: the renewed interest by NT scholars in the OT. Much of this turns on developments internal to NT scholarship. The so-called new perspective on Paul has turned its attention to Paul in his Jewish environment, with attendant fresh interest in the way the OT functions for him and his theological formulations. Several specialist accounts have been given over to describing Paul's use of the OT, with appreciation of the subtle and artful way in which the Scriptures of Israel work within his logic and arguments.[60] Richard Hays, N. T. Wright, and now Francis Watson are among the better-known names within the NT guild who have sought, respectively, to appreciate more comprehensively the way the "narrative world,"[61] the literary potentiality,[62] or the final form of the OT functions in the NT,[63] for Paul and for the basic character of Jesus's own self-understanding and mission.[64]

Whether or not it is consciously intended (this is not always stated), one could see this concern with the theological use of the Old in the New as a species of biblical theology. So one kind of decline in biblical theology may be matched by a new interest in a different guise: biblical theology as an appreciation of the theological use made by the New of the Old. Hans Hübner is one interpreter who has expressly declared this to be "biblical theology."[65]

---

60. For the theological minefield this has always been seen to be, consult the historical account of Hans Frei in *Eclipse*.

61. See my analysis of Wright's use of the OT in "Reconciliation and the Plain Sense Witness of Scripture," in *The Redemption: An Interdisciplinary Symposium on Christ as Redeemer*, ed. Stephen T. Davis, Daniel Kendall, and Gerald O'Collins (Oxford: Oxford University Press, 2004), 25–42.

62. Richard Hays, *Echoes of Scripture in the Letters of Paul* (New Haven: Yale University Press, 1989). Hays has a considerably more interesting/fruitful account of the twofold witness in his essay, "Can the Gospels Teach Us How to Read the Old Testament?" The title, however, indicates a kind of prioritizing of direction that may prove telling. More needs to be said about this essay than can be tackled here.

63. Francis Watson, *Paul and the Hermeneutics of Faith* (London: T&T Clark, 2004). Watson moves in a different direction in this volume in respect of Childs and a canonical approach than what he espoused in his earlier work *Text and Truth: Redefining Biblical Theology* (Edinburgh: T&T Clark, 1997). One finds a robust and strategic use of "canonical method" in the OT, while earlier the method of Childs was seen as misguided, measured against von Rad and others.

64. See also Ross J. Wagner, *Heralds of the Good News: Isaiah and Paul "In Concert" in the Letter to the Romans* (Leiden: Brill, 2002).

65. Hans Hübner, *Biblische Theologie des Neuen Testaments*, 3 vols. (Göttingen: Vandenhoeck & Ruprecht, 1990–95). Also, Peter Stuhlmacher, *Biblische Theologie des Neuen*

There have been dissenters to this view of biblical theology, though the reaction is not typically directed at specialist work of the kind mentioned above. Instead, it comes to the fore in the recent concern to let the OT have its own say, over against various kinds of efforts to constrain its voice. For Walter Brueggemann,[66] these stifling efforts are due to what he terms "reductionisms," and within the discipline of OT scholarship itself, these may be headed up by what he calls "historicism." The OT is hindered in making its voice heard by demands that it speak up chiefly or only through historical reconstruction of various kinds. But Brueggemann also argues there is a kind of backdraft from the NT, or from Christian theological reflection ("established church faith"), or dogmatics more specifically, that blows over the Old and obscures its "wild and untamed" theological witness.[67] The unruly character of the witness—its polyphony, etc. (Brueggemann has lots of terms for this)—ought to be left alone, and this is the ingredient most encroached upon, he argues, when one comes at the OT with theological lenses provided by the New or by Christian theology. Jon Levenson has remarked on the problematical character of this approach, so far as Judaism is concerned.[68] In less sustained ways, and for different reasons, John Goldingay (in his recently published first volume of OT theology)[69] and Rolf Rendtorff[70] have voiced similar concerns to let the OT retain its own theological voice.

I believe it is fair to say that Childs occupies considerable space between the two trends just described. For Childs, biblical theology should certainly attend to the way the New hears the Old, just as it needs to hear the New as such. When, in the final section of his

---

Testaments, 2 vols. (Göttingen: Vandenhoeck & Ruprecht, 1990–95). The titles are revealing. See the discussion of James D. G. Dunn on terminology in "The Problem of 'Biblical Theology,'" in Bartholomew et al., eds., Out of Egypt, 172–83.

66. Brueggemann, Theology of the Old Testament: Testimony, Dispute, Advocacy (Minneapolis: Fortress, 1997).

67. Ibid., 107.

68. Levenson, "Pluralist?"

69. John Goldingay, Old Testament Theology, vol. 1, Israel's Gospel (Downers Grove, IL: InterVarsity, 2003). See also my brief review in IJST 7, no. 2 (2005): 211–13; and C. Seitz, "Canon, Narrative, and the Old Testament Literal Sense," Tyndale Bulletin (2008): 27–31.

70. Rolf Rendtorff, "Toward a Common Jewish-Christian Reading of the Hebrew Bible," in Canon and Theology (Minneapolis: Fortress, 1993), 31–45.

book on Paul's use of the OT,[71] Hays holds Paul up as a hermeneutical lesson for our imitation or edificatory modeling, to the degree to which this is meant to count for biblical theology, Childs finds the approach faulty if not eccentric.[72] It is not possible to adopt the pneumatological stance of Paul, even if one thought this a good idea. Paul's stance on the OT is one in which there has yet to be formed a two-testament canon, and Christian theological reflection entails this material (canonical) reality, a reality that for Childs is foundational. Another problem involves the NT *as canon*. To stand with Paul would be to isolate his voice over against the other voices of the NT witness (it would also likely entail accepting the historical-critical canons of what with confidence we can attribute to Paul to begin with) and so to wrongly construct a category of biblical theology called "Pauline theology" (on an articulated historical grid). And then there is as well the problem of whether identification with Paul's pneumatological freedom is to misunderstand what the task of biblical theology outside the apostolic circle genuinely looks like.[73]

Now to spot the problems with this particular understanding of biblical theology is not the same thing as saying just how the OT's theological witness is to sound forth, both for its own sake and in the light of a subsequent witness (the NT) in which its voice has been taken up (*Vetus Testamentum in Novo receptum*). Here Childs has referred to the "discrete voice" of the OT. He was earlier criticized by Francis Watson for, among other things, describing a dimension of the witness of the OT in ways that are indebted to historical-critical investigation.[74] Presumably, the innocent and proper worry here would be that such a

---

71. Hays, *Echoes*, 178–92.

72. Childs, *Biblical Theology of the Old and New Testaments*, 84–85.

73. Much fuller reflection needs to be undertaken on this issue. There is often a readiness in Christian circles to collapse the church into the NT without further ado and then to think of the OT in clear contrast to this (the difference at this point with Aquinas's commentary on Psalms, for example, where Christ prays for his church, is instructive). A canonical understanding of the role of the Scriptures sees the church, for different reasons and to different degrees, in a less direct relationship to both Testaments and certainly not in one which amounts to conflation or simple contrast. More on this in chapters 2–4 below.

74. See his discussion in *Text and Truth* and in an exchange with myself in *SJT*: "Christological Interpretation of Texts and Trinitarian Claims to Truth," *SJT* 52 (1999): 209–26; Francis Watson, "The Old Testament as Christian Scripture: A Reply to Professor Seitz,"

(historically retrieved) account of what the OT has to say could then never be attached to the New's reception of it, because this latter phenomenon goes on without recourse to historical-critical categories or assumptions.[75] The live question, however, is whether this is what the discrete voice of the OT actually is *for Childs*, and here we are back again to the topic addressed above: how do historical-critical methods function in a canonical approach? It has been argued above that a "canonical approach" as adopted by Childs gives priority to the final form of the text, and this final form is what Childs means by the "discrete voice"; this approach by no means holds the final form hostage to historical-critical reconstruction, even as such methods might help us grasp it. To say this is to address the worry that a category is being invented ("the discrete voice") that cannot attach itself to the New's hearing of it.

The problem with Watson's earlier approach has now shifted to the opposite front: by issuing a warning against hearing the discrete voice of the OT, the voice of the OT may end up being only what moves uncomplicatedly into the New's version of its own witness.[76] That kind of "anti-discrete" move would mean a silencing of much that is in the OT, on the one side; and it would also threaten to misunderstand the way in which what the New has to say *is genuinely new and fresh and provocative.* This is an irony, in some ways, because this latter dimension had been the source of much focused interest and theological shoring-up in Watson's earlier works, and in his understanding of the relationship between the Testaments.

SJT 52 (1999): 227–32. See as well Childs's evaluation of Watson in *Church's Guide*, 128–31 (brief discussion above in n26).

75. This point has been made at another place by N. T. Wright, and it appears congenial for several reasons with a canonical approach. In a volume that included treatments of the suffering servant by OT scholars, Wright posed the question: why did they not ask "how Isaiah might have been read by Jesus' own contemporaries?" (W. H. Bellinger, W. R. Farmer, eds., *Jesus and the Suffering Servant* [Harrisburg, PA: Trinity Press International, 1998], 282). See my discussion in "Prophecy and Tradition-History," 38–39.

76. *Paul and the Hermeneutics of Faith*. In this volume Watson seeks to show that Paul hears the canonical shape of the OT better than his contemporary interlocutors do. The Pentateuch endorses the "second (theological) use of the law"—the law as death dealing. This is fine for portions of the Pentateuch—one thinks of the golden calf episode—but the "birth of the new" emphasis of Numbers and Deuteronomy is oddly muted in a reading said to attend to the canonical form. See Dennis Olson, *The Death of the Old and the Birth of the New: The Framework of the Book of Numbers and the Pentateuch* (Chico: Scholars Press, 1985).

The simple point is that the "discrete voice" (as Childs means it) is not a voice that cannot sound forth in the New due to historical-critical privileging of some wrong sort (a proper worry), but it is a voice that sounds its own notes just the same, in its own registers, and in so doing is fully capable of doing Christian theology. The NT can attend to this voice when it takes up the Old, even as it will transform that voice for the purposes of its own "Second Testament" witnessing to God in Christ. But this category of reflection is not determinative for biblical theology in the way that Watson suggests (or Brueggemann, Rendtorff, or Goldingay might rightly worry about). It is an ingredient in biblical theology, but it is not biblical theological reflection, either of the New or of the Old Testaments in the Christian Bible.[77]

This point was established in the 1970 volume, even at places where Childs was later to question the adequacy of his methods there.[78] Childs rightly saw in a later discussion that if one only focused on the places where the New had taken up the Old and used this for the purposes of biblical theology, the selection would be skewed and significant portions of the OT would fall silent in the work of biblical theology. An ingredient would become the full meal. But even given that probable limitation in his method, one can see in the 1970 volume how biblical theology according to a canonical approach nevertheless frees the OT to do the theological work proper to its own witnessing role. For example, Childs carefully analyzes Psalm 8's discrete voice before turning to the NT's reception and adaptation of it. As seen above, he distinguishes the canonical voice in the Old from a limiting doctrinal filtering he spots in the earlier history of interpretation. He then reflects on the NT's hearing of the psalm in its own medium and according to certain explicit christological evaluations it is seeking to make. It is important to note that this movement, from Old to New, *then reverses direction.* The psalm's high doctrine of creation is allowed to sound forth in the context of christological focus, and this assures that the incarnation and exaltation of Christ do not become isolated theological ideas, but are tied to God's ways with creation, Israel,

---

77. See Childs's comments in n26 above.

78. See Childs, *Biblical Theology of the Old and New Testaments,* 76.

and the world. The Old's voice does not somehow "correct" the New, or highlight its deficiencies—though if one read the New without this earlier witness continuing to have its proper theological effect, correction would indeed be in order. A canonical approach assures that the New's emphases remain rooted in the soil from which they have sprung. The danger is that in the enthusiasm to describe what the New is saying, modern readers simply leave unstated and unfelt what were most certainly the keen pressures and context supplied by the Old in the first evangelical efforts to account for God's work in Christ. For this, we do not have to ask what was in the mind of the authors of the New, because the OT exists as a canonical witness, showing us the horizons set forth from that witness in their own stable deliverance of them, reaching to the authors of the New and beyond to us.[79]

Another analogy may be useful here, from text criticism. If one watched what the NT said of the OT in its own Greek language idiom and sought to contrast this with the Old's own sentences in a different language, what would one be discovering? Sometimes the sense is conveyed that between two conscious choices, one is being adopted and another ruled out by the NT author, so as to make this or that fresh and determinative theological point. Priority is given both to the language of translation and to the use made of it in the New, in a two-for-one deal. But in a great many places no such conscious decision is being made at all. The New simply operates reflexively in its own translational idiom and is not making a choice for this (Greek language) text over that (Hebrew language) text—and above all not a kind of preferencing that later academic analysis engages in, observing two different languages and choosing one over the other.[80]

It is for this reason that the "discrete voice" of the OT is not to be identified with what the New makes of it, *simpliciter*. This would be giving to the New's use of the OT a kind of conscious replacing or displacing function, when there is little evidence to suggest that the

79. See the discussion of chapter 3 below.

80. And sometimes, in the Letter to the Hebrews, the author uses Greek sentences of Scripture that appear in neither an OT (Hebrew) *Vorlage* nor in any Greek recensions either. See the intriguing discussion of this and other matters in Karen H. Jobes and Moises Silva, *Invitation to the Septuagint* (Grand Rapids: Baker Academic, 2000).

NT writers actually meant to be heard as functioning in this way, over against the authoritative Scriptures they are themselves commenting on. So, can we say with any confidence that Paul intended his use of the Scriptures of Israel to determine the direction of biblical theological reflection; that is, reflection on a twofold canon of Scripture in which his own statements would be taken up into a canonical witness involving a wide variety of different genres (Gospels, Epistles of very different kinds, Acts, Revelation)? Paul is obviously unaware that a comprehensive second witness will in time appear in a now *twofold* scriptural canon, formed on analogy with the one he himself has drawn upon in the narrower sense, but now with the same authority and claim to speak as did the prophets of old. I suspect we should be expected to believe in much recent NT work that he did so assume, or that we are nevertheless right to be following his lead as consistent with this view. And yet the formation of the canon points in a direction away from simple or complex imitation of Paul as the starting point for biblical theology. Paul's use of the OT now takes place within a larger canonical witness (the NT), which is itself given a status on analogy with the first witness. A properly *biblical* theology would need to account for the two witnesses in this analogous, but also different, relationship and form.

Childs's biblical theological reflections in his 1970 work formed the ground floor of what would become a series of comprehensive investigations into the relationship between Old and New Testaments, theology, and biblical theology. In a recent work on Paul and the OT, Watson has made a clear-cut decision to inquire into how the final form of the OT might have pressured a reading in Paul—that is, a reading often otherwise credited to christological or pneumatological insights provided from outside that witness.[81] Here there appears to be some considerable movement on his part toward understanding what the proper relationship is between the "final form" laid bare by a canonical hermeneutic and the apprehension of this in the New.

---

81. Watson has a fine running discussion of the problems of J. L. Martyn's approach, in this case chiefly to be found in the magisterial commentary *Galatians: A New Translation with Introduction and Commentary*, Anchor Bible Commentary (New York: Doubleday, 1997), dedicated unsurprisingly to Ernst Käsemann. Much more could be said on this topic but it falls outside the scope of the present chapter's survey.

The irony is that there persists a concern to demonstrate this dimension only within the narrower realm of what one might call "Pauline theology," and that on at least two fronts. First, there is no attempt to register the limitations of asking about a "Pauline theology" over against NT or biblical theology; this seems somewhat strange in a work that will not tolerate any such "historicizing" moves as decisive for understanding the Old's final-form witness. So for example, "Habakkuk" cannot be understand apart from the canonical form in which it appears (the Twelve and the Prophets), yet an "undisputed" Pauline corpus, determined by historical-critical judgments, is the point of departure in the NT for investigating the Old's canonical shape. Why this discontinuity, treating the Old canonically and not (more narrowly) historically, but then reversing direction in the New? For the second problem we return to the issue mentioned above, but now from the opposite side, that is, how does the OT sound forth its theological witness? Watson wants to maximize the continuity between the Old's voice and the New's (Paul's) hearing of it, on the grounds that this is historically the case (and he can—or indeed must—demonstrate this by comparisons with literatures contemporaneous with Paul and accessible to him, as he theorizes their existence and effect on him). That is, the historical Paul read the witness available to him at his moment in history, and he argued for this or that christological foundationalism on the basis of the OT and as an accurate hearing of it, over against rival attempts to do the same (or arguably in many cases, to do something different).

What happens is complex, it could be concluded, especially in the case of the law. In an effort to secure the special hearing of Paul as coming out of the Old's canonical form, and not as the special effects supplied by the Gospel (Martyn, Käsemann), it will need to be shown by Watson that things like the law's "fading glory" are deeply embedded in the law's own plain-sense presentation of itself. In some ways what happens is that the two voices (OT and NT) are simply fused. The excesses of saying the New hears what it hears because of the overtones supplied by Christian confession, and so "reads into" the OT something that is not there,[82] are thereby constrained; so too the sense that the NT

82. A problem Watson sees in John Barton's understanding of Habakkuk's influence on Paul. According to Watson's (insightful) analysis, Barton depends upon a theory of

is arguing that the Old is a closed or wrongheaded book and cannot yield up such deep mysteries anyway. But the result is a single conflated agreement across the Testaments, at the cost of digging less deeply into the paradoxical way in which Paul is seeking to negotiate two distinct realities: the Old's plain sense and the work of Christ. The anguish that task causes him is even expressed by Paul, and rather clearly, in Romans 9–11, for example.

But even if this description does not completely capture the burden of Watson's model, what is clear is that the Old's theological witness comes alive for him only in respect of Paul's successful (as Watson has it) hearing of it.[83] At times this hearing works with a concept of intentionality one might call "canonical." At other points this is less clear.[84] One can conclude that Watson has thought deeply about the challenge of doing a species of biblical theology, and has outdistanced some weaker formulations, but that there is something eccentric or quixotic in what he attempts. There will always remain space between the New's hearing of the Old and the Old's plain sense. What is at issue is not the elimination of that space, but the careful appreciation of its character. Biblical theology will function properly when it deals with the material reality of there being two different witnesses and accepts that fact as foundational for interpretation. It is hard to see how the OT can contribute to biblical theology in the manner of Childs's handling of Psalm 8, as an example of the canonical approach, if Psalm 8 and Hebrews's use of it are maximally coordinated, for whatever reason. (Just here one sees how difficult it would be to extend Watson's project across the length and breadth of the NT canon.) Rather, both OT and NT witnesses function in a complementary way for the purpose of Christian biblical theological reflection.

Habakkuk's "intention," which Watson calls "historically naïve and hermeneutically perverse" (*Galatians*, 158).

83. In this sense, in Watson's hands, "canonical intentionality" appears to detach itself from Israel's lived life: the text refers not so much to events in its day as to a reception history yet to be known by it.

84. Watson has not entirely sorted out the problem of distinguishing Enlightenment "intentionality" from the intentionality of the final form. More cannot be said here, as it would require a greater attention to inconsistencies in Watson's otherwise ambitious discussion of "intention" than is warranted in this context.

Coercion, *Adversarius Noster*, "Untamed and Wild": The Character of the Final Form of the Text

Twenty years ago John Barton wrote:

> It is not surprising that Childs has little following in Germany. One misses in his proposals the sense so dear to the heirs of the Reformation (including many in his own Calvinist tradition) that the biblical text is something with rough edges, set over against us, not necessarily speaking with one voice, coming to us from a great distance and needing to be weighed and tested even as it tests and challenges us: *adversarius noster*, in Luther's phrase.[85]

Sweeping statements like this have a way of coming back to haunt one. It was only a year before this, at a public lecture at Yale, that Rolf Rendtorff spoke of his reaction upon reading Childs's 1979 introduction: "it was as though scales fell from my eyes." It is hard to say whether any non-German biblical scholar has ever been so thoroughly read and reacted to in German-speaking circles as Brevard Childs. Indeed, when Barton's colleague James Barr speaks of his own training in biblical studies, what seems immediately apparent is the distinguishing fact that Childs was trained in Germany and Barr in another context.[86] It would be worth a monograph of its own to investigate whether the chief differences between them turn, in Barr's case, on a very different climate of training and ecclesial

---

85. Barton, *Reading the Old Testament*, 95.

86. Barr speaks of never having divided a verse, dated a text, etc. and generally describes an Anglo–Saxon training devoid of sharp critical instincts and basking in the heyday of the Biblical Theology movement. ("I was myself never much of a historical-critical scholar. I do not know that I ever detected a gloss, identified a source, proposed an emendation or assigned a date. . . . On the contrary, scholars who thought that these matters were the essence of exegesis . . . were laughed at and looked upon as fossils from some earlier age. The cutting edge of Old Testament study, and its impact upon theology, seemed to lie in the concepts of biblical theology," *Holy Scripture*, 130). Here is another place where Barr's predictions about the field have not proven quite accurate; it is as though historical criticism is now passé, in Barr's judgment. Yet someone like Nicholson is a good example of the persistence of classical historical-critical interests and concerns, and he is quite representative in many ways of British OT scholarship (cf. G. Davies, Williamson, Barton—all proud deployers of pretty traditional historical-critical methods; for someone interested in biblical theology, I suspect one would turn to the lone Walter Moberly—not a candidate for the "James Barr prize" for things mainstream, one might have thought).

life. Barr and Barton look in on the Continental Reformation as if it is a kind of distant phenomenon, which to some extent it is for them; and so it is strange to see their often partial and intriguing use of the Reformers. This is particularly true in Barton's citation of Luther here.[87]

What Barton appears to have done in this citation is translate the observations of Luther about the content of Scripture (its *Sache* or referent) into the realm of materiality: the Bible is a kind of literary crazy-quilt, a tangle or puzzle demanding the proper critical tools to sort it out. Even when Luther uses this kind of rhetoric ("the prophets have a queer way of talking") it cannot be said that this is what he means when he says the Bible is "our adversary." Rather, he means more what Barth means when in a later day he refers to the "strange world" of Scripture. The Bible confronts us, squares up to us, with the content of its word and its address as such. It does not confront us because it has a strange, confusing, or paradoxical literality (awaiting historical-critical sorting). Barton refers to the "rough edges" of Scripture in a book on hermeneutics in the context of his concerns to keep historical-critical investigation at full employment, as a kind of necessity, given the project to which it must put its hand. Rarely, if ever, does one see the heirs of the Reformation seek to justify historical-critical work along these lines. In another context I have criticized Käsemann and Stuhlmacher for claiming that the Reformation instinct demands historical-critical quests for the "proximate."[88] But even that was not an appeal to the "rough edges" of the witness, but rather to the need to overcome what is presumed to be a theological or hermeneutical problem of access to the subject matter, due to historical distance. This kind of a problem, it can be argued, is different again from what worried either the Reformation, on the one side, or Barton

---

87. In Helmer's intriguing look into Luther's trinitarian interpretation of the psalms ("Luther's Trinitarian Hermeneutic") what one sees in Luther is an effort to find a solid footing in the semantics of Hebrew upon which to rest the church's dogmatic confession that the "Spirit spake by the prophets"—as over against the ambiguities in allegorical readings of the Holy Spirit warranted by creeds or church councils primarily, and not grounded in the scriptural clarity of the OT (which exists prior to councils and creeds). Luther is not describing an adversary here but a dogmatic ground floor.

88. Christopher R. Seitz, "Two Testaments and the Failure of One Tradition-History," in *Figured Out*, 35–47.

in his examination of canonical hermeneutics and the literary "rough edges" of the material form of the witness, on the other.

In a long series of published works, Walter Brueggemann has sought to keep the OT at some considerable distance for the purpose of explicitly Christian theological reflection, using the language of polyphony and other kindred terms, and this bears some similarity to the "rough edges" that Barton speaks about. But they are coming from very different places and end up in very different ones as well. Brueggemann worries about "christianizing" the voice of the OT, or, if a distinction can be made, mishearing or occluding the word of the Old because the interpretive lens of the New is being given precedence over it. The literary reality of the OT lines up for Brueggemann with a theological reality, making this a clear (and for his purposes, a desired) departure from traditional appraisals. The text is at odds with itself, because the God to which it refers only exists in the speech about "him" and this speech comes at us in testimony and counter-testimony. There is nothing about the "final form" of the text that points to a settling down of the *"hin und her"* highlighted by Brueggemann. Just because this is so, it follows naturally that the reader must seek some understanding of the text's address, must read it out of the "wild and untamed" literary witness before us, and the idea that Brueggemann is *choosing freely* to hear what he hears and see what he sees is an idea on his terms without genuine alternative. I suspect the most that could be said in a methodological sense is that the text *can* be read this way and so this is the way Brueggemann chooses to read it. Such would be all that could be required, one assumes, on this kind of postmodern playing field (though why *any* reading is not possible, and also impossible to adjudicate as good or bad, remains somewhat unclear).[89]

It is Childs's notion of a final form, a stable witness, a "discrete voice," that runs in a direction Brueggemann finds unacceptable. Historical criticism gave us a sense that the texts go through various phases of development. This is fine. The danger for Brueggemann is taking this fact and then constructing something behind the text,

---

89. Jon Levenson, "Pluralist?" Levenson helpfully points out how complex a representative of postmodernity Brueggemann actually is.

in a history-of-religion. This is a domestication or a reductionism, on his terms. The various phases of development point instead to a point-counterpoint, and there is nothing in the text itself that gives indication of that "*hin und her*" reaching anything like a coherent final statement (even one with dialectical aspects to it).[90]

Childs has himself tried to assess this particular challenge (and widely disseminated alternative) to his approach and has done so most recently in a work on the history of interpretation of the book of Isaiah.[91] It is striking in some ways that Childs has chosen to give the work a title that also bespeaks our "postmodern" situation: *The Struggle to Understand Isaiah as Christian Scripture*. The struggle, however, is not to do with an inherent restlessness of the literature itself, as an indispensable characteristic of it; it is rather to do with what it means to seek to hear the subject matter of sacred Scripture through the medium of two discrete, if juxtaposed, witnesses. Precisely because Brueggemann disagrees with the pressure of (the necessity of) hearing both Testaments as bearing witness to one another and to Christian foundational claims as crucial to the task of interpretation, one cannot use the term "struggle" as Childs means it to describe what he is doing.[92]

On the surface, the idea that the first witness has a stable and more-or-less objective final form (even given text-critical realities we shall discuss next) probably ought to complicate the idea that we must also hear it in relationship to a second witness with the same characteristic final canonical form (comprised of various separate forms of discourse). And of course it does indeed. The "final form"

90. Christopher R. Seitz, "Scripture Becomes Religion(s): The Theological Crisis of Serious Biblical Interpretation in the Twentieth Century," in *Renewing Biblical Interpretation*, Scripture and Hermeneutics Series 1, ed. Craig Bartholomew et al. (Grand Rapids: Zondervan, 2000), 26–27.

91. Childs, *Struggle*.

92. Hugh G. M. Williamson notes in a review that Childs has a (more or less) comprehensive coverage of the history of interpretation, with the exception of some more recent commentators. That is because, he conjectures, these newer readers of Isaiah have stopped having to account for the relationship between Old and New Testaments as part of the actual "struggle" of Christian interpretation (review of B. S. Childs, *The Struggle to Understand Isaiah as Christian Scripture*, RBL [April 2005], available online at www.bookreviews.org/bookdetail.asp?TitleId=4494&CodePage=4494). Brueggemann, however, makes an explicit case for the necessity of having to stop, and so he is treated in more detail by Childs.

is neither a single narrative line (plot) nor a series of kindred genres, all lined up in a tidy way.[93] And the fact that the first witness makes final Christian sense in relationship with a second one, means there is always an act of correlation to be achieved, and for that the only proper description is "struggle."

It is crucial to keep this aspect of canonical reading clear in one's mind. At one level, Brueggemann's unruly witness is not at all unlike what Childs means when he refers to struggle; indeed, by insisting that we read the OT on its own, Brueggemann has made interior to its witness a kind of inherent "struggling" that otherwise takes place, for very different reasons, when one seeks to do Christian theological reflection on a single canon comprising two discrete (and merely juxtaposed) sections—with the latter one taking up within itself portions of the explicit semantic level of the first, and also making the delivery of its claims operative primarily at the level of "accordance" with that same first witness.[94]

This will mean that Childs has no trouble, on the one hand, speaking of the "pressure" (or "coercion") of the canonical OT text, in its final form, as a discrete and stable voice; and yet, on the other hand, of the *sensus literalis* being a sense with extension beyond itself because of the challenge of rendering the subject matter, which now entails a second accorded witness (this "extensive" character belongs to the property of the literal sense and is not merely imposed upon it). A "rule of faith" is required to help us understand another, allied, theological pressure, at the heart of the act of Christian interpretation: the two Testaments are related on analogy with the basic Christian confession that the Creator God is the Father of Jesus Christ and the Son shares the eternal glory and life of the Father who sent him (Phil. 2:9–11). Yahweh is this Triune God and we know it from the first witness itself, when its literal sense yields this up in the light of the second witness.

93. See my review of John Goldingay, *Old Testament Theology*, vol. 1, *Israel's Gospel* (*International Journal of Systematic Theology* 7, no. 2 [2005]: 211–13), who seeks to isolate kindred genres and collate these for the purpose of three volumes of introduction. The rhetorical challenge of pulling this off without tedium is enormous and may signal why the final form of the OT—among many other reasons to be sure—has resisted this.

94. Seitz, "In Accordance with the Scriptures," in *Word without End*, 51–60.

The best recent effort to describe what Childs means by the pressure of the literal sense, with sensitivity to the challenge of hearing two Testaments, is the essay by C. Kavin Rowe, the title of which gives indication of what is being sought in Childs's canonical reading: "Biblical Pressure and Trinitarian Hermeneutics."[95] In a piece of historical close reading, Christine Helmer has investigated "Luther's Trinitarian Hermeneutic and the Old Testament,"[96] and she demonstrates on the basis of Luther's understanding of Hebrew semantics how he was able to see the Trinity adumbrated, if not more fully manifested, in the OT quite apart from the traditional proof-texting. In some ways, then, we come full circle and confront again Luther's famous "our adversary." "Our adversary" is neither an unruly literality (Barton) nor a God resistant to creedal claims (Brueggemann)—indeed, on this latter point, Luther uses mature Christian confession precisely to lodge his point in contradistinction to churchly claims and pious enthusiasms both. "Our adversary" is the *Sache* of the Scriptures' plain-sense address.

When Childs speaks of "coercion" or the pressure of the literal sense, he stands far closer to what Luther meant by "our adversary" than Barton realized. The OT confronts us: as Law and, in Luther's more mature formulation, as gospel as well. It exposes, as in the famous deployment by Luther of the "theological use" of the law. It also orders our world, by telling us of God and his Christ and of the Holy Spirit, both in the Old (through its use of Hebrew and in its understanding of the Word of God) and in the New, where the literal sense of Scripture shows us more clearly the christological or spiritual referent both Testaments are fundamentally about. It is "our adversary," not in presenting us with a material form that is chaotic or whose parameters cannot be determined except by means of external aids (allegory or the ironic counterpart of this in history-of-religion or modern critical methods). It is "our adversary" in that it seeks to overcome our world and reorder it. It does this not just by catching us up for a while in imaginative construals. Nor does it do this chiefly by pointing to a world of ostensive reference that we need to reas-

---

95. In *ProEccl* 11, no. 3 (2002): 295–312. See also "Romans 10:13: What Is the Name of the Lord?" *HBT* 22 (2000): 135–73.
96. In *ModTh* 18 (2002): 49–73.

semble or make more proximate by use of historical tools. It does this by means of the final form of the text, whose words point to a fleshly and a spiritual realm both, in Luther's complex understanding. Because its subject matter is Christ—and this is sometimes quite clear and forceful, and other times oblique (as, with Luther, Israel gazes on something it cannot have or cannot yet grasp)—it disrupts and reorders our place in the world and the world itself. This is what Childs means when he speaks of the Bible's address primarily with the language of "witness."

It belongs to our specific providential place in time that we must struggle with how the Bible makes its two-testament word heard. But this has always been the case. When Childs speaks of the text's coercion or pressure, at our specific moment in time, it will be against a backdrop of challenges that did not obtain in the same form for Origen, or Chrysostom, or Theodoret, or Luther, or Calvin. Those challenges in our day have had to do with new understandings of historical reference, which make the task of hearing the "literal sense" sharpened and more finely governed by our sense of the pastness of the past. But that is simply a challenge, and it is akin to what it has meant to struggle to hear the Word of God through the medium of the historical witness of prophets and apostles in every age. A canonical method does not seek to diminish the challenge or change the subject, but it does insist that the "literal sense" can make its force felt all the same, even under the shadow of our awareness of the complex historical development of the text before us.

Still, this challenge has also come with its benefits and fresh insights. Who could read the historical back-filling supplied by George Adam Smith and not sense that the minor prophets were somehow coming alive again and making themselves heard in fresh ways, precisely because to his age had been bequeathed the legacy of newer historical methods?[97] He spoke of "fixing the indemnity" brought about by these methods, and that phrase is fraught with meaning, beyond what he might have seen, as the shadows cast by historical approaches were only beginning to lengthen.[98] The canonical approach has not

97. Christopher R. Seitz, "On Letting a Text," 151–72.

98. Iain D. Campbell, *Fixing the Indemnity: The Life and Work of George Adam Smith* (Carlisle: Paternoster, 2004).

turned its back on this challenge, nor on the "indemnification" that would be required for our age. What has emerged in the canonical approach is a text undomesticated and able to speak a word—even "our adversary," witnessing to the work of the Triune God who occasioned the speech about himself—and equipping us, by the Holy Spirit, to hear the divine word afresh in our generation.

Hebrew and Greek Canons: What Is at Stake Here?

Naturally enough, a canonical approach will be required to comment on the more traditional, material, low-flying questions of canon: which canon of the Old and New Testaments has authority for Christian interpretation and witness? But the question is immediately raised: Just what is meant by a very specific set of historical and theological/ecclesial parameters pertaining to canonicity? To speak of a canonical approach giving wrongful priority to a Hebrew versus a Greek canon (and then describing these as attaching to distinctive ecclesial bodies) is to hopelessly simplify matters. Under the rubric "Which Canon?" in *Reading the Old Testament*, John Barton's brief treatment of this issue—about which he has written at length in other publications—gives a nice series of misleading impressions. But chief among them is the statement:

> It is hard not to be swayed by the purely historical arguments of scholars such as A. C. Sundberg—writing before Childs had developed his theories—to the effect that before the Reformation there had never been a time when the Christian Church acknowledged any canon but that of the Greek Bible; so that the attempt by the Reformers to "restore" the Old Testament canon to its original limits was hopelessly anachronistic.[99]

In this summary one would be forgiven for being unaware that Jerome and Augustine had a series of important exchanges over just this issue and that the latter was forced to develop something like a theory of inspiration that could cover both "canons"—a discussion that the canonical approach has itself taken pains to point out.[100] Jerome, of course, rather famously revised the Old Latin and Greek

---

99. Barton, *Reading the Old Testament*, 91–92.
100. See most recently, Childs, *Struggle*.

translations available to him by recourse to the Hebrew text. This instinct was followed in a different day and toward a different end, by "the Reformers" (by which Barton means Luther and Calvin et al.), but this also included fresh translations by Bellarmine and others on the other side of the "Reformation." This instinct to carefully preserve the role of the Hebrew language version of the OT, and to correct extant translations on the basis of it, more than anything accounts for the concern of the canonical approach for not cutting loose the distinctive role of the Hebrew canon—alongside other matters of historical and theological argument, as we shall see.

Barton then goes on to speak of "Childs's argument that we must take the MT as our norm"[101] and here chiefly on ecumenical grounds, as he sees it. As we shall see, in the context of canonical text (including scope, language, and order) Childs has himself spoken about the "Church's ongoing *search* for the Christian Bible."[102] While a canonical approach will call for significant attention to the Masoretic tradition, it does this on a combination of grounds and not for "ecumenical" reasons only. These grounds include (1) historical/recensional reasons, (2) theological reasons, (3) the history of the OT's reception, and (4) conceptual grounds. In this latter area, Childs has argued against the sharp division of Sundberg, Barton, and others between what they wish to call canonical (scope and institutional fixation) and scriptural (some more open claim to a hearing prior to this) authority.[103]

Still, to say even this is not to valorize a kind of pristine "Masoretic Text." It needs to be made clear up front what Childs does *not* mean by calling Christian interpretation to attend to the Masoretic tradition of the OT canon. First, the MT does not have some sort of sacrosanct order to be identified over against the (emerging) different order/s of LXX texts;[104] a canon that ends with Chronicles

---

101. Barton, *Reading the Old Testament*, 92.

102. Childs, *Biblical Theology of the Old and New Testaments*, 67.

103. See also Stephen Chapman, " 'Canon' versus 'Scripture,' " in *The Law and the Prophets: A Study in Old Testament Canon Formation*, Forschungen zum Alten Testament 27 (Tübingen: Mohr Siebeck, 2000), 106–10. See also my recent contribution in *Goodly Fellowship*, including reference to the creative work of G. Steins and K. van der Toorn, both of whom set aside the distinction.

104. Against Sweeney we cannot claim to know for sure why LXX translations adopt a fourfold internal division (where they do): Is it for theological reasons (LXX leans

does not sound some sort of clear and distinctive notes over against one that ends with Malachi. There is a variety of different orders, and the final position of Malachi in English printed Bibles is a modern convention without widespread attestation in the history of interpretation (Daniel, Esther are often last; the Twelve appears with Isaiah and usually precedes it).[105] Internal order and arrangement can well be important indices in a canonical approach, but one must approach the matter with discretion and care.[106] Second, Childs's appeal to the MT is registered in no small part because of an opposite tendency, namely, the effort to prioritize a distinctive LXX text over against the Hebrew canon, in the manner suggested by Barton's quote above. It is as if the Christian Bible ought properly to be regarded as a "Greek Bible," which can in turn somehow detach itself from the MT, either because of the history of the church, which did not "acknowledge any canon but that of the Greek Bible" (a simplistic and misleading statement), or because this allows the material reality of the NT's Greek-language form to say something theologically determinative about the canon of the OT.[107] For a canonical approach, this is a category error. We have

---

toward the New—this seems unlikely; an ending in Chronicles could also be argued to "lean forward") or for lower-flying reasons of confusion and a desire to taxonomize (make the "Former Prophets" into a category of historical books and then take those from the *ketubim* which are kindred)? See his either-or approach in Sweeney, "Tanak versus Old Testament: Concerning the Foundation for a Jewish Theology of the Bible," in *Problems in Biblical Theology: Essays in Honor of Rolf Knierim*, ed. Henry T. C. Sun et al. (Grand Rapids: Eerdmans, 1997), 353–72. I discuss the matter in greater length in *Goodly Fellowship*.

105. On the variety of orders of the Christian Bible, see Earle E. Ellis, *The Old Testament in Early Christianity: Canon and Interpretation in Light of Modern Research*, Wissenschaftliche Untersuchungen zum Neuen Testament 54 (Tübingen: Mohr Siebeck, 1991).

106. In a work concerned primarily with reestablishing the coherence and proper "coercion" of the final form of books in the canon of the OT (Childs, *Introduction*), the prophetic books were treated in their MT order but with little reflection on the shape of the XII as one structured collection (this latter is now an area of considerable and fruitful investigation). Presumably there was enough to do on the first front. Still, Childs will in fact comment on the final form of the Pentateuch, for example, as against a Hexateuch or a Deuteronomistic history beginning with Deuteronomy. I have written extensively on this issue in my own publications.

107. Any amateur reading the history of interpretation (say, on a text like Hab. 3) will immediately realize that the church's alleged appeal to a single, clear, contrastable, settled "Greek canon" is illusory.

mentioned the confusion introduced by an approach that reads the OT's theological witness *in Novo receptum*. There is a text-critical/canonical aspect to this confusion as well.

We can list several issues that this prioritizing of "the Greek canon" raises for a canonical approach.

When the term "the Septuagint" is used, what is meant by this? Because of its character as a translation, Greek-language versions derived from an earlier Hebrew text did not simply fall into a single type with a fixed length or a standard internal ordering.[108]

This is also true in the history of the reception of the OT in the church. The wide variety of known Greek-language versions of the OT may be a source of excitement or exuberant shows of erudition for John Chrysostom.[109] For others it is a problem to be overcome, an irritation, or an occasion to prefer what appears to be a far more settled Hebrew textual tradition—whatever might be additionally claimed for the priority of the Hebrew on theological grounds.[110]

When appeal is made to "the Septuagint" what exactly is being said? The NT does not quote from a single LXX text; it can also quote from a (pre-) Masoretic text; and it can provide translations in Greek of the OT that are simply not known in any extant Greek

108. The Hexapla of Origen addresses this and other realities and seeks to organize the problem, if not also (it is not clear) to offer a way forward for resolution.

109. Hill writes: "Chrysostom's purpose in offering such an array (of Greek translations in his Psalm commentary) to a congregation whom he faults for lack of basic biblical knowledge escapes us, unless it is to impress them with his erudition" (Robert C. Hill, *St. John Chrysostom: Commentary on the Psalms*, trans. and with an introduction by Robert C. Hill [Brookline, MA: Holy Cross Orthodox Press, 1998], 1:7). On the problem of sorting out the manifold Greek versions, we are not helped by Chrysostom's own missteps: "His quotation of Job 31:13–15 (in commenting on Psalm 4:1) in a form markedly different from both the Hebrew and a modern composite text of the Septuagint like Rahlfs's reminds us of the diversity of forms of the LXX current at the time" (Ibid., 6). "Reading to his listeners in one hit the four verses of 7–10 of Psalm 10 plus all the variants leaves us with a picture of a preacher with a mass of material to hand" (Ibid., 7).

110. Here it is clear that the claim that the church preferred a "Greek Bible" is manifestly in error. In the actual practice of working with a book like Psalms, the history of Christian interpretation in every age sees the natural problems introduced by a translation (Greek or Latin). In researching a volume on interpretation at Antioch, I have become aware of the *sui generis* character of many Greek readings in Theodore and his colleagues (some reflecting a special textual tradition, some closer to MT readings, some to large-scale Greek traditions identified as LXX).

translation.[111] Also, it rarely—probably never—quotes from a so-called apocryphal book as if this were on par with other Greek language versions of the more restricted Hebrew canon.[112]

What does it mean to speak of the Greek (or Hebrew) language "canons" of the OT as pointing to an open canon not fixed until the Christian era? If the implication is that the OT does not function as canonical Scripture until the church or synagogue later fixes its limits, this is to misunderstand the role of the church or synagogue in respect of how it handles its sacred inheritance (on this see below). The distinction maintained by Sundberg and others between theological and literary determinations in respect of canon cannot be sustained; his is simply a piece of historical speculation simplifying an enormously complex textual and canonical phenomenon, and one with roots in the very inception of the biblical books.[113]

It derives from this that a misunderstanding about the role of the OT in the New is frequently introduced. One cannot move from a notion of relative fixity or "openness" (in terms of scope or internal orders), much less the simple expedient/necessity of maintaining the same Greek language throughout the NT (the OT is not quoted in Hebrew in the Greek language NT), to a notion of secondary and subsequent canonical authority, imposed outside of the NT's own plain-sense depiction of the authority of the OT ("the Law and the Prophets").

---

111. The point is that to speak of "The Septuagint" could confuse and oversimplify—such a text would have to be critically reconstructed. The NT is a Greek text and the Bible it quotes is a translation. When people say the NT quotes "The Septuagint" what they mean is, the NT quotes a Greek OT that could in many cases go back to a single exemplar (to be critically reconstructed), but that also diverges from this, including some interesting readings that are closer to the MT as this eventuates. See the intriguing analysis of the use of the OT in Acts 15, undertaken by Richard Bauckham in *The Book of Acts in Its First Century Setting*, vol. 4, *The Book of Acts in Its Palestinian Setting*, ed. Bruce W. Winter (Grand Rapids: Eerdmans, 1995); see also Attridge on Hebrews's use of Ps. 40 in Harold W. Attridge, *A Commentary on the Epistle to the Hebrews*, Hermeneia (Philadelphia: Fortress, 1989); and Jobes and Silva, *Invitation to the Septuagint*.

112. See the discussion in Richard Bauckham, *Jude and the Relatives of Jesus in the Early Church* (Edinburgh: T&T Clark, 1990); and my essay "Two Testaments and the Failure of One Tradition-History," in *Figured Out*, 40–42.

113. See Jeremias's analysis of the literary and theological factors—these cannot be separated—that lie at the base of Amos's and Hosea's compositional history.

This final point is a crucial one to observe. I have pointed out in another context how confusing the argument about the alleged priority of the NT's assertions vis-à-vis the Old can be. Christ does not announce that the OT has an authority because he says so, but rather acknowledges its authority, claims it is about him, and distinguishes it from the "authoritative" statements made by men about it.[114] Neither does the church declare the limits of the OT canon for the first time, as if before then it existed "only as Scripture," and so required stabilization and a statement about its authority (now as "canon") for its first-time appearance in a broader canon of Christian Scripture. The NT declares the authority of the Old, and the apostolic witness to Christ is authoritative precisely because it is "in accordance with the Scriptures." The authority of both the NT and the Christian Scripture as a twofold witness is derived from the claims of the OT—claims presupposed in the NT and asserting themselves in the milieu from which its own composition, as the "apostles" half of "prophets and apostles," is coming about.

In a rather surprising quote given the source, Adolf von Harnack chided Lessing about the latter's mistaken assumptions regarding the authority of the Second Testament, the NT, as being derived from the church (which also rendered the NT problematic for Lessing; Lessing thought something like "unmediated" witness was or ought to be available and that would be for him authoritative "truth"— if one could but get their hands on it). Harnack wanted to emphasize the independent way the NT made its force felt.[115] He might have approached the matter as did Luther, who appealed dogmatically to the creedal confession concerning the testimony of the Holy Spirit as that testimony that gave the NT its *entirely independent and unconditioned authority*"[116]—an appeal which also grounded the OT's authority, both for the NT's confession as well as for the church

114. A paraphrase from Matthew might be: "listen to teachers when they speak as Moses, but do not follow what they teach nor act as they act"; on "you have heard that it was said," see my essay "Two Testaments" in *Figured Out*, 45. Compare the more technical work of Markus Bockmuehl, *Jewish Law in Gentile Churches* (Edinburgh: T&T Clark, 2000), 1–82.

115. Adolf von Harnack, *Bible Reading in the Early Church*, trans. J. R. Wilkinson (London: Williams & Norgate, 1912). See also my discussion of this with respect to N. T. Wright's work, in *Redemption*, 25–42.

116. Harnack, *Bible Reading*, 145, emphasis original.

("who spake by the prophets").[117] Harnack defended the "entirely independent and unconditioned authority" of the NT as derived from the OT's own specific and peculiar status. He states: "This was indeed only possible because the book [NT] at once took its place alongside the Old Testament, which occupied a position of absolute and unquestioned independence because it was more ancient than the Church."[118]

In part, then, Childs's appeal to the MT is not based upon an overweening concern for one Hebrew text with fixed boundaries and special internal order and a historically monolithic transmission prior to the New. Aspects of this description may well be true, but they require considerable nuance.[119] Rather, what is at stake is the canonical authority of the Hebrew Scriptures as foundational and antecedent to Christian claims, claims that have to do with accordance and fulfillment and not with first-time establishment. The christological grounding of this perspective is given in the NT, as Christ opens the Scriptures and shows them to be everywhere about himself (Luke 24 and others).[120]

Once this perspective is secured, it helps to account for the various rationales that then guided the church as it sought to make kindred claims for the New. Too often, however, this antecedent authority, its christological confirmation and clarification, and the character of them both as influencing the church's claims about the authority of the New are forgotten. This leads to an error of enormous irony: that the Scriptures of Israel become Christian Scripture only by action of the church or by claim of the NT by transmitting them in the material form of their Greek-language expression. This puts the matter precisely in reverse.

---

117. See Christine Helmer's insightful discussion "Luther's Trinitarian Hermeneutic."

118. Harnack, *Bible Reading*, 145.

119. See my own discussion in "Two Testaments," in *Figured Out*, 35–47; *Goodly Fellowship* (my concern in this work is in showing the stability of the Law and the Prophets as a canonical grammar, whatever the scope and order of the Writings; the *ketubim* exist as their own special library and their internal order and total number are not decisive for questions of canonical authority, on the same terms as the core grammar. One can properly speak of an "open canon" and mean both canonicity and a degree of fluidity in the total number and order of the Writings).

120. See the more detailed discussion of the use of the OT in the New and a theological evaluation of this distinctive in the chapters to follow.

Brief Postscript

Mention should be made in closing about the larger canon of the "Greek Bible" and the fact that this rubric often serves as an assertion that the MT lacks the additional books which would establish its authority for Christian purposes. Much is made of the circulation of additional books in the larger canon of the LXX, though usually the statements made lack a clear proportionality for argument's sake, and this is so at a number of key points.[121]

It is frequently stated that the NT's reference to "the Law and the Prophets" indicates that only two-thirds of the Hebrew Scriptures (Tanak) are "closed" in NT times.[122] Second, it is claimed that in the "open part" would be those books that circulate in the larger canon and that one can see clear evidence of these books being cited in the NT, on par with other books. Finally, it is said that the use of these books in the Christian church means that they are important books, widely read, seen as theologically decisive, and a critical sign that the "Christian canon" is not the MT.[123] From this the conclusion also follows that the canon of the OT is not closed until the church estimates this to be necessary, and this happens late (following the development of a Second Testament, whose authority and status are then translated to Israel's Scriptures). The result is, in the language of this argument, a "Greek Bible" for Christians.

We have chosen to look behind these details to interrogate what three such assertions *may actually assume about the status of the OT as an antecedent and independent authority*. At the end of the day, arguments mounted along the lines above are not just learned assertions (which lack proper proportionality); they are the means by which one may call into question the stability of the OT—whether in Greek or Hebrew language—as an authority for Christian purposes, prior to the development of the apostolic writings and toward which the authority of the NT seeks accordance.

It should be uncontestable that the density of citation of books from the Hebrew canon in the NT vastly overshadows even alleged

---

121. See Barr, *Concept*, 563–80.
122. Barton et al.
123. Barr, *Concept*, 576–80.

citations of non-Hebrew books, by a factor of enormous proportion. Arguing for an allusion here or background noise there, measured against the phenomenon of direct citation ("proof text"), ought in reality to warn against any effort to compare at all. Appeal to "Law and Prophets" for the purpose of showing that only two-thirds of the Tanak is "closed" has been quite clearly shown to be a speculation at best, and without secure warrant.[124] And we have seen that the tendency of the history of reception is to be conservative in respect of the Hebrew textual legacy. To put it differently, no Christian proponent of the "Greek Bible" cautions against appeals to the Hebrew *because the former has more books or because the NT cites it in a form that shows the Hebrew canon was not closed.* At that point, modern argument and ancient convention part company.

If there were indeed a larger and "open" canon of the OT, the paucity of reference in the NT to books in it would be staggering and require explanation. This observation is tantamount to a declaration that the additional books are somehow secondary and insecure, or poorly circulating, and so forth—for reasons we can only speculate about.[125] More economical is a view that the OT canon is relatively stable, with exceptions to this picture in the NT very few and proving the rule.[126] Such an observation has nothing to do with Protestant versus Catholic proclivities, ecumenical hopefulness, or whatever. Jerome did not invent a distinction between Hebrew and Greek books (the latter to be read for edification but not doctrine). At a number of levels and for several good reasons—not least the plain-sense witness of the NT itself—he observed one.

---

124. Most recently by Stephen B. Chapman, *Law and the Prophets*. See the earlier work by T. N. Swanson, "The Closing of the Collection of Holy Scriptures: A Study in the History of the Canonization of the Old Testament" (PhD diss., Vanderbilt University, 1970).

125. See Bauckham's careful discussion in *Jude and the Relatives of Jesus*.

126. On the stability of the Law and the Prophets, see Seitz, *Goodly Fellowship*; and Roger T. Beckwith, *The Old Testament Canon of the New Testament Church* (London: SPCK, 1985). Beckwith's argument for a single Genesis-to-Chronicles order has NT warrant in the "Abel to Zechariah" theme (Matt. 23:35; Luke 11:51), and in my view the influence of Chronicles on the shape of the Gospel of Matthew needs further study. I am less confident than Beckwith, however, on a single Genesis-to-Chronicles Hebrew exemplar for reasons explained in my new work, having to do with the character of primary associations in the Scriptures of Israel and a proper assessment of the *ketubim* (*Goodly Fellowship*).

In sum, the church did not bestow authority on the OT, but acknowledged it and explained its character for the church, following the dominical warrant. The church was the place where the confession was registered that the authority of the OT was from the Holy Spirit "who spake by the prophets." Following Augustine, a canonical approach will acknowledge the Holy Spirit's activity in both Hebrew and Greek canons, which guide and constrain the church's reflection and confession. What is more properly at issue is the antecedent and independent authority of the Scriptures of Israel, in accordance with which, in the earliest Easter confession, Christ died and rose again.

Canon as Witness

Speech-act theory may be a way to negotiate (or finesse) problems associated with divine and human authorship of Scripture, whose last uncomplicated expression may have been that of Calvin.[127] Modern biblical interpretation "complexified" the matter considerably, not just because it may have found itself allergic to claims of "divine authorship" in the wake of Kant. With the rise of modernity, the more compelling region of complexity was *human authorship itself*, as the various biblical books "gave up the ghost" of the human authors said to be authorizing them (Moses, Isaiah, Jonah, Daniel, Paul's Letter to the Ephesians, Colossians, etc.) and breathed their last.

A canonical approach, it has been argued, has detached itself from a view of human or authorial intentionality.[128] The situation has,

127. See Childs's discussion in *Struggle*, 209–13; cf. David L. Puckett, *John Calvin's Exegesis of the Old Testament* (Louisville: Westminster John Knox, 1995).

128. Lindbeck in the Childs 1998 Festschrift writes: "Even biblical scholars such as Childs and Hays assume that the canonical sense of Scripture is to be determined as much as possible without reference to what was intended by either God or its human authors" ("Postcritical Canonical Interpretation: Three Modes of Retrieval," in *Theological Exegesis: Essays in Honor of Brevard S. Childs*, ed. Christopher R. Seitz and Kathryn Greene-McCreight [Grand Rapids: Eerdmans, 1999], 48). I confess never to have heard this statement made in Childs, and certainly not with the kind of transparency this quote suggests. Lindbeck continues, "Fear of the intentional fallacy, it seems, prevents them from recognizing that their exegetical practice is (fortunately) full of appeals to authorial intention." Perhaps Hays runs afoul of intentional fallacy concerns, but it has

however, been seen to be far more complex than that.[129] One can indeed speak of "canonical intentionality" and find oneself back in the domain of the final form of a biblical book, with an "authorial intention"—to use the language of the debate at hand. Isaiah "authored" the book associated with him, or, as we shall prefer to say, the Holy Spirit "inspired" through Isaiah an intended word. Intentionality persists even as the older views of authorship have had to be adjusted to account for the unique character of biblical books, authors, and authorizing.

The problem of speech-act theory at this point is its level of abstraction, by virtue of introducing a philosophical construct to handle the theological problem of divine-human discourse.[130] The problem is also deeply historical, to put it in more concrete terms. It may be possible to say that God commandeers human language toward a specific intended end, but then to say practically nothing at all about the constitutive, historically real, indeed "elected and providentially chosen" manner of speaking through Moses and the prophets and Israel as such. Does the commandeering *depend upon prior, genuine, historical inspiration and human electing and acting*? What role does this dimension play? It would be an odd (if rather exalted) form of inspiration (speaking dogmatically) which insisted on divine intention and discourse, but which reduced the agents of that speaking to Origen's plucked instruments—now on the other side of the Enlightenment and with the aid of a philosophical insight about language and communication.

The canonical approach has not released itself from the historical dimension of inspiration. It has broadened this considerably to

---

not been a feature of Childs's discussion in any obvious sense I am aware of. It would be my argument that a canonical approach is a modern effort to rethink the relationship between human and divine authorship. Focus on the human author—on the right and on the left of the theological spectrum—fails adequately to deal with the surplus that results from divine inspiration, which in turns leads to an extension of the original proclamation as a truthful hearing of God's Word: both within the OT itself and as the NT hears the. OT in the light of Christ.

129. Christopher R. Seitz, "Changing Face," in *Word without End*, 80–82; Brett, *Biblical Criticism*; Noble, *Canonical Approach*; Barton, *Reading the Old Testament*.

130. Nicholas Wolterstorff, *Divine Discourse: Philosophical Reflections on the Claim That God Speaks* (Cambridge: Cambridge University Press, 1995).

include the entire process and especially the consolidation of that process consisting in the "final form of the text."[131]

There is an inspired and coherent Word of God to Israel and to the world, which arises from the historical speech of Amos and Hosea, in the canonical form of the Twelve, but which entails a "history" they saw only partially (and which God over time was revealing in his history). The canonical approach seeks to describe that process, and "success" is less in getting every diachronic detail right (that would be a wrong tack and would end in an "eclipse of biblical narrative"—to use Frei's language) and more in accounting for the present structure and presentation of the Book of the Twelve, to choose but one example, as it now sits before us (or in front of us). The historical dimension of God's real speech with real men and women is not eliminated. Amos preached a message to the northern kingdom and to Amaziah the priest at Bethel, and he likely did this before Hosea and probably certainly before Joel. A canonical approach wishes to understand this inspired speech in all its historical and human particularity. Those who shape the books associated with them and the collection of books within which they now reside did not treat them like "plucked instruments" or like the girl (was it a girl?) on the swing whose sweet (but fortuitous) singing converted Augustine.[132] At the same time, they did seek to hear in their words the abiding and accomplishing Word of God, and so human authorship was always tied up with divine authorship and with the providentiality of the Holy Spirit's knowledge and work.

Calvin may have been able to move easily between these two realms, but for him the nature of the task was far easier (however we judge

---

131. Lindbeck's criticism is at this point over the clarity of what Childs is achieving. If he were clearer, would this meet with Lindbeck's approval? He writes of Childs, "his primary vocation is to interpret Scripture for the canonical shaping of its content. To lump this highly diverse content together with the rubric 'witness,' however, does not add clarity to his task" ("Postcritical Canonical Interpretation," 34n7). My response would be to question whether a "highly diverse content" is as Lindbeck characterizes it; others have viewed the canonical shaping identified by Childs as *too* tidy. Canonical intentionality can more easily connect to a view of "witness" than Lindbeck seems to suggest. See below.

132. The account assumes a signal position in the evaluation of divine discourse provided by Nicholas Wolterstorff in *Divine Discourse: Philosophical Reflections on the Claim That God Speaks* (Cambridge: Cambridge University Press, 1995), 1–8.

his success at it). The biblical books and their human authors had yet to come apart (though Calvin is beginning to sense that a problem exists). It is difficult to say whether the ease of movement seen in him, between the realms of divine and human inspiration, turned on such an economical and as yet uncomplicated view of biblical authorship. What is easier to say is that, with the rise of critical methods, and with a severe complication introduced into this tidy picture, the organic character of inspiration came undone, and with a vengeance.[133]

Speech-act theory may feel it can enter this realm of confusion and tidy it all up.[134] Whether it was intended for this kind of operation is another question altogether; I rather doubt it. The biblical witness is carrying too much historicality in its bosom, and it is difficult to see how this dimension will not get shortchanged by philosophical constructions being deployed, even if for good reasons and with a prudential concern to guard against something going wrong. A canonical approach retains a specific concern with historicality, and it judges the season of critical inquiry we have been in to be one that both cannot be avoided and that also brought with it a set of concerns that shed light as well as shade—even at times pitch darkness.

Providentiality covers the seasons of interpretation as well as the seasons of original, historical inspiration. The season we are presently in has raised the acute question of historicality and is sensitive to the

133. See chapters to follow. When, for example, Calvin says that David "prophesied Christ" in Ps. 2, does he mean that David's mental apparatus as human agent grasped the details associated with Jesus's future coming and life, or does he mean that God inspired David to speak about such details truthfully and without an attendant need on Calvin's part to explain how that could be so via the human agent divorced from that divine intention? It is difficult to avoid the impression that the problem does not have the same urgency or contour for Calvin as it will later in the eighteenth century and into the modern period, where the category "anachronism" becomes more compelling.

134. See the discussion of Brevard S. Childs, "Speech-Act Theory and Biblical Interpretation," *SJT* 58 (2005): 375–92. He concludes, "Wolterstorff's application of speech-act theory to biblical interpretation is deeply flawed" (391). He then continues, "I would also hope that it has become apparent just how high are the theological stakes in this debate. Many of us can recall, often with much pain, that generations of Reformed theologians, especially in North America, were led astray in the late nineteenth and early twentieth centuries when Charles Hodge and B. B. Warfield sought to defend Christian orthodoxy within the framework of Baconian philosophy. It would be sad indeed if a new generation of evangelicals would once again commit themselves uncritically to a new and untested philosophical model, allegedly designed for the twenty-first century" (391–92).

sheer temporal distance of the events the Holy Spirit occasioned in prophets and apostles both. New is newer than Old, to be sure, but the relative character of that cries out for resolution. Käsemann spoke of "proximity to reality" as guaranteed by historical methods.[135] A canonical approach insists that the inspired witness is building a bridge to us, which is sure and which has our seasons in mind. The character of canonical Scripture is precisely that it overcomes one account of past-present-future and so anticipates the reader and seeks to situate the reader in its own account of time. We are not prophets or apostles, but the canon appreciates this reality with all its witnessing majesty, as we are brought fully into the range of the Holy Spirit's work by virtue of the canon's shape and character as witness.[136]

Childs has used the general rubric "witness" to organize in an underdetermined way the genre of scriptural testimony. "Divine discourse" has been viewed as a hopeful improvement on this genre by Lindbeck.[137] Lindbeck likewise contrasts "witness" in the canonical hermeneutics with a third "classic" approach (his language), which he associates with Richard Hays and others ("reading for narrative world").[138] It is not the place here to comment on the taxonomy or the way in which both Childs and Barth fare in such a description.[139]

Witness has to its credit the possibility, as a "classic approach," of attaching to older dogmatic insights. Chief among these is the work of the Holy Spirit. The Holy Spirit "witnesses" to the Father and the Son and so gives a truthful trinitarian account whose purpose is to order our lives in his body. As Luther argued in another

135. See the discussion in Seitz, *Figured Out*, 39–44.

136. The phrase "we are not prophets or apostles" is Childs's. See my discussion in *Word without End*, 102–9, and in chapter 2 below.

137. See his essay in "Postcritical Canonical Interpretation." He calls this "interpreting for authorial discourse."

138. The phrase he uses, "Interpretation for Narrationally Structured Symbolic Worlds," is more ambitious, if not more problematic ("Postcritical Canonical Interpretation," 33). Hays finds himself rubbing elbows with Wayne Meeks and others here, and not just the Karl Barth he hoped to meet in his "strange new world."

139. Lindbeck says, for example, of Barth, "It should be observed that the Bible on the verbal level is for Barth chiefly 'God's word in written form' rather than 'witness.' That this verbalization is not in accord with the content of Barth's position is, however, strongly argued by Wolterstorff" ("Postcritical Canonical Interpretation," 34n7)—and it would appear that Lindbeck is in agreement with this view.

context, the OT has an authority grounded in the succinct creedal claim that the Holy Spirit spoke by the prophets. For Luther, this meant that David could actually see into the divine mystery and by the Holy Spirit could describe the relations between Father and Son in the inner trinitarian life—this all accomplished by the semantics of Hebrew language. What was at stake in this elaborate account was the authority of the OT deeply precedent to the church's recognition and confession of it, crucial though that would be, because grounded in the reality of God himself.[140]

For our age, less controversial than Luther's exegesis ought to be his claim to understand how the OT Scriptures do their work. Historical agents are inspired to speak of things—to Israel, in Israel, from Israel—that both pertain to their day and also pertain to things the Holy Spirit alone can see and bear witness to, as an extension of what is vouchsafed to them.

One problem of appeal to "narrative world" is, in the end, "just whose world?" Typically, for normative purposes, this world will end up in the hands of someone like Richard Hays, "the narrative world of Paul," who is then taken to be a normative model for Christian exegesis and faith and life. Who could dispute the sincerity and commendable character of this?

The problem is that, in the realm of a biblical theology of the Christian Scriptures as a twofold witness, the OT threatens to be swallowed up into Paul's confessions and construals about it (or in an imaginative reconstruction of a narrative world said to be influencing him, by deduction).[141] This narrative world is an abstraction derived by recourse to historical tools, and it exists apart from the canonical form of the Pauline Letter collection and the influence this form has on interpretation.[142] Apart from the problem of reifying such a "narrative world," it is also not clear whether Paul would accept the laurels bestowed on him. Why should his "narrative world" (as

---

140. Helmer, "Luther's Trinitarian Hermeneutic." See now also Heinrich Assel, "Der Name Gottes bei Martin Luther. Trinität und Tetragramm—ausgehend von Luthers Auslegung des fünften Psalms," *EvT* 64 (2004): 363–78. I have an extended treatment of this in the entry on "The Trinity in the Old Testament" for Oxford University Press (forthcoming).

141. See chapters 2–4 below.

142. See Childs, *Church's Guide*.

reconstructed by Hays) speak over the manifold witness of the OT said to be generating it? What for Hays is a narrative world exposed by his careful analysis of Paul or the Gospels[143] is a reduction of what can be said about the witnessing work of the Holy Spirit "who spake by the prophets" in the OT scriptural attestation. The OT generates its own christological and trinitarian doctrine, using its own specific idiom. Paul taps into this potentiality. He does not exhaust it, nor is his example at this local point the warrant for a wider choosing of the NT's use of the OT, thus restricting the church's tapping into the literal sense of the OT at its maximal length and breadth, on the terms of its own delivery, as Christian Scripture.

Conclusions

In this chapter I have sought to give an account of the canonical approach that does justice to its extraordinary range. Much more could be said, of course. Childs is unique, to my mind, because he has worked at a sophisticated and creative level in areas that are usually the domain of one scholar only, and he has done so with an amazingly integrative touch. New Testament, Old Testament, church history, reception history, text criticism, theology, and the practice of Christian ministry are but a sample of what he has sought to control and integrate. The canonical approach entails very specific concerns regarding interpretation, but these concerns have been at the service of Christian theology at the most basic and the most comprehensive levels. A canonical approach is an effort to read texts in a fresh way, to engage in questions of historical, theological, practical, and conceptual significance, and to keep the lines of communication between the Testaments, between the Bible and theology, and between them both and the church, open and responsive.

I have not dwelt in great detail on matters of historicity or the final form of the text, and I have only given a brief analysis in the overview above. The explanation for this is that I have written a good deal on these topics in other places and feel that the resources for discussing these topics intelligently are widely available. I also tentatively con-

---

143. Hays, "Can the Gospels Teach Us How to Read the Old Testament?"

clude that in a good many ways, Childs's proposals on final form and on matters of historical reference have actually met with consent (or curiosity and respect) and are presently bearing fruit in commentary treatments and in other areas. I suspect forty years ago no one would have imagined that treatments of Isaiah that did not deal with the challenge of the book as a totality would be peripheral and minority accounts. Even Childs himself did not push a detailed canonical approach in areas like the Book of the Twelve, though at present scholars as diverse as Jeremias, Nogalski, Sweeney, House, Schart, and Steck would be dumbfounded if this approach were not pursued with diligence, and if the delicate matters of historical reference were not front and center, and requiring a careful assessment. Work in the Psalter is similar and one could go on indefinitely at this point. Even in NT studies, where the resistance has been manifest (by design or by omitting to notice), canonical approaches and concern with the effect of arrangements and final literary presentation are making inroads. New Testament studies are often content to stay with specific fixed and well-known issues, and to cover them again and again, perhaps aided by some new data recently available, and there is a kind of innate conservatism in the field that is hard to account for. The sociology of knowledge and its relationship to NT studies is a topic of enormous interest, to my mind, but it cannot be pursued here.

With a greater appreciation of the effect and sophistication of the final form—a sophistication made even clearer on the other side of our seasons of historical reading—we are now in a position to dismantle the single most decisive claim made by historical-critical reading. And as much as some have sought to describe the historical-critical method as an ingredient in the Reformation, and its indispensable genius, gift, and fruit, this conclusion is far from clear. For the disentangling of general Renaissance and Enlightenment cultural developments from appeals to things like *sola Scriptura* is exceedingly fraught and requires multivolume treatments in the history of ideas with deep learning and enormous sensitivity to the challenge to hand. As time passes and one comes to terms with the exegesis of men like Luther and Calvin, it seems clearer that they inhabit a universe quite distinct, if not unbridgeable, from the one that historical-critical methods bequeathed us in their heyday. Indeed, what would "the Reformers" *really* make of projects like dating the Yahwist, or the Q phenomenon, or even anodyne accounts of the history of Israel or the Greco-Roman milieu—areas in which we know more than the prophets or apostles themselves, for what that may be worth.

The decisive claim of historical-critical methods, to be able to provide an appreciation of the historical dimension of the Bible never before available, also meant a Promethean intuition that what had gone before was inherently limited because it lacked proper historical fact-finding, or just old-fashioned because it was premodern and so unable to tackle the tasks at hand. The canonical approach has not turned its back on the findings of historical-critical inquiry, but it has put these under a light and asked what is really being said that helps with interpretation of the literal sense of the text. Given the season in which canonical approaches work, it must be no surprise that a canonical appreciation of the final form is not the same thing as what Thomas Aquinas described as "the literal sense" in Psalm 21 [MT 22]. But the point is: a canonical approach can detect something like a kindred set of concerns linking the reading of Aquinas and its own sense of what is crucial in interpretation, and *it is persuaded that this capacity is crucial to its own success as a method for our day, because of and not in spite of historical-critical questions.*

It is for this reason that in the above I have chosen to look in greater detail at matters of (1) the relationship between the Testaments, including text-critical considerations, (2) the possibility of "doctrinal lenses" (or, the obverse, the impossibility of theologically neutral reading), and (3) biblical theology. In my judgment, because of the concerns of dealing with a two-testament scriptural witness, a canonical approach has had to make sensitive forays into the area of text criticism. It has done this not because it seeks to give some overstated priority to the Hebrew (Masoretic) text, but because a proper understanding of the relationship between the Testaments, as a piece of Christian theology, demands assuring that the choices are not made too stark. Of course, the Christian Bible has circulated with fuller and narrower reckonings of books ("the Apocrypha" et al.). What is at issue is not a (relatively interesting) piece of church history, but instead treating the relationship between the two Testaments of Scripture, for the purposes of Christian theological reflection, in a flexible and nonmonolithic fashion. Efforts to reify a "Septuagint" often come in the name of seeking to prioritize the NT's hearing of the Old—where said "Septuagint" is alleged to be crucial—over a sensitive account of how the OT actually does Christian theology from its own plain sense. That is why the issue is crucial from the standpoint of canonical approach: because of the need to account for the OT as Christian Scripture, where its own trinitarian doctrinal potential is not constrained by a new trend in historical-theological NT studies. What one sees in the history of interpretation is a genuine sensitivity to the "plus" the OT offers in the realm of basic doctrinal reflection, and a canonical approach wants to be sure that the truth of that basic intuition is not lost in the name of a biblical theology generated chiefly on the back of historical-critical developments of the past two centuries.

As for the second topic, doctrinal predisposition, what Levenson has shown in his discussion of Brueggemann, and in his own way, in Brueggemann's analysis of James Barr, indicates that it is simply impossible to defer in any honest way the very necessary movement, back and forth, between plain-sense reading and a larger theological account of God and his relationship to the dual witness of Christian Scripture. In my judgment, canonical approaches have foregrounded this concern, and rightly, precisely because Christian interpretation will confess that one cannot read the Testaments apart from one another, and that because of this, first-order doctrinal claims will and must surface. Here Brueggemann, Levenson, and Childs actually all agree, even as they go their own ways, or start with different concerns and contexts. In the case of canonical approaches, the coincidence with postmodern and reader-response instincts is largely just that. All this means that the long and diverse history of interpretation of the Bible is no longer annexed in the name of theology-free reading, or due to the enthusiasms, now waning, of an objective historical approach.

The canonical approach, with its capacity to listen to, appreciate, and penetrate to the abiding theological concerns of a long history of interpretation, now has a long horizon stretching out in front of itself. Because it has not made Promethean claims on the order of older historical analysis, in respect of the inadequacies of the history of biblical interpretation, and because it has been prepared to make adjustments and acknowledge blindspots and attenuations,[144] the canonical approach will always have as its chief task the theological interpretation of the plain-sense witness of two Testaments, and that task is unending. It is hard to imagine what the next season will throw up, under God, as its main challenge. History has been the ingredient most calling out for attention in our past season, and a canonical approach has, to my mind, handled that challenge with proportion and insight.

The area calling out for greatest clarity, at least in the guild of biblical scholarship, is just what is meant by the turn to *theological interpretation*. I have chosen in this chapter to focus on what several popular NT scholars are presently interested in, which is accounting for the role of the OT (Hebrew Bible) in generating NT thought, exegesis, and even ecclesiology. All of this is quite hopeful, and it arguably benefits from the inroads made by a canonical approach to Scripture—*but only or chiefly on the OT side of the canon.* This deficit must be corrected, for the result could be serious: the OT could function in its final form, for theological purposes, but what Childs has meant by "canonical shape" could become nothing more than a piece of reception history, seen from the standpoint of a NT utilization, theorized by recourse to a standard kit of historical-critical tools now put to a new purpose by NT scholarship.

More crucially of concern, and we have dwelt on this above, is the threat posed by using the second witness's theological exegesis of the Scriptures of Israel, or a historical reconstruction of the narrative world it is said to be impressing upon key NT figures, as a normative category of Christian theology. The threat is potent because so very subtle. New Testament use of the OT is indeed a species of what might properly be considered biblical theology. But it is important to reiterate that Christian theological reflection on the OT has a life

144. Having finished writing a commentary on Isaiah, Childs writes in the preface of his next published work: "I have recently finished a technical, modern commentary on the book of Isaiah. The task of treating the entire book of sixty-six chapters was enormous, but in addition, the commentary had necessitated restricting the scope of the exposition. That entailed omitting the history of interpretation and relegating many important hermeneutical problems to the periphery of the exegesis. *After the commentary had been completed, I was painfully aware that many of the central theological and hermeneutical questions in which I was most interested had not been adequately addressed*" (*Struggle*, ix, emphasis added).

proper to itself. That this has fallen out and become largely a species of history-of-religion is a sad fact traceable to developments in the wake of historical-critical inquiry. Correcting this through appeal to a "canonical shape" is not intended to encourage a reinstatement of the OT, now as a piece of reception-historical utilization seen from the standpoint of a NT historical analysis. This improperly delimits the OT from functioning as a major doctrinal source for Christian reflection on God, and obscures or forecloses on the ontological thinking necessary for understanding Christ's work in accordance with an entire scriptural witness. It also releases NT scholarship from the obligation to think through what it means to read the second witness *as a canonical witness* and to reflect theologically on the entire shape of the NT before attempting biblical theology in the comprehensive sense.

And here the turn to the prior history of interpretation will serve a welcome purpose, not just for reading the OT theologically, but also for reminding ourselves how the OT and NT *together do theology.* Such an examination will not serve to give us role models to imitate step-by-step for our day: that would be driving with the rearview mirror. What the history of interpretation teaches us is how certain critical interpretative instincts come into play when a variety of factors are demanding constant monitoring and attention, history being but one of these. The vast doctrinal potential of the OT in an earlier history of reflection serves as a warning not to believe that the best way to hear the Old is either through historical questions primarily or by letting the NT filter out what is most crucial on this score. On the other side of our great experiment in historical acuity, it is time to take stock and be sure that what we are discovering actually aids us in the task of hearing the plain sense and of relating that sense to the larger figural landscape of God's work in Israel and in Christ, across a dual scriptural witness. History will not evacuate itself in such an endeavor. It will find its proper place as God has intended, by virtue of learning all over again just what the word "history" actually means.

We take up in the chapters that follow the concerns articulated here at the close of this evaluation of the canonical approach, especially the use of the OT in the New. The term "rule of faith" has also found its way into recent accounts of canon and theological interpretation. Because we view a proper assessment of this rule as crucial for the theological handling of the OT at a time when the New is under construction, we will conclude the present study with an appraisal of the term's use in the ante-Nicene period. It is to be hoped that the rule's use in the early period will help us understand and appreciate the theological contribution of the Scriptures of Israel, and especially as this emerges without concern for the NT's own hearing of the Old. Only in this way will the centrality of the exegesis of Proverbs 8:22–31, for example, find explanation, as arguably one of the most significant testimonies to the identity of Christ in the early church, which at the same time transpires without extensive NT development or appeals to the use of the OT in the New.

2

BIBLICAL THEOLOGY AND IDENTIFICATION WITH CHRISTIAN SCRIPTURE

"We Are Not Prophets or Apostles"

This chapter will look at the question of identification by the Christian church with the NT and OT. It seeks to raise basic introductory questions and to provoke general reflection on assumptions about the specifically two-testament witness of Christian Scripture and how we relate to this material given the character and form of the witness. It questions whether it is too simple a matter to say that the church identifies with the NT more naturally than the OT. This of course raises the question as to just what is meant by identification as such; the phrase "we are not prophets or apostles" locates the issue by distinguishing between kinds of revelatory perspectives within the canon and then contrasting these both with the church's own providential location.[1] The chapter also questions whether identifications

---

1. Childs, *Biblical Theology of the Old and New Testaments*, 70–79, 242–44, 378–83. In 1970 Childs could put the issue in this way:

are properly made with apostolic witnesses in the NT, specifically at the level of their use of the antecedent witness of the OT. Finally, it urges that use of the OT by the NT is not a substitute for Christian theological reflection on the OT in its own formal integrity.

At the conclusion of this study we will devote a chapter to the rule of faith in the early church. This is because it is important to understand how the Scriptures of Israel functioned when the canonical NT was still in formation. At such a moment, it will be argued, the rule of faith was crucial especially for stipulating the character of the authority of the Scriptures of Israel, the "Law and the Prophets" (that is, what will in time be called the "Old Testament") for the formulation of basic Christian belief (e.g., Jesus Christ died and rose again "in accordance with the Scriptures" [1 Cor. 15:3–4 NRSV]; "Jesus Christ is the eternal Word of God"). At this particular moment in the church's life—with a single scriptural authority and a second developing one—it is easier to grasp how the church understood its relationship to the Scriptures of Israel in a very direct, if complex and controversial, way.[2] When the NT eventually takes form, this relationship to the OT is unchanged in the early period, and if anything the nature of the relationship be-

---

It is a widespread error to recognize the historical conditioning of the Old Testament, but to conceive of the New Testament as "the timeless interpretation" that has transcended historical limitations. The modern Biblical theologian cannot share uncritically the witness of the New Testament any more than he can that of the Old. His context is just as different from that of the New as it is from that of the Old. The formation of a canon of Scriptures is a recognition of the need for a context, different from both Testaments, in which the Christian Church continues to wrestle in every new age with the Living God who continues to confront his people through the ancient testimony of the prophets and apostles. (Brevard S. Childs, *Biblical Theology in Crisis* [Philadelphia: Westminster, 1970], 113)

As we shall see below, certain recent efforts to give precise historical contextualization to the use of the OT in the NT also result in a hermeneutical privileging that is, ironically given its claim to historical precision, its own kind of "timeless interpretation." The NT becomes the ultimate phase of reception history, to be directly imitated by the church, instead of a canonical witness in complex relationship with the first witness, that is, the one that gives it foundation and continues to speak forth in its own special idiom of Christian theological reflection. That the NT uses and depends upon the first witness is not a warrant for a developmental understanding that threatens to void the ontological theological claims of the first. That is the thesis of the present work.

2. On the character of the scriptural witness of Law and Prophets, see Seitz, *The Goodly Fellowship of the Prophets: The Achievement of Association in Canon Formation* (Grand Rapids: Baker Academic, 2009).

comes crucially a matter of understanding the way two Testaments are united in delivering the subject matter appropriate to them both, not of privileging one witness over another on a developmental understanding. That such an understanding has become popular since the rise of historicism has frustrated our ability to properly understand how the church relates to the Scriptures in their specifically two-testament form. At stake in particular are the ontological claims of Scripture in respect to the nature of God and the way the OT is fundamental in comprehending them.[3] The church, it will be argued, is differently proximate in relationship to the respective testament of Christian Scripture, and in no way is it possible to think of the Second Testament either without the First, or as more decisive than the First, when it comes to basic talk or dogmatic reflection about God, creation, the church, and the world.

Biblical theology in the modern period has had a specific concern for the way the church appreciates the character of Christian Scripture as twofold in its witness. It is necessary therefore to enter into the discussion of the church's relationship to Scripture through the lens of efforts to do biblical theology in recent generations.

What Is Biblical Theology? The Canon and Biblical Theology

It will have to be conceded at the outset that "biblical theology" is an elastic and imprecise term. An assessment of recent efforts to think theologically and hermeneutically about the Bible as efforts to do "biblical theology" will therefore face the question: Just what kind of biblical theology does this or that recent effort seek to represent? Many approaches could be said to think of themselves as making a contribution to biblical theology or as embodying this as such, and still leave to the side just what kind of biblical theology this results in. I will seek to bring clarity to biblical theology as a term by speaking of a canonical approach to the discipline and will seek to distinguish

---

3. See Gerald Bray, "The Church Fathers and Biblical Theology," in *Out of Egypt: Biblical Theology and Biblical Interpretation*, Scripture and Hermeneutics Series 5, ed. C. Bartholomew et al. (Grand Rapids: Zondervan, 2004), 23–40.

this kind of approach from others that want to think theologically about the NT, OT, or both together.

Indeed, it also should be clarified up front that this chapter seeks to evaluate biblical theology from the standpoint of efforts that place in the foreground *the character of the relationship between the Testaments* as that aspect which is most central in any biblical theological treatment. This will help focus the evaluation. Left to the side will be approaches from history-of-religion or tradition-history, insofar as these may be said to soften the sharpness (or dispute its character altogether) of the formal distinguishing feature of Christian Scripture as consisting of two discrete Testaments. Christian theological reflection on the canon of Scripture as twofold in essence is the main task of biblical theology.[4] One can say this without rendering a judgment about the appropriateness of such approaches, and that is the position of this chapter in a more restricted sense.[5]

That considerable confusion exists about what is meant by the term "biblical theology" is readily apparent, and is itself frequently the subject of reflection. James Dunn is representative in opening a recent treatment of the topic by indicating that the term "biblical" alone could mean several different, if not contradictory, things.[6] He speaks of works by Hübner and Stuhlmacher (which describe themselves as biblical theology) as efforts that foreground the use of the OT in the New as ingredient ("a major explanatory key") in biblical theological reflection.[7] This is to be contrasted with efforts, like that of B. S. Childs, which mean by "biblical" a completed Christian Bible made up of two entities, which are the subject of theological reflection in

---

4. On the problems of tradition-history, see Seitz, "Scripture Becomes Religion: Two Testaments and the Failure of One Tradition-History," in *Figured Out: Typology and Providence in Christian Scripture* (Louisville: Westminster John Knox, 2001).

5. See the extended discussion in James Barr, who prefers a history-of-religion emphasis (*The Concept of Biblical Theology: An Old Testament Perspective* [London: SCM, 1999]).

6. Dunn, "The Problem of 'Biblical Theology,'" in *Out of Egypt*, 172–84. An earlier version appeared as "Das Problem 'Biblische Theologie,'" in C. Dohmen and T. Söding, eds., *Eine Bibel—Zwei Testamente: Positionen Biblischer Theologie* (Paderborn: Ferdinand Schöningh, 1995), 179–93.

7. Hans Hübner, *Biblische Theologie des Neuen Testaments*, 3 vols. (Göttingen: Vandenhoeck & Ruprecht, 1990–95); Peter Stuhlmacher, *Biblische Theologie des Neuen Testaments*, 2 vols. (Göttingen: Vandenhoeck & Ruprecht, 1990–95).

their own right and together.[8] Yet even this distinction proves to be of limited use when Dunn proceeds to describe the former as meaning by "biblical" the OT: "But since for the New Testament writers there was as yet no New Testament as such, 'Bible' here denotes only the (Jewish) Scriptures."[9] This is probably pressing things too far, since what Hübner and Stuhlmacher surely mean is: biblical theology is NT theological reflection that makes some serious effort to understand the role of the OT insofar as the New uses it to do theology or uses it more generally in the delivery of its subject matter. If this be true, then "biblical" does not mean OT (or Jewish Scriptures) at all, but rather that how the OT makes theological sense is primarily (Stuhlmacher) or only (Hübner) on the basis of how the New brokers this. Biblical theology is NT theology. On this account, a clear decision is being made to do biblical theology and to have in the foreground the nature of the relationship between the Testaments, in which the New's voice is the means of hearing the Old, in either what is seen by the author to be a very robust and constructive sense, or of one that is more restricted on this front.[10]

In the 1992 volume *New Directions in Biblical Theology* one sees a similar set of problems articulated by the contributors.[11] The nature of the problem is similar because the volume consists entirely of treatments of "biblical theology" undertaken by NT scholars. They want to speak about the "biblical theology" of various NT books, and chiefly as these NT books use the Scriptures of Israel to do theology. A. J. M. Wedderburn is not alone in sensing the problem of using a term like "biblical theology" to speak of the NT's appropriation of the Scriptures (of Israel).[12] Anticipating from a very different direction some

8. Childs, *Biblical Theology of the Old and New Testaments.*

9. Dunn, "Problem of 'Biblical Theology,'" 173.

10. See Stulhmacher's own analysis, "Biblische Theologie des Neuen Testaments— eine Skizze," in *Eine Bibel,* 275–90. Compare T. Holz, "Neutestamentliche Theologie im Horizont der ganzen Schrift. Peter Stuhlmachers Biblischer Theologie des Neuen Testaments," in B. Janowski, N. Lohfink, eds., *Religionsgeschichte Israels oder Theologie des Alten Testaments, Jahrbuch für Biblische Theologie* 10 (Neukirchen-Vluyn: Neukirchener, 1995), 233–45.

11. Sigfred Pederson, ed., *New Directions in Biblical Theology: Papers for the Aarhus Conference, 16–19 September 1992* (Leiden: Brill, 1994).

12. A. J. M. Wedderburn, "Paul and 'Biblical Theology,'" in *New Directions,* 24–46.

of the concerns of Childs, he notes the inappropriate or anachronistic use of a term like "biblical theology" when applied to "Paul and his contemporaries," because "they knew as authoritative writings only those of the Old Testament, however its extent was defined at the time."[13] Over against Hübner's and Stuhlmacher's congenial usage, Wedderburn sees a potential problem with the term, since it could well be the case that " 'biblical theology' is defined as an attempt to tie together both Testaments as one 'Bible' and to seek the unity within it."[14] Leaving aside the final qualification, we see again something of the problem pointed out by Dunn, but now without defining "biblical" along the confusing lines he does in his effort to disentangle Childs from Hübner and Stuhlmacher. For Wedderburn, "biblical" does not refer to NT theological reflection in its own right and as it uses the OT, but follows along the more natural sense of the term, that is, having to do with the entire biblical witness, OT and NT.

In the same volume, Otfried Hofius speaks of doing biblical theology "in the light of the Letter to the Hebrews."[15] This points in a rather different direction than what has been described thus far, because biblical theology is not (even anachronistically) what the NT does with the OT, but only something that happens "in the light" of such a description—and which indeed may depart from it, as it does in the case of Hofius's own understanding. Note the way the following sentence is formulated: "Biblische Theologie, die den Spuren des Hebräerbriefes folgen wollte, wäre zweifellos eine dezidiert *kritische* Disziplin."[16] Hebrews demonstrates a decidedly critical attitude toward the OT it reads, for which Hofius gives the description, "eine erstaundliche hermeneutische Kuhnheit"—and one might well conclude, as does Hofius, not just hermeneutical but also theological audacity. Biblical theology, then, follows with a critical analysis of its own, and it may judge the critical decisions found in the Letter to the Hebrews as themselves in need of critical biblical theological evaluation. Biblical theology "follows the tracks of the Letter to the

---

13. Ibid., 41.
14. Ibid.
15. Otfried Hofius, "Biblische Theologie im Lichte des Hebräerbriefes," in *New Directions*, 108–25.
16. Ibid., 124.

Hebrews," but it then marks out its own terrain and goal. In such an evaluation, the OT ceases to have its voice constrained by the (sympathetic or critical) use made of it by individual authors in the NT, for biblical theology will have to judge the character of that witness from the standpoint of Christian theological reflection on some other basis. For Hofius, as he understands this, one must now proceed from "historisch-kritischen Voraussetzungen."[17]

It will be necessary to return to this essay shortly and to what is meant by an appeal to "historical-critical presuppositions," and also what this looks like in Hofius's actual deploying. It will be important to understand the basis upon which he brings a critical eye to the exegesis of Hebrews and how he is able to do that. For now what is to be noted is the way in which "biblical theology," undertaken even from the standpoint of the NT's use of the OT, diverges from one proponent to the next. Even within a shared commitment to understanding the NT's theological use of the OT as somehow central to biblical theology, very different accounts are possible. It is not just a matter of terminological imprecision, even as that does exist, but of a more substantive evaluative stance, especially as this entails the relationship between historical description and theological significance, and an assessment of how the voice of the OT actually does Christian theological work.

The Obviousness of Identification with the New Testament over the Old Testament

Due in part to an understanding of the priority of the NT for Christian theology, and the self-evidence of this, and therefore, of necessity, of understanding the OT as leaning toward the NT or being heard chiefly on the basis of it for theological purposes, it should be possible to conclude firmly that the church stands in a more direct relationship to the NT than the OT. It can be noted in passing that the self-evidence of this is of such a nature that it has precluded any genuine inquiry into just how the church may be thought to relate itself to the NT (so, does one "identify" with

17. Ibid., 125.

Paul and his use of the Scriptures or with the audience Paul is addressing as apostle? how does the Pauline corpus relate to the NT canon more broadly?). This explains for example why something like a "biblical theology of the New Testament" is presumed to be clear language for an obvious project. The fact of there being two Testaments, and the naturalness of the assumption that the First is in a more complex relationship to the church than the Second, has been allowed to run interference for the fact that in reality *we must think very carefully indeed about the way in which the church is related to the NT canon more narrowly*. On the face of it, it is surely true that the church of Jesus Christ may be thought of as more naturally affiliated with the church depicted in the NT, when this is set over against the OT. But even my statement of affiliation and identification requires testing against other possibilities.[18] How this relatedness takes form actually differs markedly from interpreter to interpreter, and at a specific level, not much is genuinely said that sheds light on the character of the claim. Moreover, for some the NT declares its subject matter at the level of basic existential communication, and talk about the church encroaches on this universality and probably says too much about the NT as

18. So, is this to do with temporal proximity (we are closer to the New than the Old), religious development (the New speaks of a better religion than the Old), cultural realities (most Christians are not Jews), or just a general sense of progress and development, for which modernity wins the prize? Bray helpfully points out that for the early church, older realities were taken to be more impressive, and to carry greater weight, than newer ones. Consider the prominence of Prov. 8 and Gen. 1 in the first four centuries of Christian theological reflection (Prov. 8's centrality is all the more astonishing, measured against modern instincts, when one considers how little a role it plays in the NT). And if the economic is not to cancel out the ontological in basic Christian theology, can one not see that the OT is significant in its own right, because it tells of the work of Christ in latent if not patent terms (this is the view of Irenaeus, Tertullian, and Origen, and later of Augustine in his famous expression) and grounds trinitarian logic (see Richard Bauckham, *God Crucified: Monotheism and Christology in the New Testament* [Carlisle: Paternoster, 1998]; C. Kavin Rowe, "Biblical Pressure and Trinitarian Hermeneutics," *ProEccl* 11, no. 3 [2002]: 295–312). If this dimension be granted, then the "advance" of the NT is in part including the outsider in the work of Christ in the dispensation of Israel and bringing the voice of the OT into the life of the church. Luther could speak of the Scriptures of Israel as a kind of will and testament, read aloud after the death and resurrection of Christ by surprised beneficiaries, a position based upon Luke 24 and kindred texts. The alternatives were seen clearly by Marcion and set forth with enthusiasm and conviction.

a canonical totality as well. One must hunt for good and poor existential claiming potential in a "canon" containing them both (so, e.g., R. Bultmann).

At stake is how identifications with the NT are in fact proposed, either explicitly or as is more likely, implicitly, by interpreters interested in biblical theology. At ground, it is this presumption of identification, and the imprecision that it masks, that is to be interrogated in this chapter. This means that when Childs makes a statement like "we are not prophets or apostles"[19] what is striking at one level is the assumption of a kind of equivalence of distance that entails the church's relationship to both Testaments, not just the one or the other. Given what has just been said, this equivalence requires detailed comment and justification. Given the inclinations that mark biblical theological treatments of the canon as just noted, how can such a claim be lodged and defended?

At stake here, we shall hope to show, are all manner of assumptions about why we choose to make identifications with biblical authors or redactors at all, and when one then factors in the reality of the Bible being comprised of two Testaments—each with individual authors, historical settings, and implied audiences—it simplifies things enormously and probably misleadingly to allow a graded sense of relatedness to say more than it can, the second being somehow clearer about this than the first when it comes to the church's identification.[20]

It should again be noted in passing that, especially in recent studies, this is why the character of the relationship between church and synagogue, between Jewish and Christian communities of faith,

19. Relevant sections in Childs, *Biblical Theology of the Old and New Testaments*, where this concern is voiced include 70–79; 242–44; 378–83. "The Christian Church today possesses a canon of Scripture consisting of an Old and a New Testament, both of which bear witness to Jesus Christ. In this regard, its situation differs theologically from that of Paul for whom only the Old Testament was the Church's *graphe*" (244). See also Christopher R. Seitz, " 'We Are Not Prophets or Apostles,' The Biblical Theology of B. S. Childs," in *Word without End: The Old Testament as Abiding Theological Witness* (Grand Rapids: Eerdmans, 1998), 102–9.

20. For a treatment of different models for appropriating Scripture, including the experiential-expressive one (where "identification" is prominent), see George A. Lindbeck, *The Nature of Doctrine: Religion and Theology in a Postliberal Age* (Philadelphia: Westminster, 1984).

frequently makes an appearance at the conclusion and calls for attention.[21] For yet again, this is an obvious but an overly simplified way of thinking about the problem of identification and relatedness (Jews read the Tanak in this way; Christians read the OT in that way), and it is attractive precisely for this reason. Jews themselves must frequently point out that there is nothing all that obvious about modern Jewish identification with the OT anyway, even of a kind that makes Christian differentiation from all that tidy an affair.[22] There is certainly a challenge to be confronted concerning the fact that the Bible is shared by different communities with different claims about its component parts. But to move too quickly to this topic is to run right by the problem captured in Childs's terse phrase, and that is, that the church's identification with and relationship to the Bible is not self-evident *for either Testament.*[23] This means that on my ear at least, the idea that one can conceive of and undertake a project and then call it a "biblical theology of the NT" is sitting right on the problem. So the previous discussion about terminological lack of clarity is not just a matter requiring a kind of tightening-up of the terms of description. It is a matter of theological significance of the first order, having to do with the relationship between the Testaments and the relationship of the church to the canon in all their conceptual richness and challenge.

21. This is particularly true in recent German-language treatments. See the discussion of Childs in "The Canon in Recent Biblical Studies: Reflections on an Era," *ProEccl* 14 (2005): 26–45. For further consultation, among others, see Rolf Rendtorff, "Toward a Common Jewish-Christian Reading of the Hebrew Bible," in *Canon and Theology* (Minneapolis: Fortress, 1993), 31–45; Christoph Dohmen and Franz Mussner, *Nur die halbe Wahrheit? Für die Einheit ger ganzen Bibel* (Freiburg: Herder, 1993); Erich Zenger, *Das Erste Testament. Das Jüdische Bibel und die Christen* (Dusseldorf: Patmos, 1991); Christoph Dohmen and Günter Stemberger, *Hermeneutik der Jüdischen Bibel und des Alten Testaments* (Stuttgart: Kohlhammer, 1996); Christopher R. Seitz, "Old Testament or Hebrew Bible? Some Theological Considerations," *ProEccl* 5 (1996): 292–303.

22. Seitz, "Old Testament or Hebrew Bible?" 292–303.

23. Consider for example the ruling of Acts 15 and the Western text's changes in the proscriptions laid down on gentiles. Here is a case where the difficulty of identification, after the parting of the ways, manifested itself and encouraged a wider biblical theological reflection. Prohibition of murder and the love commandment do duty in the light of a wider grasp of the canon's two-testament sense, appropriate to the church's life after the parting of the ways. See my essay, "Dispirited: Scripture as Rule of Faith and Recent Misuse of the Council of Jerusalem," in *Figured Out*, 117–29.

It might be said at this point, so as not to confuse, that at one level the church's identification with the NT is indeed a more obvious one than with the OT, insofar as "church" is distinguishable from its type "Israel"—though even this needs to be said with care.[24] What we hope to show, however, is that precisely this obvious character tends to run interference for much deeper questions about the NT canon as a total theological statement, and about the relationship between apostolic witness and the church. It will also emerge as our thesis that for the purpose of Christian theological reflection, the OT and the NT simply do their work differently, and not crudely developmentally, such as would lead one to conclude that the NT is more suitable for theological reflection than the OT in the very nature of the case.

Identification with Christian Scripture

The particular expression "we are not prophets or apostles" has found its way into the evaluative atmosphere of NT studies, concerning basic hermeneutical and theological presuppositions.[25] It has also been used in the context of OT studies, and I have myself sought to clarify the expression in the more specific sense of Childs's biblical theological

24. George A. Lindbeck, "The Story-Shaped Church: Critical Exegesis and Theological Interpretation," in *Scriptural Authority and Narrative Interpretation*, ed. Garrett Green (Philadelphia: Fortress, 1987), 161–78.

25. See David M. Williams, *Receiving the Bible in Faith* (Washington, DC: Catholic University Press, 2004). Williams concludes: "Interpretive techniques and principles that the NT writers employ in dealing with the OT, which Childs recognizes as an important element of their witness, are rejected as models for later Christian practice with little more explanation than 'they were Apostles, we are not'" (105). The discussion by Childs of this decisive hermeneutical and theological concern is nowhere near as scanty as Williams's own brief account would give one to believe. As such it raises questions about the intelligence and coverage of Childs's massive contribution by Williams when in a doctoral dissertation summary of under thirty printed pages he could confidently conclude, "This consistent lack of attention to important theological issues raised by his own thought can only bring the entire structure into question" (105). Childs does not state that discontinuity is what marks the apostolic and the subapostolic readings of the OT, but that failure to attend to the canonical implications of the New Testament as a totality causes historical contextualization of a sort that differentiates the modern inquiry into "the use of the OT in the NT" from the reflections of the early church. So it is not simply that the early church had two Testaments and the apostles just one, but that the apostolic use of the OT exists now within a New Testament canonical whole and must be evaluated theologically on account of that.

concerns.[26] Given the concerns of this chapter with the way use of the OT in the NT has become a major category in the inventory of biblical theology, analysis of the phrase is properly located in the first instance with NT studies. Also, because a recent study on biblical hermeneutics[27] has challenged the claims of Childs on this front, on the NT side of the canon; because the challenge comes in the context of Childs's concerns with a project associated with Richard Hays; and finally because that project is part of a much wider interest at present in NT studies, it is appropriate that we begin at one point where the hermeneutical and theological issue of identification with the NT was finely sharpened and proceed from there.

Mention has already been made in the previous chapter of the work of Richard Hays, *Echoes of Scripture*, and the conclusion of that work, where Hays took up a central and provocative question of how his historical and literary findings about Paul's use of the OT might be useful for the church. The context of concern he raised allows the present chapter to argue for a general compatibility in respect of the question now being posed: how can the church properly use the NT and identify with it? This is the question Hays posed, and it is to his credit that he realized that an investigation of Paul's use of Israel's Scriptures might reasonably raise in the minds of his readers the modern hermeneutical question: just what are we to do with this description of Paul's interpretative approach, now that an intelligent and probing interpreter has so ably laid it out for us? That Paul was using the first part of the Christian Bible, which at the time was the only "Scripture" warranting the name, might logically be seen to raise a pertinent, modern, analogous question: how do Christians, or how does the church, read its "Scripture"—now

26. "Precisely what gives the Church its identity and its unique standing is that it orders its life according to a canon of biblical writings; to state it crudely, characters in the Bible had no Bible in the same sense. To say, as Childs does, that 'we are not prophets or apostles' is neither to denigrate the Church as 'latecomer' nor to encourage a nostalgia for a sort of 'pure revelation' vouchsafed to the original men and women, somehow indirectly analogous to our own experience of God (on this, see John 20:29–31). Rather it is to recognize that a fundamental feature of the canonical process is its capacity to transform a tradition-historical process into a final stabilized text, a lively 'charter document' against which the Church can measure its common life . . . based upon the foundational legacy of apostles and prophets, whose experience of God is different in kind, but not in substance, from that of all succeeding generations" (Seitz, *Word without End*, 90n11).

27. Williams, *Receiving the Bible*.

comprised of two parts, OT and NT? I phrase the question in this way because it points to a real complexity, not really dealt with in Hays's more limited account (viz., Hays focuses on Paul's use of the OT as a model for Christians and does not apply this hermeneutic to Christian use of the NT more globally, that is, with attention to Acts, the Pastoral and General Epistles, Hebrews, or Revelation). We will take this up in a moment in our discussion of the recent treatment by Andrew Lincoln of the Letter to the Hebrews.

The questions that follow from this complexity are numerous. Can one identify with Paul as an interpreter? What does identification really mean? Does one do as Paul did? Or does one judge Paul's work to have a kind of finality or authority or truthfulness in respect of the OT, urging one to identify more with the singular achievement and authority of Paul's work than with Paul himself as interpreter, with certain exegetical instincts (recovered by historical inquiry), whom we are also to imitate in our own day and in our own way, somehow following his example? And then a further question must be faced. Does our identification with Paul entail a judgment about the OT canon, allowing us to identify with his interpretations of the OT Scriptures—in either of the manners just described—meaning that we do like Paul does, or accept as truthful what Paul has done, and so now have some strong clue about the status and meaning of the OT as Christian Scripture by virtue of standing alongside Paul and seeking to do as he does in respect of the OT? Paul's (invariably) selective use of the OT, that is, guides our notion of canonical authority inside that first witness.

Then the corollary must be followed up, and here is where we touch directly upon the status of the NT as canon: if we identify with Paul in this way, and so get inside the NT canon at a moment of identification en route to its own status as "Scripture" (on analogy with the term's alignment with the writings Paul is interpreting), would not consistency demand that we proceed in the same way with the NT when it becomes Scripture, that is, selectively and charismatically interpret the NT based upon the concerns in the "community of faith" as Paul is held to have done?[28] The alternative would be

28. More on this below. See Andrew Lincoln, "Hebrews and Biblical Theology," in *Out of Egypt*, 313–18.

accepting that we have made an identification in the second part of Christian Scripture that is in the very nature of things piecemeal and fragmentary, calling into question just what it means to call the NT "canon" or "Scripture" and so treating it in a way that was derived on analogy with the first part of Scripture—namely, a claim regarding scope, arrangement, stability, and the totality of its witness and effect?[29] This results in a kind of asymmetry in canonical terms, which at the starting point renders the enterprise's reliance on a concept of authoritative Scripture questionable, and which at the exit point calls into question just what it means to have an authoritative NT canon, such that we visited it for such an investigation at all, on the grounds of not just its historical but also its authoritative theological claim on the modern Christian community or church.

These are formal matters and I have touched on several of them in the preceding chapter. Here our concern is additionally with the question of the status of the canon and the effect of that, hermeneutically, on our access and identification with Scripture in the church. I have already pointed to one problem in the analysis of Hays, having to do with just what is meant by identification or, to use his term, "imitation." The discussion he undertakes is limited in part by the interlocutors he chooses to set in contrast with his own position, and the foreshortening of the genuine issues that results from that. But leaving that limitation to the side, just what are we to make of linking a concern with normativity and truthfulness on the one side, and with imitation and identification on the other? To his unintended credit, Richard Longenecker manifests in his own effort the difficulty in wanting both aspects to sit next to each other and also in trying to extricate them one from another—an endeavor whose problematic Hays exposes.[30] But this only begs a question. If Paul's interpretative efforts are in some sense to be understood and commended as true and final accounts of the OT's sense in Christ,

---

29. K. Kertelge, "Biblische Exegese im Kontext katholischer Theologie," in Walter Kasper, Eberhard Schockenhoff, and Peter Walter, eds., *Dogma und Glaube: Bausteine für eine theologische Erkenntnislehre: Festschrift für Bischof Walter Kasper* (Mainz: Matthias-Grünewald-Verlag, 1993), 88–99.

30. Richard N. Longenecker, *Biblical Exegesis in the Apostolic Period* (Grand Rapids: Eerdmans, 1974).

which Hays seems to want to say, then it is difficult to know on what terms we might be thought to be on a proper tack of imitation. If ours were strictly speaking replications of the conclusions Paul has drawn, why would we be in a position to be doing anything except bare repetition, and just what might that mean in a context other than Paul's own? Hays appears to try to cover for this by saying that in our imitation efforts, we would need to be true to the account he—Hays—has given of the way Paul does what he does, and so would be like him in that our conclusions would rather invariably end up matching his—Paul's—own.[31]

But here we touch on the problem of the canon from another direction. Assurances that we are doing what Paul is doing can really only be given by Hays, as he is the one who has tried valiantly to understand what Paul is doing and how he is doing that and by what rules of engagement, and so how he has reached the decisions he has (and which he—Hays—might therefore additionally be in a position to conclude are right and true accounts of the sense of the OT). That is, the canonical NT does not really give us an exhaustive (or even simple) account of what Paul believes he is doing when he reads the OT, in terms of exegetical methods (hence the need for Hays's project). It simply shows Paul doing it. Our "doing likewise," or imitating Paul, could then only be judged as appropriate by Hays, who has reconstructed the account of what it means to do this according to certain rules or constraints, and also what it means to do it in a way he—Hays—judges to be a truthful and imitable account of the OT as such. Either we have charismatic imitation of Paul, which leads to fresh readings different than the ones reproduced in the NT, or we have imitation of Paul's exegesis, which amounts to replication. These are not the same things and indicate the problems with an imitation appeal. The fact that Andrew Lincoln appropriates the first leads in the direction of freedom in respect of the NT's own voice and the

---

31. Hays writes against Longenecker: "I would argue that the only theologically appropriate answer is . . . Paul's readings are materially normative (in a sense to be specified carefully) for Christian theology and his interpretive methods are paradigmatic for Christian hermeneutics. His letters help us understand both what the Old Testament means and how it should be read. I hasten to add, however, that these affirmations must be understood in the light of the findings of the foregoing pages" (*Echoes of Scripture in the Letters of Paul* [New Haven: Yale University Press, 1989], 183).

church's warrant or mandate to correct the witness of the NT when
it comes to cultural realities it judges crucial.

Two further canonical issues arise here. The first is very simple and
it derives from the fact that the sense of the canonical OT remains
intact and is never "erased" in the complete sense of the term, by
virtue of its simple persistence in a formal canonical status. The OT,
read and interpreted by Paul, and judged in this form to be truthful by
Hays, never disappears: its plain sense remains what it is. It requires
an external judgment, which could go in different and opposing directions, as to what the relationship between Paul's sense of the OT
is (*Vetus Testamentum in Novo receptum*) and what it remains in its
present canonical form (*Vetus Testamentum per se*). The intractability
of the difference means that accounts like Hays's of Paul can only
ever be well-meaning judgments and can never exist independently
of such judgments. For this would require not only a statement of
explicit finality, registered at the level of the NT's plain sense (the OT
only "means" anything by virtue of what is being said about it), and
the concomitant decision, canonically speaking, to loose the second
witness from the first and cut it free.

The second issue also arises at the level of the plain sense of the
NT as canon. Hays offers as a concluding rubric for his hermeneutical reflections a verse from 1 Corinthians 4:16, "I exhort you,
then: become imitators of me." The natural sense of imitation in the
context of the admonition proper is concern for teaching the ways
of Christ as Paul personally embodies these. Imitation (of Christ)
is followed by imitation (of Paul). There is certainly no suggestion
that what Paul is encouraging is reading the OT according to the
patterns discovered by Hays or, if it were available, as this might be
delivered in the plain sense of the NT, according to teaching about
such interpretative methods and goals, undertaken by Paul himself
and obvious to all readers of the NT on account of that. Paul does
of course frequently commend the Scriptures as capacitating this
or that reading that he has adopted, or that can be adopted more
generally (Rom. 4:22; 15:4; 16:25; 1 Cor. 9:9; 10:11; 2 Tim. 3:14).
But this is a general warrant to be followed and it falls short of the
clarity necessary for the case to be made that what Paul chiefly means
when he speaks of imitation is a concern on his part for the exten-

sion of his methods of reading the OT to those who will come after him.[32] We can also leave to the side an investigation of whether the earliest efforts at reading Scripture in the church, outside the NT canon's own range, did so on the basis of faithfulness to such an admonition from Paul, or according to a concern for matching his conclusions. The answer in chief is no. Early Christian reading of Scripture—OT or NT—proceeds without need of endorsement from Paul as to how specifically to do exegesis of the Scriptures. Where there is a similarity, it does not rise to the level of faithful adherence to an admonition from Paul.[33]

32. In preparing a commentary on Colossians, I have been made aware of yet another kind of challenge. Why are there letters that lack direct OT appeal altogether? Explanations can be given (the Colossians are gentiles and have no awareness of Scripture or scriptural appeal; Paul wants Christ to be Torah; the letter is not by Paul; the later Paul prefers allusions), but one can see how difficult it is to coordinate Paul the interpreter of the OT with the NT canon and its presentation of Paul. At the close of the letter Paul speaks of encouragement and he mentions the psalms. Does he mean: read them as I have read them, or read them in Christ, whom you have put on? This is an example of the challenge when one holds up Paul as model for imitation. See Brevard S. Childs, *The Church's Guide for Reading Paul* (Grand Rapids: Eerdmans, 2008). He has an evaluation of the more recent contribution of Hays as well on 36–39 (Hays, "Can the Gospels Teach Us How to Read the Old Testament" *ProEccl* 11 [2002]: 402–18). On Colossians and the possible explanations for scriptural citation, or lack thereof, see C. A. Beetham, *Echoes of Scripture in the Letter of Paul to the Colossians* (Leiden: Brill, 2008).

33. One thinks again of the centrality of Prov. 8 in Christian theological reflection in the first four centuries. Those who work closely with the claims of this text, in formulating christological confession, might refer to Col. 1:15–20, but equally might not: the text is doing its own theological work independently of whatever interpretative methods one might argue are Paul's and imitable for that reason (pace Williams, *Receiving the Bible*). The more typical move is concern for understanding Prov. 8 in relationship to Gen. 1 (C. F. Burney, "Christ as the ARXH of Creation," *JTS* 27 [1926]: 160–77). Prov. 8 is being read Christianly, and it is held that its true literal sense, heard in conjunction with Gen. 1, establishes christological confession. Richard Hays rightly notes that the early church could commend Paul as helping to understand the OT. The point at issue is rather different. Does Paul specifically ask us to be imitators of his exegetical instincts and to read the OT along the lines he does, or does the wider witness of the NT canon commend the Holy Spirit as teacher in these matters more generally, an appeal going back to the authority of Christ in opening the Scriptures? See Hays, *The Conversion of the Imagination: Paul as Interpreter of Israel's Scripture* (Grand Rapids: Eerdmans, 2005), viii. Paul may have, according to Origen, "taught the Church which he had gathered from among the Gentiles how to understand the books of the Law" (*Homilies on Exodus* 5.1). That is not in dispute as a historical fact; the NT indicates that Paul taught gentiles how to understand the books of the Law, etc. The hermeneutical and theological issue is what that means for how an interpreter like Origen, or a modern interpreter, now uses the OT

The Apostolic Circle and the New Testament Canon

A related matter should also be filed at this juncture, and this has to do with Paul's own apostolic office and the self-understanding that animates Paul in the faithful exercise of that office. Though he may not have expressed the issue with the kind of acuity Hays was looking for, Longenecker also touches on this issue, though from a different perspective. The question could be posed thus: In what sense does Paul judge his interpretation of the OT, for the purpose of his proclamation in the context of its delivery, as belonging inside his apostolic office and appropriate to and constrained by that?[34] If it is strictly speaking a function of his apostolic office and derived from that, we might also find explanation for why he does not choose to commend his scriptural interpretation for general imitation. First, it is interpretation appropriate to the singularity of his office and so not a matter of general Christian hermeneutics (even of the most imitative sort one might presumably imagine). Second, within the scope of the exercise of that office, Paul's exegesis is directed to a purpose constrained by all other apostolic testimony to Christ (which will eventually comprise the NT canon) and an assessment of that in its entirety. Paul is an apostle amongst other apostles.[35] Paul's readings of

---

to commend Christ, or how the book of Exodus makes constructive theological claims for the church. Paul may indeed be quite useful here, but the history of interpretation reveals that the church did far more than imitate him, or see him as an exhaustive guide, in respect of his material use of the OT in the NT. See chapter 4 below. One also needs to reckon with the reality, seen in the early church, that heretics claimed to be keen followers of Paul and imitators of him—precisely where they appeal to personal spiritual revelations said to be warranted by selective readings of Paul's own letters, where his experiences of special revelations are intimated.

34. This is a different point to the otherwise salient one raised by Childs, viz. that Paul's "Bible" is only the first witness, while the church stands before a two-testament canon.

35. The point can be sharpened by considering Marcion, who tried to have a "Scripture" consisting of "Gospel" and "Apostle." Most assume Marcion meant by this Luke and Paul. One effect of the canon—Acts in particular—is to link the "letter writing Paul" to the other apostles, precisely so that he will not be read as an isolated witness—even an exemplary one—if that should come at the cost of separating his apostolic witness from that of the other apostles. The appeal to canon is an appeal to apostolicity in this scripturally catholic sense. The difficulty with historical accounts of this or that figure's use of the OT is both hermeneutical and theological, as well as historical. History, including the dimension of apostolic and canonical maturity, and trying to get below this without reattaching what is found within the wider canonical reality, runs into problems the church encountered in

the OT must be set alongside all that can be taught of Christ, across the apostolic witness, and must be finally measured by Christ's own self and work (Rom. 14:14–15).[36] Here is where the logic of imitation might rightly be said to operate. In this regard, Paul's OT interpretation also must then confront a further canonical reality, namely, that the plain sense of the OT has not been cut loose in the cause of proclaiming Christ, but continues to operate according to its own idiom. Paul's apostolic reading can never exist apart from, or displace, the prophetic witness to Christ (OT). It is a further question altogether whether, apart from the fact of the canonical existence of the OT in continuous Christian usage, Paul himself believed that his readings of the OT were somehow definitive of its sense, even Christianly conceived and directed to his audience in an explicit sense. Public commendation of Scripture in the Christian assembly, and failure to make demonstration of his reading principles and conclusions a central part of his apostolic ministry, for imitation and extension, could imply that Paul genuinely did not so believe. His readings inhered in his apostolic office, and in this he was a true follower, with the other apostles, of Jesus Christ himself (Luke 24).

We begin at last to touch, then, on one kind of distinction that might profitably be detected between the church and the canon, at a very basic level, as this relates to the matter of identification and relationship. The church will and does observe the use of the OT in the NT canon more broadly, and the patterns—many indeed they are—of basic Christian appropriation of the OT for the purpose of commending Christ "in accordance with the Scriptures." The stabilizing of the NT canon, in time, would usher in a sense that the church's reading of Scripture would not be imitation of the NT only, but would take on its own life, as the entirety of the OT, and not just those portions commented upon

---

Marcion. See the discussion of J. Knox, "Acts and the Pauline Letter Collection," in *Studies in Luke-Acts: Essays Presented in Honor of Paul Schubert*, ed. Leander E. Keck and J. Louis Martyn (Nashville: Abingdon, 1966), 279–87; and the analysis of Kavin C. Rowe in a recent discussion, "Literary Unity and Reception History: Reading Luke–Acts as Luke and Acts," *JSNT* 29, no. 4 (2007): 449–57. See as well B. S. Childs, *Church's Guide*.

36. Michael Thompson, in a public lecture, pointed to Paul's concern for imitation of Christ as more crucial in the context of Rom. 14 than just getting a specific exegetical formulation right, at the level of consistency and logic. Imitation of Christ pointed to a concern for charity greater than principles otherwise strongly held on matters of the Law.

in the NT, was opened up for kindred Christian reflection. Paul's reading of the OT inhered with his office as apostle and was constrained in that sense, now to be measured against the witness of the NT in its entirety. The canonical and historical realities exhibit here a degree of overlap, and we know this from the NT's frequent assertion that Paul was an apostle in association with other apostles.

Paul's canonical status did not mean that the church was operating in something like the same space as Paul, for in time this would be a formal impossibility: the church would have a twofold canonical witness, and Paul had only the Scriptures of Israel, his "it is written." It belonged to Paul's apostolic moment and Paul's apostolic office that he read the OT as he did, in the service of the proclamation vouchsafed to him. The church would not understand its status outside the canon as requiring a strict imitation of Paul on the matter of the reading of the OT because it was neither in the place of "apostolic witness" nor did it have the same scriptural inheritance on the same terms as did Paul.[37]

This did not mean it was in some kind of impoverished time, missing out on the kind of inspired proclamation that belonged to Paul and the apostles. Far from it, the church had the apostolic witness in the fullness of its account of Christ, and it had a prophetic witness whose riches had only begun to be mined, and which would never cease delivering up its riches.[38] What Paul said of this witness would be heard alongside the canonical NT in a broader sense, and the density and distribution of this NT use of the OT prevented any simply unilateral replication of this or that NT voice. It also encouraged an awareness that in the light of a new Christian Scripture, OT and

37. Calvin can refer to the use of psalms by Paul as the apostle "rendering freely" and mean by that a specificity of application that must be tested against the psalm's literal sense as a Christian sense. See below, n44.

38. In a fine analysis of Scripture in Irenaeus, Denis M. Farkasfalvy describes the versatile way in which the church father appeals to prophets and apostles, each with their own distinctive character of inspiration, that of the second derived from, and based upon, an understanding of the Holy Spirit's work in the OT, and the Logos active in those dispensations. This perspective is threatened when one uses a historical method to gain a sense of the logic of Paul when it comes to his exegesis of the OT and then attempts to theologize this, with the hermeneutical exhortation for the community of faith to be imitators of Paul. The ontological claims of Scripture—especially the OT as prophetic witness—can in such a manner lose their inspired and providentially given character. See Denis M. Farkasfalvy, "Theology of Scripture in St. Irenaeus," *RBén* 78 (1968): 319–33.

NT, new ways of hearing the witness to God—Father, Son, and Holy Spirit—were to be the central work of Christian explication of the Bible in its entirety, under providential ordering of the selfsame God, inspiring the developing canon and the church both.

Conclusion

It is very much to Hays's credit, and this must be emphasized, that he concluded his descriptive work on Paul with hermeneutical and theological reflections. Often these go unstated, as though historical/descriptive work in biblical studies can take place with no obligation to account for theological and hermeneutical issues it has provoked; with the notion that this can be avoided altogether because "historical work" can successfully carve out for itself a zone of obviousness and self-containment (a problem of the sociology of knowledge); or because the task is in the nature of the thing preliminary if one is thinking about theological significance, and conclusions it derives must be handed over to *others* who then use *different* tools to pry out meaning. Or maybe historical work on the biblical material is just self-evidently the same thing as theology.

Hays has brought firmly before us the theological problem of hermeneutical application, and vice versa. He is bold to use terms like "normative" and "exemplary" as well as "freedom" and "constraint." For our purposes, by emphasizing "imitation" (of Paul) he has put the question of identification by the church squarely at the center of the discussion. We want now to look at a more challenging NT example in order to give some proportion to the question of identification and the NT canon. In order to interrogate the dimension of equivalence suggested by the phrase "we are not prophets or apostles," it will also be important to bring some OT examples into the discussion. In conclusion we will make some general observations about identification and the church, as this is ingredient in any account of biblical theology of OT and NT understood from the perspective of a canonical approach.

3

AN ILLUSTRATION OF
THE CHALLENGE

The Letter to the Hebrews, Biblical Theology, and Identification

We may now to turn to a second example, from within the NT. We have thus far left to the side the thorny issue of what it means to focus on Paul for identification (in the manner of Hays or otherwise) given (1) *questions about the extent of those letters to be associated with him* and (2) the way in which any historical account of his use of the OT will raise a question about the relationship and kinship of this use of the OT *across even those letters held without dispute to be his own*. We will take up these matters after we look at our second example, because it should help sharpen the issue. We have chosen the Letter to the Hebrews.

Why Hebrews?

It is important to say something about this choice. Why Hebrews?

1. Because the "exegetical freedom" toward the OT modeled by Paul and commended for imitation by Hays can be said to mark the author of Hebrews, this immediately raises the problem of what is meant by "freedom." What is the "constraint" on this freedom, especially when Hebrews appears to display a more extravagant or critical use of the OT than the letters of Paul (see the description of Hebrews by Hofius in the previous chapter). Since Hays has raised the issue of Pauline imitation, what questions does this present given another exegetical practice in the NT, that of the Letter to the Hebrews? Ironically in this regard, the widespread assumption that Hebrews was not written by Paul turns on just something like the awareness that his use of the OT does not match—is not imitative of—what Paul does.

2. Because the "exegetical freedom" manifested in Hebrews does not occur outside the canon, in the "community of faith" (Hays), but inside it, this raises more acutely the canonical question of internal (apostolic) and external (churchly) witness.

3. The imitation ("do likewise") notion of Hays has also proven a hermeneutical rule in the case of the Letter to the Hebrews, but not with the suggestion that the author's freedom toward the OT is a model in the "community of faith" (and here see the problems of point 1 above), but that such freedom is a model in respect of *the entire Bible, the NT included*. We raised the question above of whether this might prove an inevitable consequence of Hays's model, and in a recent essay Andrew Lincoln has focused the issue in a way not easily rejected in Hays's own canvassing of hermeneutical options.[1] So Hebrews focuses the canonical and hermeneutical issue in an especially sharp manner.

---

1. Andrew Lincoln, "Hebrews and Biblical Theology," in *Out of Egypt: Biblical Theology and Biblical Interpretation*, Scripture and Hermeneutics Series 5, ed. C. Bartholomew et al. (Grand Rapids: Zondervan, 2004), 313–38.

4. The Letter to the Hebrews has also evoked an opposite judgment from similar premises, that is, the use of the OT is a model of critical appraisal in terms of biblical theology, and we should follow this lead, but precisely *not* on the terms that the author of Hebrews operates; to do so would be to misunderstand, hermeneutically, the transfer from a description of practice to direct imitation (something Childs in other places terms "biblicism"). Rather, it is the critical perspective, theologically speaking, we can learn from, not the conclusions being drawn in the exegesis of Hebrews as such. So Hebrews provides a good place to test what it means not to imitate a practice of the NT when it comes to the OT's *per se* sense. Hofius will be set in contrast to Lincoln here and the distinctions between them carefully noted.[2]

5. And finally Hebrews is a good choice for evaluation of the question of church and identification because the matter of identification is different when the canon presents a book where clarity about the actual historical author, and therefore the possibility of a larger collection to be associated with him, is not forthcoming, and is likely never to be so by virtue of simply working harder at historical description and reconstruction. This in turn raises the question about the self-evidence of churchly identification with biblical *authors* full stop when it comes to the NT. This issue (authorship) has always been a place where the OT goes its own way and so may prove to be a place where the OT is especially relevant when it comes to understanding the hermeneutical implications of a canonical approach to biblical theology for the NT.[3] A separate chapter will investigate this question below.

Rather than looking point-by-point at these issues, the discussion will be focused by examining two recent treatments of Hebrews that

2. Hofius, "Biblische Theologie im Lichte des Hebräerbriefes," in *New Directions in Biblical Theology: Papers for the Aarhus Conference, 16–19 September 1992,* ed. Sigfred Pederson (Leiden: Brill, 1994), 108–25.

3. See my discussion of Mosaic "authorship" in *Word without End: The Old Testament as Abiding Theological Witness* (Grand Rapids: Eerdmans, 1998), 113–29.

also are concerned with biblical theology. We trust the various facets of the challenge of Hebrews referred to above will be covered by the conclusion of this examination.

Hebrews as Exemplary Biblical Theology: Andrew Lincoln

In a volume of diverse essays dedicated to the theme of "Biblical Theology and Biblical Interpretation," Andrew Lincoln offers a study of "Hebrews and Biblical Theology."[4] The choice of Hebrews for an examination of biblical theology is for him something of a self-evidence, for as he puts it, "of all the New Testament writings Hebrews provides us with the most focused and explicit treatment of the relationship between the new revelation in Christ and God's previous disclosure."[5] The lack of precision about why the NT is a good place from which to consider models for biblical theology at all is covered by the remark, "One has to start somewhere and, if one's starting point is at the New Testament end of the canon . . ."[6]—a comment that just about sums up why an analysis of biblical theology is being undertaken in the present work. This being said, by the end of the essay we see more precisely why the claim that Hebrews is a uniquely suited book for biblical theology also means that, for Lincoln, it has the potential for doing a kind of biblical theological handling of the OT that is quintessentially paradigmatic not just for the OT but for the Bible itself, NT included. Hebrews is unique and in that uniqueness it can claim a priority for biblical theology.

The bulk of Lincoln's essay is a fairly workmanlike account of the various ways the author of Hebrews uses the OT. This is undertaken for its own sake and also to demonstrate the degree to which scriptural (OT) citation is crucial to a NT book's argument, character, and rhetorical success. Again, this is why Hebrews is a good place, according to Lincoln's purpose, to consider biblical theology, for "Scripture and the relation of old and new in revelation permeate the structure and

---

4. Lincoln, "Hebrews and Biblical Theology," in *Out of Egypt*, 313–38.

5. Along this kind of narrow range of consideration, he also notes that others have drawn the same conclusion (he cites Moody Smith and Otfried Hofius as representative), ibid., 315n8.

6. Ibid., 315.

rhetoric of Hebrews."[7] When Lincoln turns to the matter of biblical theology and hermeneutics, he is able to summarize the use of the OT by the author of Hebrews in the following way, and also to draw a conclusion based upon this description of how Hebrews offers a model for our own utilization:

> If Hebrews can relativize and critique parts of its authoritative Scriptures in the light of what has happened in Christ . . . should not any biblical theology that adopts its approach be prepared to critique and relativize parts of its Scriptures—including now, of course, the New Testament, in the light of its central confession about the gospel of the crucified and risen Jesus?[8]

Lincoln sets up this way of doing things by emphasizing an authorial situation in which he imagines there to be a kind of adjudication of key issues before the community with the aid of biblical (OT) texts. "The writer selects certain texts or passages of Scripture because they are perceived to be appropriate to his pastoral task," a task that entails "the pressing needs of a specific situation in the lives of a particular group of believers."[9]

We will leave to the side the functionalist implications of such a view of Scripture (why capitalize [S]cripture and also speak of "authoritative texts" if one is prioritizing functional concerns in the community?) and also the notion that what the author of Hebrews is doing is best understood as relativizing and critiquing the OT, because our focus here is on the question of biblical theology and the idea that the church imitates the practices of biblical authors. As they read the OT, so we read the Bible: selecting passages in response to pastoral needs.

It is of course possible to characterize the use of the OT by Hebrews in a different way to Lincoln. At one point at least he does recognize that when it comes to exhortation (a mode of discourse rather different in kind than pastoral concern for "needs" in the community), often the author uses the OT in strong continuity with its original form. What is more crucial to note is the way in which historical description

7. Ibid., 317.
8. Ibid., 333.
9. Ibid., 330.

shorn of NT canonical reflection is particularly open to a totalizing tendency, when one moves into the area of hermeneutics. As we noted in the discussion of Hays and of Paul's use of the OT, it is important for both historical and canonical reasons to be forced to relate what Paul is seen to be doing, according to a historical investigation of his exegetical practices, with what he does elsewhere, and with the received canonical presentation of Paul as an apostle amongst other apostles. By turning Hebrews into a unique book—a potential that is latent on other grounds because of the lack of explicit connection of the book to a clear canonical author—and then by absolutizing its use of the OT in accordance with a historical theory from our modern stable, Lincoln has detached the book from any constraints from within the canon and from any association with other uses of the OT in the NT. The stage is then set from the beginning for a reading that is held hostage to his own historical analysis of techniques of reading the OT and assumptions in the area of the history-of-religion about pastoral practice in antiquity (assumed but not really argued on the same historical grounds), combined with a claim to canonical uniqueness, which is then turned to a kind of totalizing hermeneutical purpose in the late-modern classifying of biblical theology.

In passing, early in the essay, he notes that Childs also views Hebrews as a book with interest in what he is terming "biblical theology," and he quotes with approval a sentence from the 1992 study where Childs writes, "the book of Hebrews represents an important theological attempt at resolving the relationship between Old and New Testaments."[10] Anticipating the conclusions he intends to draw on hermeneutics and biblical theology, and their rather sharp divergence from Childs's own views, he is forced to assess the difference between his and Childs's method. This latter he believes is the result of a defensive move, on the one hand, and an inconsistency, on the other. Childs had once seen the NT's use of the OT as a "central category for biblical theology,"[11] but then he was forced to "backtrack" on this view because in Childs's later work (1992) it was the discrete voice of the OT he was compelled to "overemphasize." It is for this

---

10. Quoted from *Biblical Theology of the Old and New Testaments* in ibid., 312.
11. So Lincoln, "Hebrews and Biblical Theology," 316n10.

reason that Lincoln finds Childs's view on Hebrews, quoted above, "interesting to observe."[12]

It will be important to examine Childs's early view of biblical theology, for on the face of it Lincoln does seem to spot a change in approach—not least because Childs himself helpfully acknowledged it in the later work. We are fortunate in that the example Childs works with in *Biblical Theology in Crisis* focuses specifically on the issue at hand, namely, how Hebrews reads the OT (in the case of Ps. 8). It will also be necessary to look at this treatment because it bears some resemblance to the way Hofius handles Hebrews and the question of biblical theology done in the light of his example, and also because Lincoln quotes Hofius with approval as operating with something of the same position as his own.[13]

At this point it is instructive to look at Childs's treatment of Hebrews in the later work, which itself is indebted to his lengthier introduction in *The New Testament as Canon*, specifically in the area in question: biblical theology and hermeneutics.[14] Lincoln is right in noting that Childs sees Hebrews as representing something like an incipient biblical theology; it would be difficult to imagine any treatment of Hebrews that did not emphasize this point. Having seen this, however, Childs draws very different conclusions. He compares Hebrews with Barnabas, on the one hand, and with the other examples of OT exegesis

12. Childs returned to Hebrews in his final work, *The Church's Guide for Reading Paul* (Grand Rapids: Eerdmans, 2008), 237–52. This includes an evaluation of Lincoln as well.

13. Lincoln states, "The writer of Hebrews is clearly critical in his theological reflection, wrestling both with the issue of where the continuity between the two stages of revelation lies and where the discontinuity between them is such that the parts of the former have to be critiqued and pronounced no longer applicable. Biblical theology which takes Hebrews as one possible model for its work will need to be critical in the same way" ("Hebrews and Biblical Theology," 332); he then footnotes with approval Hofius as invested in "biblical theology in the light of the Hebrews as a critical discipline" (332n21). But Hofius views the author of Hebrews as requiring a critical appraisal because his instincts are not to be followed when it comes to theological declarations based upon material use of the OT in his argument. Lincoln seems to have convoluted the point Hofius was making in order to endorse a quite different method of liking what the author of Hebrews is doing (as he sees it) and then wishing to do likewise with both OT and NT (critiquing, spotting discontinuities, and eliminating where needed, etc.).

14. Brevard Childs, "Hebrews," in *Biblical Theology of the Old and New Testaments* (Minneapolis: Fortress, 1994), 308–13; Childs, *The New Testament as Canon: An Introduction* (Philadelphia: Fortress, 1984), 400–418.

in the NT, on the other, especially Paul. Whatever Hebrews is doing in the area of "biblical theology" (the term is properly anachronistic) cannot be directly transferred from historical description to herme-neutical imitation, however precisely or imprecisely one accomplishes the first, without acknowledging the canonical perspective in which these exegetical practices now are located. Hebrews marks a kind of outer limit, beyond which Barnabas goes, in respect of a Christian understanding of the OT (especially in the area of cult and law). We do not simply imitate the practice of an individual author, because this fails to reckon with the fact that such a witness is available only from within the context of a NT canon.[15] We will need to say more below about the matter of authorship from a canonical perspective, in the case of Hebrews, but it remains the case that simply isolating the exegetical practice of a single author and describing it in better or worse historical terms and then saying, "go do likewise," requires an illegitimate transfer at a wide range of levels. We noted above the asymmetrical pairing of (what is considered to be) historical and lit-erary precision, with sociological universals like community needs, especially when the literal sense of Hebrews is not the best broker of a precise account of the community being assumed by Lincoln. Here is but the tip of the problem-of-identification iceberg.

Hebrews and Biblical Theology: Otfried Hofius

Hofius, like Lincoln, also offers a brief account of Hebrews with an eye toward biblical theology. He too notes the radical character of the author's critical theological appropriation of the OT. For Hofius, however, the author of Hebrews does not provide us a model for imi-tation, except to the limited degree that he himself must be open to *Sachkritik* (evaluative assessment). In the specific area of the author's handling of the OT, moreover, Hofius explicitly judges several of his exegetical moves as remaining fully under the shadow of the original sense of the OT, which in this original sense better serves the purpose of Christian theological reflection on the two-testament canon. How

---

15. See n19 in the preceding chapter. Cf. *Church's Guide*, 251–52, where the effect of reading Hebrews in relationship with Colossians and Ephesians is evaluated.

does Hofius render this judgment, which sounds like strong avoidance of what Childs calls biblicism? His explicit appeal in the case of hearing the OT is "unsere historisch-kritischen Voraussetzungen." Leaving aside for a second the suitability of this criterion, or even what it means in Hofius's estimation, it is clear that Hofius wishes to acknowledge that a transfer from ancient setting to modern setting, for the purpose of hermeneutical application, can be no naive matter. We stand at a considerable distance from the community and the author of Hebrews, and there is no simple way to bridge that gap. Indeed, one might say that it threatens to become, in Hofius's hands, somewhat unbridgeable.

We will need to come back to the question of the propriety of a historical-critical criterion as we search for an alternative to either Lincoln or some fresh application of "our historical-critical presuppositions." What goes unstated by Hofius in his evaluation of the potential for Christian theology in the OT is just how he knows this. Does this come from the application of historical-critical presuppositions? Well perhaps, as broadly conceived by him. But the sentence in question is at this point worth examining. At issue is how Hofius can determine that what Hebrews does with the OT needs reexamination in the light of the OT's own plain sense and its own potential for Christian theology. I have phrased the issue in this way because it presses the question of whether Psalm 8, for example, reveals this theological potential due to an application of historical-critical methods, or whether alternatively these methods are the reason for Hofius's own judgment *theologically* in the NT. At the place where the issue is sharpened, Hofius writes:

> Der 8. Psalm etwa wäre eine solcher in seinem ursprünglichen Sinn rezipierbarer Text, sind seine Aussagen über die Hoheit des von Gott geliebten Menschen doch durch Christi Einsatz für den Menschen endgültig in Kraft gesetzt und als wahr erwiesen.

I would offer this loose paraphrase: Psalm 8 is an example of a text whose original sense is received as confirming the work of Christ, who has established the dignity of mankind in accordance with what is expressed there, and so its voice remains fully alive.

In my judgment Hofius gives approval to Psalm 8 over what he calls the christological reinterpretation of Hebrews 2:9 simply because he is able to appeal to a larger set of theological convictions, which guide his evaluation of Hebrews's argument.[16] These make their force known, in my view, at the level of what we are arguing is the *canonical constraint of the NT in its entirety*. Here is the level at which Hofius gleans what he calls a "historical-critical" evaluative stance, though he does not speak of it in canonical terms and might indeed resist such a characterization. By determining the referent of Psalm 8 in too strict a fashion as Jesus, Hebrews would produce a reading which runs afoul of a criterion Hofius feels warranted in appealing to, on the basis of what is believed about the work of Christ more broadly conceived. Hebrews must be read theologically, not only according to its own discrete logic where care must be taken in understanding the use of the OT, but according to theological judgments that are rendered more broadly. For Hofius these center on the fact that Jesus Christ has acted decisively for humanity and conclusively bestowed the dignity Psalm 8 was adumbrating from its own limited perspective. Hofius knows this, presumably, based upon his comprehension of the canonical witness of the NT and the congruence of the wider logic of Hebrews with it.[17]

16. In what follows it would also be possible to question whether Hofius has properly grasped what the author of Hebrews is doing, but the specific issue at this juncture is imitation of a move by a biblical author when it comes to use of the OT in the NT. Our point is that Hofius and Lincoln are doing very different things when it comes to an assessment of the voice of the OT and hermeneutical application. Hofius follows the view that the author of Hebrews intends a christological interpretation of Ps. 8 that, in some sense, distorts a potential it has for theological construction. Our concern is to know how he can say this (as against Lincoln's method). An alternative is that the author of Hebrews uses the plain sense of Ps. 8 (its "ursprünglich" sense) to indicate that dominion has not been accomplished for humanity in general, as the psalm had promised, but that Christ has done this (suffering for a little while but then crowned with glory). One can then argue that the psalm is used in a productive way and that the author of Hebrews has adopted an inferential model of exegesis that cooperates with the psalm and does not read it in a displacing, christological sense, but in a model integrative way. This understanding can be seen in the translations of NEB and NRSV, for easy reference. See the note to follow.

17. The author of Hebrews uses the OT not for the purpose of indicating its exegetical intention, in the same way that Hays may seek to interrogate the exegesis of the OT in Paul and ask us to imitate him in our use of the OT; nor is the author of Hebrews somehow setting aside the plain sense of the OT and relativizing it in the manner of Lincoln. In chapter 1 the author provides a list of texts from the OT to show that angels are not intended by

It is not the purpose at this juncture of the argument to evaluate the judgments Hofius is here rendering, and it would be difficult to do so in any event because the comments he makes are much too lapidary. At issue is illustrating the difference between the approaches of Hofius and Lincoln, and demonstrating that any resemblance is actually superficial. Hofius is able to exercise a theological *discrimins* that judges the readings of Hebrews as it diverges from the OT's plain sense and also presumably more broadly. The OT then retains its *per se* voice, and in this way can better be connected to Christian theology, in this particular instance. At other places, Hofius is very clear it just falls to the side. But the way in which such judgments are

---

God, but he does not move forward to declare that the only sense of these passages, in the literal intention, is to refer to Jesus. That would be possible only by inference. This same inferential appeal occurs in chapter 2. He uses a passage from Psalms (very loosely attributed, it is to be noted—"someone said somewhere") where angels are more clearly ruled out—a distinction operative in the psalm in ways more explicit than in the texts in chapter 1—as a referent and contrasted with mankind (*'adam*). But since the dominion to be exercised has not happened in time, the author of Hebrews points to Jesus Christ as filling this space—not because Ps. 8 intends this in some straightforward way according to the intention of its human author (hence "someone said somewhere"), but because Jesus has done what Ps. 8 promised would be the case of *'adam*. This use of the OT is such that a space opens up and the author argues Jesus Christ fills it. But this is not an effort to replace one referent with another, by virtue of exegetical argument. It is simply a theological argument about the work of Christ made possible by reference to the OT's plain sense and a larger divine intention. Lincoln misses the point badly when he argues the use of the OT is some kind of adaptation of its sense based upon the needs of the community. The sense of the OT remains what it is, and then the author moves to his theological purpose with the aid of it. Ps. 8 spoke rightly of dominion by humanity. Christ set that in motion by his work for us. Childs does a far better job grasping how the OT continues to function alongside the use made of it by the author of Hebrews. (The view above regarding lack of dominion in *'adam* in contrast with Christ's dominion is held by F. F. Bruce, Westcott, R. McL. Wilson, E. McKnight, and others; see the discussion in Philip E. Hughes, *A Commentary on the Epistle to the Hebrews* [Grand Rapids: Eerdmans, 1977], 86–87.) The discussion of Calvin is illuminating on the matter of use of the OT in the NT (*The Epistle of Paul the Apostle to the Hebrews and the First and Second Epistles of St. Peter*, trans. W. Johnston [Grand Rapids: Eerdmans, 1963], 22–23). Seeing the divergence with Ps. 8 (and without recourse to an argument via the LXX), he writes, "I answer that it was not the purpose of the apostle to gave an accurate exposition of the words" (22) and "the apostle has no intention of overthrowing this meaning ['a little lower'] or of giving it different turn . . . he does this more by alluding to the words than by expounding what David meant" (23). So whether the exegesis of Hebrews sees a contrast of the dominion of Christ with that of humanity according to Ps. 8 (see the NRSV translation), or speaks of Christ's future dominion, it remains the case that the psalm's meaning is not evacuated by the NT use, nor is its true sense revealed by a subsequent argument extraneous to that sense.

rendered is not chiefly a function of the material use of the OT in the NT, nor does it amount to a steady preference for the NT's take on the OT. Some other criterion must be employed, and in our judgment, Hofius here departs from both Hays and Lincoln by refusing to let the voice of Hebrews be restricted from a necessary influence from the broader NT canonical dimension. Hebrews simply cannot be asked to carry the biblical theological weight Lincoln wants to give it, for it lacks any *sui generis* claim to this.

Hebrews is, however, an excellent candidate for showing how complex the matter of the use of the OT in the NT genuinely is. To take the OT example here at issue: First, Hebrews quotes an OT text in a form that diverges from the MT (angels instead of "*elohim*"; little while instead of a little less—in v. 7 this is a potential rendering; cf. v. 9). In this form, and because of certain potentialities it manifests, the author then determines the referent in a way that moves beyond the OT's own strict frame of reference. So there are least three levels of sense transfer: textual, semantic/temporal, and referential. Does the author of Hebrews self-consciously exercise a judgment that turns on choosing one text tradition over another, one now familiar to us from the OT in MT form and elsewhere, and subject to our critical awareness that choices actually exist? This is highly unlikely. It has been argued that the OT reading in the MT could actually make the point better at the final level of referential transfer (God instead of angels), though this is obviously a judgment call and the issue is already a challenging one within the Psalter at other places, precisely in the MT tradition.[18] Once the matter of an alternative textual filter comes into play, it makes it difficult to speak of the NT as offering a critical reading of the OT subject to our concern for biblical theological usage or imitation. It is for this reason that in much of the earlier history of interpretation, it was easier to conclude that the NT author was rendering freely, or in some other way "embellishing" the OT, and yet with no need to sharpen the matter in the manner of biblical theological preferentiality.[19]

18. Hughes is bold to argue that the LXX makes sense where the MT does not, here and elsewhere where 'elohim appears (LXX Ps. 97:7; 138:1; 82:1, 6)—see Hebrews, 86. Cf. Harold W. Attridge, A Commentary on the Epistle to the Hebrews, Hermeneia (Philadelphia: Fortress, 1989), 71.

19. See the discussion in chapter 4 below. This is Calvin's view, as in n17 above.

In a great many cases it is concluded that each text (OT and NT), at a variety of levels (Hebrew, LXX, NT interpretation), is doing its own specific theological work. Measured against this kind of theological and textual sensitivity, any method that seeks to restrict choices so as to produce a judgment that a single NT witness is providing a kind of evaluative lens in the area of biblical theology would have to be judged faulty or foreshortened.

For this reason it is now important to revisit the conjecture of Lincoln, that Childs's methodological judgments (in Hebrews and in biblical theology more generally) were altered because of defensiveness about the "discrete voice" of the OT (if that is what Lincoln is implying). The conjecture, as noted, is reasonable enough at one level, but our interest is not so much in exonerating an individual's methods as in testing what is at stake for biblical theology in a proper hearing of both Testaments. Childs has clearly thought a good deal about this matter, and Hebrews is one place he has tested his own views.

Hebrews and Biblical Theology: Brevard Childs

Lincoln rightly sees that Childs himself registered a caution about using as a central category for biblical theological reflection the use of the OT in the NT.[20] But he does not mean this in the way Lincoln implies. In 1970, Childs wanted to model a form of biblical theology that took seriously the exegesis of the OT, where this occurred in the NT. At issue was the general dismissal of such exegesis, either on the grounds that it was eccentric or did not line up with "historical-

---

20. "There is no literary or theological warrant for assuming that the forces which shaped the New Testament can be simply extended to the level of biblical theology involving theological reflection on both testaments" (Childs, *Biblical Theology of the Old and New Testaments*, 76). This is a consistent position Childs has held, over against Hays and others. It marks his final conclusions in *Biblical Theology in Crisis* as well, as the discussion of Heb. 8 there shows. So when he makes the next statement, it refers to the dangers implicit in his starting point, not to the motives Lincoln attributes to him. "In this regard, my earliest attempt at using the New Testament citations of the Old Testament as a major category for biblical theology stands in need of revision and is an inadequate handling of the problem." That is, danger existed in the restriction of the model to only occasions where the OT was used in the NT, not in the larger conclusions he draws about how to handle both Testaments—conclusions very different to those of Hays, Lincoln, and others.

critical" methods, or, where it was appreciated, it was only from the standpoint of a history-of-religion and not theologically. The entire argument of this section of *Biblical Theology in Crisis* started with this background concern.[21]

As I am writing over two decades later, a new front has emerged. Now the exegesis of the OT in the NT has become *salonfähig*, and the danger in Childs's former palliative concern is manifesting itself on the biblical theological front. Only examining OT texts for biblical theological purposes where they appeared in the NT would threaten to restrict the range of constructive theological work the OT is intended to do as Christian Scripture. There is nothing in principle wrong with doing biblical theology with texts from the OT that appear in the New—especially if one chooses the kind of challenging texts Childs decided to interpret with this selective interest. But in the long run, it would be necessary to take up the unfinished business of the OT as Christian Scripture in its entirety. Whatever else it means, attention to the "discrete voice" is a caution about restricting the OT's range as Christian Scripture.

In point of fact, when it comes to the specific case of Hebrews and biblical theology, what is remarkable is the degree of continuity marking Childs's serial engagements as he looks at the book with a variety of different overarching concerns animating his evaluation.[22] I have mentioned in passing the way concern for the canonical form of the NT has influenced his treatment of Hebrews. I have also suggested that at least in some very brief remarks, Hofius's own biblical theological judgments about Hebrews appear to operate with similar

21. Childs indicates that by focusing on the actual use of the OT in the NT he hopes to avoid abstractions or a method concerned with theological loci (*dicta probantia*); "history or theology apart from the witness itself" (*Biblical Theology in Crisis* [Philadelphia: Westminster, 1970], 115). He notes that this provides only a selection of the OT and is therefore limited—although selections often imply larger contexts. But I suspect his chief concern is with the charge that this kind of attention to the OT in the NT will yield only the "incidental and curious in application" (117) and it is this modern idea that he believes is faulty and attenuated. Childs wishes to reassess this dimension, over against what is valued by historical-critical canons, but then he also cautions: "it remains the exegete's responsibility to distinguish between levels of seriousness in the interpretation offered" (117). Childs is not interested in precritical or biblicistic imitation, any more than he is interested in deferring only to what is yielded in a certain kind of historical-critical investigation.

22. Now we must include as well *Church's Guide*, 237–52.

restraints. I left to the side Hofius's own claim that in what he was doing he was chiefly reliant on historical-critical presuppositions for his judgments, though I offered the conjecture that the term "critical" in this instance meant with an eye toward the entirety of the canonical witness and not imitating local exegetical moves in an unreflective sense (this is why he says earlier that biblical theology is a "decidedly critical discipline"; see chapter 2).

When one turns to Childs's own 1970 biblical-theological account, one sees that historical-critical sensitivity is but one dimension Childs brings to the interpretative task. In classical fashion, he allows the various questions posed by historical criticism to arise, and then seeks to determine their proportional corrigibility and usefulness for handling the plain sense of OT and NT, individually and then together. On this latter point Childs emphasizes the need for more than historical clarity or methodological rigor, when one moves to theological interpretation. The task here is of listening carefully and, in some sense, of knowing which instruments in an orchestra need to be dampened and which brought into sharper timber or increased volume. Psalm 8 must be heard in its proper critical context, and against the orchestration of the OT more generally. Hebrews uses the psalm, but not in such a way that our attention is chiefly on what one can allege is different to the OT's own usage, at the level of the psalm itself, but rather within the logic of the author's own argument in the canonical shape of his letter. "Difference" functions to illustrate the argument of Hebrews, not in order to get us to focus on changes in the psalm more narrowly, some of which belong at a different level of intentionality. The OT's focus is on humanity and creation. No starting point of identification can simply be assumed for interpretation. The voice that speaks in the psalm speaks of creation, but from within Israel's purview and confession. The church does not live within and alongside this voice in any natural sense, but is brought to the voice in the OT by the man Jesus Christ, whose own incarnation is both a means of access and of measurement. Hebrews does not "correct" the psalm but, using a Greek-language rendering of it, seeks to understand how Jesus Christ has brought about the proper subjection of creation that was the subject of praise of God in the psalm to begin with. The psalm's voice does Christian theology in something of the manner urged by

Hofius, but with more explicit attention to the way this happens in concert with the discrete voice of Hebrews.

The summary given needs to be filled out by careful attention to Childs's original essay, but the point for our purposes has hopefully been established. One can make identification with the author of Hebrews by seeking to understand his use of the OT, and by conjecturing about the setting in which this occurs and the purpose for which it is done; one can even contemplate this as a model for our imitation once all the speculation is filled out, and the model can be extended to modern application of biblical texts from both testaments according to perceived needs in a faith community. From a canonical perspective, Hebrews shows us more clearly than does the use of the OT in Pauline materials the challenge presented by a NT witness with a high capacity for individualization. The very forces that might helpfully secure a high degree of historical particularization, with no internal canonical affiliation, are also those that threaten to push interpretation into a hermeneutical and theological *aporia*. Hofius is able to guard against this because biblical theological concerns are still in some kind of proportional relationship to historical-critical reading, and his sense of orchestration is still balanced by a number of constraints—perhaps not all of them obvious to him. But the collateral influence of NT theology brings Hebrews within its compass and frees the OT also to sound its notes. In my judgment, Lincoln's interpretation, to pursue the orchestra metaphor, is like a long blast from a single tuba: penetrating sound but not awfully good music. In that sense, focus on the particular challenge presented by the Letter to the Hebrews helps illustrate the problems of hermeneutical application shorn of proper canonical or wider theological constraints.

Hebrews and the New Testament Canon

We noted at the outset various reasons why an evaluation of Hebrews's use of the OT might sharpen the question of identification by bringing proportion to an account that was more narrowly concerned with Paul as exegete. In the case of Paul, and of Hays's account of the use of the OT by him as a model for Christian imitation, it would be necessary to ask how such an account would deal with Paul in a comprehensive way. Here the relationship between historical and canonical dimensions is by no means straightforward: if we are imitating Paul, would we not be doing this best by assuring that the maximal amount of material was brought into discussion? The best imitation of Paul is surely the least partial one, and here the historical question is acute. How do we know which letters are Paul's only? If imitation becomes a kind of desideratum in commendation, why would we restrict letters that might by critical standards even be considered deutero-Pauline, for ought they not also be constrained by the same imitation concern?[23] Just what is the canonical Paul, as well, and how do we judge this dimension for the purpose of hermeneutical reflection?[24]

The Letter to the Hebrews helps sharpen these questions because, of the various books of the NT canon, the matter of its authorship is the least straightforward. This has meant that its capacity for affiliation and correlation is more of a challenge. It is not just that various contenders for authorship are possible (Paul, Luke, Timothy, Barnabas, Apollos) but that the issue is likely unresolvable in the nature of the case; as Origen famously said in response to the question of authorship, "God alone knows."[25] And yet, the conclusion of the book signals that some kind of affiliation is intended, however we are to understand that.[26] The fact that its canonical position has been the least fixed[27] indicates that affiliation has never been easy, and Jerome's attribution to Paul, though comprehensible in some ways, only served to sharpen the critical eye of those who would later see the genuine problems with this conclusion from the learned church father. The

23. See the remarks concerning Colossians in the epilogue below.

24. See the fresh discussion in Stanley E. Porter, ed., *The Pauline Canon* (Leiden: Brill, 2004), and the posthumously published work of Brevard Childs, *Church's Guide*.

25. See the thorough treatment of Hughes (*Hebrews*, 19–30) or Harold W. Attridge, "Hebrews, Epistle to the," in ABD, ed. David Noel Freedman (New York: Doubleday, 1992), 3:97–105.

26. Childs, *New Testament as Canon*.

27. Robert W. Wall, "The Function of the Pastoral Letters within the Pauline Canon of the New Testament: A Canonical Approach," in Porter, ed., *Pauline Canon*, 36; David Trobisch, *Paul's Letter Collection: Tracing the Origins* (Minneapolis: Fortress, 1994); Childs has a brief treatment of the issue with reference to Metzger, Gamble, Bornkamm, and others (*Church's Guide*, 3–7).

vagueness surrounding the authorship issue is also matched by the intended audience: just who are "the Hebrews"?[28]

Questions like these are unavoidable once one asks what the hermeneutical implications of a canonical approach to biblical theology are. Lincoln presumed that several factors were true about the application of OT texts to pastoral care in the context of Hebrews, but there is genuinely no way to verify this (indeed the appeal to pastoral concern for a community's needs is one crucial place where Lincoln's reading lacks actual historical-critical or history-of-religions precision). By the singularity of its rhetoric and use of the OT, Hebrews asserts itself in a way that serves to contrast it with the letters of Paul. From a canonical perspective, the lack of contextual particularity, really asserted or editorially supplied (the title and conclusion do not help much), functions in my view *to urge that the book is to be affiliated in the broadest possible way* with the remaining NT books as a whole. Not having any obvious kin, it ends up being best interpreted in relation to them all, requiring flexibility and theological reflection.[29] This does not mean that the search for contextualization is flawed or that it cannot produce better or worse results; indeed, it is usually the case that the search may even be accelerated in proportion to the lack of hard referential linking. It is just that the canonical form must itself be respected for what it does, and does not do, as its own piece of historical data.

In this sense, the Letter to the Hebrews operates with some of the same features as do the Gospels in contrast to the letters of Paul. Recent work on the fourfold Gospel collection has pointed to the hermeneutical, literary, and historical problem of recreating the setting of the author/redactor or audience of an individual Gospel and making this decisive for interpretation.[30] In that particular case, the character of affiliation requires an account of the effect of the fourfold Gospel form—in evolution or in final form—and the theories rushing in to help especially on the former question are legion.

28. On this, see Childs's discussion in *New Testament as Canon*, 406–7.

29. Childs pays attention to the relationship between Hebrews and the Pastorals, and to Ephesians and Colossians (*Church's Guide*, 251–52).

30. Bauckham, ed., *The Gospels for All Christians: Rethinking the Gospel Audiences* (Grand Rapids: Eerdmans, 1998).

Reacting from a different set of concerns, Kertelge has recently questioned the preoccupation of NT scholarship with authorial intention as a predominating influence in interpretation.[31] In the case of Paul in particular, should interpretation identify less with the mind of the author and more with the implied audience of his address? Much could be said here about the way such a concern might link up with a canonical approach. At one level, however, Kertelge appears to be concerned with the overarching question of this chapter, which is with the relationship between the church and Scripture, and how identification is properly to be made with the NT. Because this touches for him on the relationship between tradition and Scripture, especially in a changing Roman Catholic perspective, we will need to return to Kertelge's essay at the close. Kertelge wants to give priority to Scripture, but at the same time the tradition-historical approach to the NT has opened up for him a dimension of scriptural authority that again raises the question of the difference between tradition-history inside the NT and tradition as the lived life of Scripture in the history of its reception.

What has not yet been sufficiently noted is the way in which the appearance of the OT in the NT affects precisely the question raised by Kertelge about an author-centered approach to hermeneutics. There appears to be the potential for the construction of an analogy between NT authors and the church, occasioned by the fact that the former read and interpret the OT and the latter stand before a similar task in respect of the Bible as a whole, which has encouraged identification with NT figures, now with a fresh urgency and warrant. One determines what they are doing by recourse to various versions of careful historical analysis and says "do likewise" either

---

31. After acknowledging the intention of the author as important, he goes on to write: "Dabei hat der Exeget zugleich auch den *Adressaten* des Textes in den Blick zu nehmen. Wem galt dieser Text, in welcher Situation galt er ihm? Wie ist die Aussage bzw. die Intention des Autors angenommen? Welche Wirkung hat der Text gehabt? Hat der Text seine Botschaft übermitteln können—wenn nicht an die ursprunglichen Adressaten, dann an 'Adressaten' einer späteren Generation?" (K. Kertelge, "Biblische Exegese im Kontext katholischer Theologie," in *Dogma und Glaube: Bausteine für eine theologische Erkenntnislehre: Festschrift für Bischof Walter Kasper,* eds. Walter Kasper, Eberhard Schockenhoff, and Peter Walter [Mainz: Matthias-Grünewald-Verlag, 1993], 93). We intend to examine this dimension in chapter 5 on canonical shaping in the OT.

in respect of the OT or of the Bible in its entirety. In one recent version in particular, what this requires is for the OT to be read strictly according to its canonical shape, with the same demand for strictness going in the reverse direction in the NT, which is unaffected by the pressures of a canonical hermeneutic and must be so.[32] On our view this is not just simple methodological inconsistency, but strikes at the heart of what it means to speak of a canonical approach to biblical theology.

There is a further dimension to the issue. Close attention to canonical shaping in the OT ought not just absolve one from methodological inconsistency in the basic sense of that. It might also prove crucial for providing a historical warrant for believing that the NT took form by conscious attention to precisely the same kinds of canonical arrangements and interpretative concerns as have been noted—even by NT interpreters of the use of the OT in the NT—in the OT itself. It will therefore be necessary to turn briefly to several examples of canonical shaping in the OT, with an eye toward seeing whether they might usefully illumine questions of identification and theological appropriation in the NT. If so, the equivalence implied in "we are not prophets or apostles" might have more going for it than one might first have thought. Our canonical location is not that of prophet or apostle; the relationship of the church to Scripture, in view of its material division into OT and NT, contains similar and continuous features as well as distinguishing ones. It is to this delicate balance that we must turn in conclusion.

Before we do that, we wish to stay with the now popular trend of producing a historical reconstruction (often very sophisticated) of what is happening with the use of the OT in the NT (strictly speaking, a concern with inner-biblical *Receptionsgeschichte*) and then in turn using this to commend such a perspective for modern Christian theological appropriation of the OT. We will assess whether this dimension, unique to the two-testament character of Scripture (that the second witness is indebted at the literary level to the first), was seen in the same way in the earlier history of interpretation. Our treat-

---

32. Francis Watson, *Paul and the Hermeneutics of Faith* (London: T&T Clark, 2004). In the following chapter we discuss this work in greater detail.

ment will conclude with an analysis of the rule of faith in the early church, prior to the full consolidation of the NT canonical witness. At the earliest period, the Scriptures of Israel are the only "Scripture" strictly speaking, and the sense of their difference, their privilege, the indebtedness of the second to the first witness, and the necessity of reading the OT prophetically (in figure as well as in promise) and as revealing of the trinitarian character of God are all in the foreground. It is crucial that this perspective find fresh appreciation if something like a strong alternative to modern developmental understandings can again animate the theological appropriation of the entire Christian Bible, OT and NT. That the NT uses the OT at the level of its literal sense proclamation ought not, ironically, result in a silencing of the first witness at the very point where its own unique Christian voice makes itself heard: in figure, promise, and basic level theological discourse—everywhere presupposed in the second.

4

THEOLOGICAL USE OF THE
OLD TESTAMENT

Recent New Testament Scholarship and the
Psalms as Christian Scripture

Preliminary Observations: The Old Testament as Christian Scripture, in Light of a Two-Testament Canonical Form

Christian Scripture is unique in content but also especially in form. The fact that the account it gives is comprised of two Testaments is a matter of considerable importance and challenge. The Second Testament does not give record of what it seeks to tell in a detached idiom, even as its language and structure (Greek; Gospels, Acts, Epistles, and Revelation) depart from that of the First Testament (Hebrew/Aramaic; Torah, Prophets, and Writings). It speaks of a special action in time, but it can only describe this action with reference to prior acts recorded in the First Testament. In order to do this persuasively and formally it grandly takes up the language—allusively, or by citation of specific words, phrases, sentences—of the First Testament. The status of the Second Testament is therefore a deeply accorded one: it says what it says by recourse to the language of the first, in order to state what it judges to be the decisive act of God.[1] The First Testament, because of its obvious anteriority, does not use the Second Testament's language on any analogy. How one might properly speak of its *forward* relationship to the New falls at a different level of accordance (more on this below).[2]

This fact is of considerable significance, for it means that the status of the OT is both what it is, as a discrete literary witness, but also what the New has made of it. It exists in its own right, but it also exists as part of the plain sense of the New's discrete witness. We speak here *only of a special literary fact*, as one confronts Christian Scripture as a particular formal reality, consisting of two Testaments with different and separate canonical characters.

Moving beyond this literary observation, how might one evaluate the challenge of reading the OT as Christian Scripture, given this basic fact of its formal status?

First, one could argue that the OT demands to be heard apart from the New's use of it, but still as Christian Scripture, for theological reasons—that is, because God has acted in the OT and spoken; and because there is no foundational sense of the Second Testament's challenge to this most basic theological claim, the Christian is obliged to hear the OT as a discrete witness, whatever she or he might then also say about the New's use of it.[3] Indeed, at some basic level, the fact that the New takes up the Old in the proclamation of its subject matter means that for the Christian interpreter who accepts the claims of the Second Testament as constitutive, the Old's voice is inherently relational. Much hangs on this claim, of course, and much must be developed from it. But it does need to be said up front that any serious attention to the discrete witness of the OT—without prioritizing the New's actual use of it, or using such usage as a primary lens on the

---

1. Christopher R. Seitz, "In Accordance with the Scriptures," in *Word without End: The Old Testament as Abiding Theological Witness* (Grand Rapids: Eerdmans, 1998).

2. We can leave to the side the controversial business of Christian glossing of the First Testament and projects like that of the Hexapla, meant to bring order to the texts being discussed by Christians and Jews.

3. See Childs's essay "The Old Testament in the Christian Church," in *Biblical Theology in Crisis* (Philadelphia: Westminster, 1970).

Old's own voice—is not a claim to hearing a voice that is somehow non- or pre-Christian.[4]

Much confusion has entered the picture by the claims of certain forms of (recent) historical inquiry into the OT. These seek to focus on the retrieval of an authorial intention behind the witness of the Old, in the events of history to which the text is said to refer, or in the religious life that either gave rise to the literature or is somehow related to it, as an independent sphere of reconstructive interest. Insofar as these areas of inquiry defend themselves on the grounds that they are attending to the discrete witness of the OT, apart from the New's handling of it, they move to the side of what is being described here.[5]

What is at issue is a discrete voice that acknowledges as crucial the claims of the NT about the witness of the Old, but that does not believe the New's material use of the Old can be the primary or the comprehensive means to think about its theological witness as Christian Scripture. Indeed, it has been said that what is faulty in such an approach is the very fact that the New's use of the Old is a perspective that can only be occasional or provisional, insofar as the New is only on its way to becoming a Second Testament.[6] When, on its pages, a Paul or a Jesus is identifying the sole Scripture's word of address, the "New" Testament has yet to emerge as a second witness in its own right. Only when such formal status is granted will one be able to take the New seriously as a second comprehensive witness, formed on analogy as Scripture by virtue of the antecedent authority and form of the OT. It follows from this, therefore, that *any properly biblical theology would of necessity be about letting each mature witness do its specific work as Scripture, in that completed form, and then as a coordinated witness of both Testaments together.* To use the New's material deploying of the Old as a totalizing lens would be akin to declaring Augustine's use of the NT determinative of its

4. As we shall see below, in debate with Marcionites, gnostics, and various efforts to absorb or redirect the force of the OT, this dimension is particularly crucial for the early church fathers.

5. One thinks of the popular theological accounts of the OT provided by Walter Brueggemann and John Goldingay.

6. Childs has made this point consistently. See among other publications, *Biblical Theology of the Old and New Testaments* (Minneapolis: Fortress, 1994).

plain-sense witness; the relationship between the Testaments for the purposes of basic theological work is different in kind than that, and is not a matter of unidirectional reception-history. The OT retained its specific form and construction as a discrete witness—even though the Second Testament made heavy and intrinsic formal use of it— and that canonical reality is crucial.[7] So, in sum, a theological claim was formally reinforced by the canonical decision to set the New off as a discrete witness, while retaining the Old in its received form. To observe the heavy use made of the Old in the New ought not to mean—in some deep irony—a disqualification of the Old's ongoing, discrete theological word, or an insistence that what a second voice says about it as it renders its subject matter comprehends the former's theological horizon. The New itself speaks of the capacity of this sole Scripture to instruct, sufficiently, through its own literal sense. That instructing takes places at a wide variety of levels, of course, precisely because of the way its potential as Christian Scripture is opened up (more on this below).

A second objection to focusing on the New's use of the Old as a primary theological category *entails the status of the Second Testament as canonical Scripture in a more specific sense.* Much attention to the New's use of the Old must of necessity be piecemeal, measured against the New's own canonical standard. That is, specialist studies of Paul's use of the OT, or Jesus's perceptions of his place in time over against Israel's history, are what they are: technical, historical accounts of this or that moment in the religious awareness of key Christian figures, indeed of "historical Jesus" himself.

Important though these may be, they do not typically worry about whether what they see of the New's use of the Old is *limited* by virtue of not handling the entirety of the NT witness at this same level of reflection. Instead of a canonical investigation of the varieties of use of the OT in the New, which would aim at theological comprehensiveness, what we usually find are accounts that focus on this or that key figure or book of the NT. So, "Paul's use of the OT" turns out to be

---

7. On the status of the OT canon and flexibility in respect of order and scope, centered on a grammar of "Law and Prophet," see Christopher Seitz, *The Goodly Fellowship of the Prophets: The Achievement of Association in Canon Formation* (Grand Rapids: Baker Academic, 2009).

"consensus NT scholarship's accounts of who Paul is" and not the actual letters of the NT canon associated with him, and much less these works and those many others that exist alongside them in the NT as a canonical whole.[8] The problem is that a historical account of how Paul is doing this or that with an OT text is hindered by a failure to account for the NT as canon. In the NT as canon, Paul's individual exegetical decisions form part of a canonical witness and need to be understood within the canon's understanding of the apostolic office and how the parts of the NT relate to one another.

The argument could be made that if a truly comprehensive view of the canonical NT's use of the OT were provided, then one might well find represented the entire scale of exegetical insights into the OT as a properly Christian theological witness. But even then, one would be driven back to the OT as a comprehensive material witness and the task of interpreting it as a canonical whole, because nowhere does the NT claim to say all that can be said about this witness in its present total shape. To say such a thing would be to turn the OT inside out and make it nothing more than a document poised for necessary and subsequent disentangling, and silent without a second word about it. An unintended ricochet, moreover, could result in the New's use of the Old becoming something akin to a rabbinical tract, intending only to point out how something old remains relevant, without which the anterior witness would simply be an archaic, if treasured and valuable, artifact—chiefly on the grounds of its antiquity as such. But here one would cease to indicate the way the NT is different than a rabbinical tract and how it claims to be an equal though different canonical witness, whose authority is derived from the final-form status of the very witness it is itself commenting upon.[9]

In sum, one might well ask for a comprehensive account of the many ways the OT is used in the New, and one could learn much thereby about why certain instincts for reading the Old quickly become

8. How, given the concerns for "historical Paul," does one deal with the use of Scripture in the Pastorals, or in Colossians and Ephesians, and integrate that into a NT reflection?

9. See my lengthy quote from Harnack on this point in Carl E. Braaten and Christopher R. Seitz, eds., *I Am the Lord Your God: Christian Reflections on the Ten Commandments* (Grand Rapids: Eerdmans, 2005), 36–37n27.

dominant in the early church, if not also distinguishable in certain crucial ways from rival Jewish (non-Christian) and other commentary of the period. But this would still leave open the necessity of extending what one learns of these methods of reading, as the New handles the Old, to all those portions of the OT not explicitly commented upon in the New. Here one needs only recall the central place a book like Leviticus can have in early Christian commentary (or Proverbs, Ecclesiastes, and the Minor Prophets) to realize that nowhere does the instinct assert itself to say: comment only on what the NT itself declares as decisive in the OT, and comment in the same way the New comments. Quite the contrary, one could argue that precisely the possibility of hearing God's Word afresh from portions of the Old Testament, not commented upon by the New, encourages rather than restricts earlier Christian commentators.[10] What the NT does not explicitly comment upon may well be regarded as fertile ground for hearing God's Word and also for assuring that nothing that needs to be heard will fall to the ground because one relied on the fortuity or expediency of what may or may not be commented upon in the second witness to God's actions in Jesus Christ.

This leads to a final comment before we look at recent NT scholarship and the scriptural witness of the OT. Luke 24 is revealing, as much for what it does not say as for what it does say.[11] Clearly the account asserts that the church of the risen Christ receives from him

10. See Rolf Rendtorff's discussion of Childs and the theological confession regarding the Creator God, fully assumed from the OT and not developed afresh on the basis of some further delimitation, in "Revelation and History: Particularism and Universalism," in *Canon and Theology: Overtures to an Old Testament Theology*, trans. and ed. Margaret Kohl, 1st English ed. (Minneapolis: Fortress, 1993), esp. 122–24. He takes particular exception to the formulation of Pannenberg, within the larger atmosphere of Bultmann and his students: "In the history of Israel Yahweh has not shown himself to be the One God of all human beings. He has only shown himself to be Israel's God" (Wolfhart Pannenburg, *Offenbarung als Geschichte* [Göttingen: Vandenhoeck & Ruprecht, 1961], 98). See the excellent account of biblical theology in Neil B. MacDonald, *Metaphysics and the God of Israel: Systematic Theology of the Old and New Testaments* (Grand Rapids: Baker Academic, 2006). It is as Israel's God that we learn of creation and the LORD God of creation.

11. Compare Richard Hays, "Reading Scripture in the Light of the Resurrection," in Ellen F. Davis and Richard Hays, *The Art of Reading Scripture* (Grand Rapids: Eerdmans, 2003), 229–32; R. W. L. Moberly, *The Bible, Theology, and Faith: A Study of Abraham and Jesus* (Cambridge: Cambridge University Press, 2000).

the Scriptures of Israel and is taught how to see in them all the things that pertain to Christ. The text is critical for asserting the dominical referentiality of the Scriptures of Israel and also for the fact of these Scriptures being brokered by him as special teacher (what on dogmatic terms will prove to be a work of the Holy Spirit in a more comprehensive sense).

What is crucial to observe is *that just how that referentiality was spotted,* and *where it manifested itself,* is never declared in the plain sense of the NT witness. Luke 24 is decisive for indicating that such a "Christian reading" is available across the witness of the Old Testament and that the warrant for this comes from Christ himself, and also intrinsically from the old witness: it is a sense that is there; it is a sense that is disclosed for what it is; it is not a sense that is added on, exteriorly, *a posteriori.* The things about Christ are really there in Moses and all the prophets and Christ can point to them. But nowhere does the Gospel of Luke feel constrained to offer specific examples of just how the church of the risen Christ is meant exhaustively to know how the plain sense of the Old will yield up its treasures. This means that when Acts provides examples, it is following a more general warrant and not a specific template (incidentally, this fact is made clear when one observes the variety of usages of the OT in Acts, and the variety in the rest of the NT confirms this). It would be mistaken to conclude, moreover, that what is given there is meant to either constrain or exhaust what Christian exegesis of the OT will say. As we shall see below, precisely here Luther ran into a problem. But ever the protean interpreter, he would simply move on and find room to discover other senses when the lead of Acts proved to be too limiting. How and why he did that, one can conjecture about. But in many ways, he was allowing the spirit of Luke 24, and especially its careful constraints of a different kind (silence about the specifics of "christological" reading and the location of where this voice makes itself heard across the OT) to lead the way.

This opening section has sought to give a general picture of what is at stake in Christian handling of a Scripture in a two-testament form: a form in which the Second Testament makes widespread material use of the First. Its intention has been perspectival and orientational. We now turn to the specific instance of NT scholarship's assessment of the use of the Old in the New.

Recent New Testament Scholarship and the Old Testament

One can see something of a cottage industry in NT scholarship's recent interest in the OT. Three examples will suffice. All are well known interpreters and one properly associates these scholars with important trends in biblical studies.

For N. T. Wright, interest in the OT has to do with the narrative world (of which it forms the central part) said to be influencing the intentions and purpose of "historical Jesus," as Wright seeks to reconstruct these.[12] For Francis Watson, the OT in its canonical form helps formulate for Paul key convictions concerning the law and justification by faith.[13] If one can talk about a two-way dialogue between Paul and Scripture, it appears as though in Watson's recent work it is less the New making sense of a rather inchoate or indirect[14]

---

12. The works of Wright are well known. I have offered a brief response in "Reconciliation and the Plain Sense Witness of Scripture," in *The Redemption: An Interdisciplinary Symposium on Christ as Redeemer*, ed. Stephen T. Davis, Daniel Kendall, and Gerald O'Collins (Oxford: Oxford University Press, 2004), 25–42.

13. Francis Watson, *Paul and the Hermeneutics of Faith* (London: T&T Clark, 2004).

14. This word ("indirect") appears on occasion in Watson's book and points out some serious conceptual problems with intentionality and the "mental states" of OT figures. In the St. Andrews seminar on Scripture and Theology, one student observed:

> Watson's initial discussion of the "indirect" character of the OT witness to Christ begins in his introduction (21). From the outset it is already evident that he does not clearly distinguish the issue of the OT's witness to Christ from the issue of what OT writers themselves personally know of Christ. As far as I can tell, the reason the OT witness is "indirect" for Watson lies precisely here. Speaking in reference to Paul's usage of OT texts in Romans 9, he stresses that the christological reference of such OT texts is "indirect" and then offers the following rationale: "It seems that Paul respects the fact that the scriptural authors he cites—Moses, Isaiah, and others—are not in a position to share in the distinctively Christian confession of Jesus as Lord. Their testimony to God's saving act in Christ can only be indirect. They anticipate something of the logic of the future divine action, but they know little or nothing of its concrete form. . . . Scripture testifies to the gospel, but, since its testimony is indirect, it requires the apostolic interpreter to identify the conjunction of the two" (*Paul and the Hermeneutics of Faith*, 21). It appears that Watson is here conflating what these writers knew with their (scriptural) testimony. This sort of confusion resurfaces repeatedly in the book, a few of the more notable examples being found on 38–39, and esp. 161, where he links this confusion with what he thinks 1 Peter 1:10–12 is saying. [More on this in the next footnote.]

It is doubtful that 1 Pet. 1:10–12 is offering a deep hermeneutical theory; it is certainly an exhortation to Christian readers to consider the privilege of their place in time. "Mental states" of OT figures have been replaced in the recent work with the "canonical sense" of the OT, but it remains necessary that the NT speak some final extrinsic word about even this sense.

OT witness, and more an honest dialogue, with both partners taking one another seriously.[15] Watson, however, reserves the right to declare which dialogue partner is getting the better of it, so in point of fact he turns out to be an equally crucial—one is tempted to say, determinative—dialogue partner adjudicating the Old to New movement.[16] Finally, one should mention the work of Richard Hays. In an earlier publication, *Echoes of Scripture in the Letters of Paul*, Hays pressed ahead in the final section of his work to declare Paul's reading of the OT normative for Christian interpretation in our day.[17] That is,

---

15. In response to a review of his book, Watson writes this about the OT:

In the light of Easter Day, the law and the prophets can be seen as preparing the way for what has come to pass. But this only becomes apparent *retrospectively:* the prophets themselves had only the haziest knowledge of the future event to which, for Christian hindsight, they bore witness (1 Peter 1:10–12). Christian Old Testament interpretation is therefore a re-reading, a second reading which clarifies and re-orders the first reading. A re-read text (a novel for example) is a text read in the light of a prior knowledge of the whole—a knowledge as yet unavailable to the first time reader. The second reading does not repeat the first reading, but neither does it erase it; it preserves within itself the knowledge that, although the end or goal is now known, this was not the case at first. Old Testament texts should therefore initially be interpreted within a purely Old Testament context, with distinctly Christian concerns temporarily bracketed out. The "discrete witness" that emerges in this way is only a preliminary and provisional witness whose scope will be clarified and expanded by the second, explicitly Christian reading. But the initial preliminary and provisional witness remains an indispensable foundation for the re-reading." ("The Old Testament as Christian Scripture: A Response to Professor Seitz," *SJT* 52 [1999]: 229–30)

This re-reading model is not what has been understood as a Christian reading of the OT in the earlier history of interpretation, and as we shall see, the *sensus literalis* of the OT was taken to be an intrinsic and not a retrospective sense as described here by Watson. The point here is that the 2004 work has appeared to shift away from the "mental states" conception to a canonical sense. See also the evaluation of Childs, *The Church's Guide for Reading Paul* (Grand Rapids: Eerdmans, 2008), 128–31.

16. He valorizes the "canonical shape" of the Old and carefully establishes what this is, so as to say its "intentionality" is crucial in the Twelve (Habakkuk in the XII, not the mental state of Habakkuk, the concern with which he calls "hermeneutical perversity" in the hands of John Barton), but then, if the last chapters of Deuteronomy, which belong to its canonical shape, are not helpful to the point he is trying to establish, he justifies this by saying Paul did not focus on them in his NT argument. This is why he is the main "dialogue partner" in an otherwise quite technical, close reading. Another inconsistency is why one declares as "perversity" an interest in the mental states of OT figures—a problem he himself has not escaped—but then happily works with such a concept in the NT.

17. Richard Hays, *Echoes of Scripture in the Letters of Paul* (New Haven: Yale University Press, 1989).

for him the hermeneutical/historical and the prescriptive/theological dimensions are related projects requiring self-conscious reflection, correlation, and commendation. One might even declare Hays's approach a "biblical theology" when it comes to understanding the relationship between the Testaments, because for him, what the New says about the Old, and how it goes about saying it materially, is a theological guide for the Christian interpreter.[18]

It would be unfair to say that these popular accounts of Paul and the more general NT appropriation of the Old intend to exhaust what can be said about the OT as Christian Scripture or about the task of biblical theology. *The failure to be explicit on this front, however, can lead to confusion in respect of modern application* (here Hays is at least clear). What can be said is that it is possible to see such interests in the OT as somehow critical to the task of Christian reflection on the OT and not just as an interesting historical exercise.

That this is so turns on the fact that we are not freezing the frame of "takes" on the OT with a church father; or with a non-Christian reading in general; or with James or Peter or the disputed letters of Paul; or even with the NT as a canonical whole; but rather with the key figures of Jesus and Paul (Paul here being the Paul of historical-critical retrieval, of a fresh but familiar kind; likewise Jesus).[19] It is

---

18. See Richard Hays, "Can the Gospels Teach Us How to Read the Old Testament?" *ProEccl* 11 (2002): 402–18. Childs offers a brief critique in his new work on Paul (*Church's Guide*, 32–42). Hays is seeking to redress a misunderstanding of the OT as Scripture (he gives a particularly unflattering modern example). He does this, as he sees it, by showing that the NT delivers its sense with specific, often underestimated, reference to the OT, the appreciation of which helps us hear the NT in clearer sense. This is fine as far as it goes, but the significance of the OT as Christian Scripture precedes the use made by it in the NT's material form. See Harnack's remarks (reference in n9) and the treatment in the final chapter.

19. In Watson's case, however, this issue is muddled. One can identify in his work the historical-critical legacy of assuming these and not those letters of Paul to be appropriate to investigate for their use of the OT. But then when it comes to Paul's dialogue partners, as a matter proper to historical contextualization, he stands aloof; he needs not to establish for historical reasons that Paul actually knew the writings of those he is said by Watson to be in dialogue with. And finally, when there is the factor related in the NT of Paul being in dialogue with other apostles, this dimension falls out entirely as well. One could fault him on canonical grounds for not hearing "all of Paul" or "all of the NT witness" (particularly as he prizes this dimension in the OT and chides others for not so doing). But there is in addition the problem of Paul's historical relationship to other apostolic voices. Both go missing.

difficult to avoid the impression—and in Hays's case we really should not—that as Jesus and Paul do, so should we as well.[20] Can one suggest otherwise and not look somehow un-Christian!

In N. T. Wright's popular publications, the significance of the OT would appear to lie in how Jesus used it to conceptualize and direct his mission. This raises several questions. Is his imaginative reconstruction a good guide for Christian theological reading of the OT as such? The question may be sharpened precisely by considering the centrality of the OT for Wright's popular accounts of Jesus and his mission. Just this centrality raises the question of whether what Jesus is doing—as Wright reconstructs it—is somehow invariably going to be a contender for the "gold standard" of OT use in Christian hands. One might be forgiven thinking that the OT's essential purpose is revealed in Jesus's use of it, or more accurately, in Wright's speculations about such use.[21]

When one turns to the history of interpretation of the psalms against this specific set of questions about biblical theology and the use of the Old in the New, what insights can one gain? That will be the focus of this brief treatment. By observing theological interpretation being done by classic Christian interpreters, perhaps when they look like they are doing something other than the Jesus or Paul of recent scholarship, we will take comfort in resisting the hermeneutical suggestions explicitly or implicitly made in these recent works.

The Psalms in Christian Interpretation

Like the book of Isaiah, the psalms are widely received in the NT and all premodern interpreters register this awareness and comment on it. Indeed, over against most modern scholars, they are united in

20. Note for example the centrality of Luke 24. Watson comments, "As the Lucan Emmaus Road story shows, *the Christian reading* of Jewish Scripture as 'Old Testament' is a re-reading of a Scripture that is already read and known, in the light of the completed event of Jesus' life, death and resurrection" ("Old Testament," 229, emphasis added). Even the use of a specific phrase like "the Christian reading of Scripture" is highly problematic. It is probably significant that Luke 24 never spells out what such a reading actually looks like.

21. I evaluate the theological significance of the canon for proper handling of exile and restoration—key N. T. Wright categories—in "Reconciliation and the Plain Sense Witness of Scripture," in *Redemption*, eds. Davis, Kendall, and O'Collins, 25–42.

believing that this is their chief labor, and the implications of this for the fact of distinct disciplines of Old and New Testament scholarship could not be more important. The Bible refers to itself across two discrete Testaments, and here is where the main theological density is manifested and so also where the chief work of interpretation occurs. How does the fact of the Old appearing *in Novo receptum* affect the interpretations of the Old as Christian Scripture? Does the Old's *per se* voice find explicit clarification and guidance for interpretation by virtue of what is said about it in the Second Testament? These questions are material ones, and they lead straight into an account of who God is and how his will is made known in Israel, his Son, and the church.

In more recent work by NT interpreters one would be forgiven for gaining the sense that, while there may be a dialogue between the New and the Old, the crucial thing is (1) paying attention to the dialogue as such and not to the discrete voice of the Old as itself doing Christian theological work, or (2) focusing on what the latter voice is saying about the former and how it uses this witness to make its arguments. This is in part a function of the parameters of the questions being asked, and the fact that NT scholarship is the one doing the asking, to be sure. But why these parameters? Can one justify on theological grounds using such a historical investigation as a preliminary exercise, unless the next steps are explicitly taken (Hays) or anticipated, clarified, and defended?[22] What we hope to see by examining the history of interpretation is how such an inquiry classically fit within the larger task of Christian interpretation of the OT.

A simple thesis would appear to commend itself at this point: historical analysis of the use of the Old in the New threatens to create a disproportionate picture of what theological use of the OT by the Christian church should actually look like. And in so doing, it has also failed to reflect on what it means to speak of the NT as canon. Unless one coordinates a historical inquiry into what this or that voice in the New makes of the Old, with what the New as a canonical whole has to say, the danger is real that the Old is treated in its final canonical

---

22. Here the assumption of some "neutrality" in commenting is exposed as more a matter of timing than of substance; eventually, all readings intend something more than "neutral" observation and this is particularly true of the Bible, given its subject matter.

form—but only as this works itself out in a history of reception—while the New is handled historically and not canonically on the same terms. The lack of analogy in handling the two Testaments ought to serve as a warning that something has only reached a threshold stage of inquiry, and more work remains to be done. The truth of this also is borne out by examination of the earlier history of interpretation, where these kinds of narrower historicist handling of the canon were still to the side.

Voices in the Earlier History of Interpretation

We begin with Calvin. In respect of the OT, by saying the apostles "render freely" Calvin is free to honor the discrete voice of both witnesses. The NT does not tell us how to read the Old. It shows us how the NT renders freely when it relates the subject matter that is proper to the presentation of its testament. That it does this with the OT is appropriate (the use of Ps. 40:6–8 in Heb. 10:5–7). This is no warrant for Calvin to "go and do likewise." And it is certainly no warrant for letting the NT's use of the OT determine the theological sense of the OT, as if that usage determines what it means to speak of the OT as Christian Scripture. The psalms are Christian Scripture, and the use of them in the NT is but one incidental by-product of that larger theological fact.

Calvin is committed, as a consequence of his theological perspective on covenant and God's work in Israel, to letting the Hebrew canon's literal sense maintain its own specific integrity, even where he is aware that a Greek version of the OT may have a variant reading. What is striking here is that the NT's recourse to such variant readings (some of which we come eventually to see in what many NT scholars uncomplicatedly refer to as "the LXX")[23] does not upset Calvin's overall judgement in respect of the "free rendering" of the NT. That is, it matters not to Calvin that the NT witness may here

23. See the intriguing discussion of Greek renderings of Psalms, the text of Hebrews, and "the Septuagint" in Karen H. Jobes and Moises Silva, *Invitation to the Septuagint* (Grand Rapids: Baker Academic, 2000), 195–99. In a provocative analysis, they conclude about the author of Hebrews, "it was he rather than the LXX translator who came up with *the pars pro toto* metonymy as a means of highlighting the messianic significance of the psalm" (197).

and there appear to confirm a reading that is found in "the LXX." The burden remains to let the literal sense of the OT have its specific say. So even when a NT author may not be "rendering freely" but is in fact handling a different textual variant, for Calvin this does not amount to a significant difference. The plain sense of the Hebrew text remains the focus of his theological attention even where the NT's rendering of the OT goes its own way. Yet one will also rightly observe that Calvin's reading of the psalms is resolutely connected to Jesus Christ and his church. He thinks of the relationship as variable in character, involving exemplification, figuration, prophecy, and promise—depending upon the literal sense of the psalm under discussion.

Luther wrote much commentary on the book of Psalms, and for many different occasions, making it perilous to seek to synthesize something like "Luther's approach." One can see that he often uses the NT (Acts) to provide a clue as to how to read David in the psalms as prophet (the practice can be seen in early patristic commentary, even of the Antiochenes, in Ps. 2).[24] By this Luther means that David did not speak primarily to contemporaries about things that were chiefly to do with them. Instead, he spoke about Christ, and the NT confirms this when it says that David did so speak (as in Acts). On some occasions then, and when it suits his purposes, the referentiality of Psalm 2's literal sense is revealed only in the NT.[25]

On a very different tack, Luther can use the semantic level of the OT in the NT (Ps. 110) to argue for a doctrinal potentiality in the OT, having to do with the persons of the Trinity. But Luther does not view the NT's actual literal appropriation of OT texts as hermeneutically valuable in any way at all. He returns to the OT and allows it to make

---

24. The Psalms lectures of 1513–15 are found in Hilton C. Oswald, ed., *Luther's Works*, vol. 10, *First Lectures on the Psalms* (St. Louis: Concordia, 1974).

25. There is a difference to be noted in the heavy christological reading of Ps. 1 in the first lectures and what one finds in a second exposition published in 1519 (see *Luther's Works*, 14:287–311). The commentary on Ps. 2 has not changed much. In 1513 Luther appears to be influenced heavily by the portrayal of Acts and the notion of David speaking of the details of the conflict between Jesus and the Jewish authorities. The wicked in Ps. 1 become quite specifically the Jews. In the latter treatment this very strict *in Novo receptum* perspective has fallen out. Aquinas and Augustine never push their understanding of the plain sense to the extreme of Luther's earlier treatment.

the doctrinal point off its *per se*, literal witness. This *per se* witness, Luther is at pains to insist, provides the pneumatological warrant for viewing David as the vehicle of the Holy Spirit's declaration of the trinitarian subject matter of the OT as such. For Luther's purposes in his debates with opponents, it is *crucial precisely that the OT make this trinitarian claim in a way that is unique to its own witness and without necessity of replication* in Novo receptum *on those same terms.*[26] In other words, the OT makes uniquely Christian claims, and these are unique precisely because they cannot be tracked into the material use made of the OT in the New. This is what it means for Luther to affirm that the Holy Spirit "spake by the prophets."

In his commentary on Psalm 22, Thomas Aquinas argues that a certain species of historical reading offends against the theological implications of Scripture's "literal sense."[27] The literal sense must be

---

26. Christine Helmer, "Luther's Trinitarian Hermeneutic and the Old Testament," *ModTh* 18 (2002): 49–73. See also my essay, "The Trinity in the Old Testament" for an Oxford University Press publication (forthcoming).

27. In a pregnant comment at the opening of his discussion of Ps. 22, Aquinas articulates the relationship between the figural, the literal, and the historical:

As was said above, just as in other prophecies, so too is it here a question of some present events at that time, insofar as they were a symbol of Christ (*figura Christi*) and pertained to prophecy itself. And for that reason, matters are sometimes set forth which pertain to Christ, which surpass, as it were, the power of the narrative (*virtutem historiarum*). This very Psalm, among others, treats of the passion of Christ in a spiritual manner (*inter alia spiritualiter*). And for this reason, this is its literal sense (*hic est eius sensus literalis*). Therefore, Jesus referred to this psalm particularly during his passion when he cried out "Eli, Eli, lema sabacthani", that is, "My God, my God" as begins the psalm. Thus, although this psalm speaks figuratively about David, nevertheless it is especially referred to Christ in a literal sense (*ad literam*). At the Synod of Toledo, a certain Theodorus Mopsuestenus, who was explaining this psalm literally with respect to David, was condemned, because of this approach, and for many other reasons; he ought to have explained it with respect to Christ. Let it be known this is treated of abundantly before the passion of Christ, of which this very Psalm is the first. (Made available online by DeSales University as part of their Aquinas Translation Project [http://www4.desales.edu/~philtheo/loughlin/ATP/Psalm_21.html])

Having stated that the danger is a specific kind of limited history, he does not refrain from commenting upon the psalm as it made its force felt in Israel and what the expressions mean according to comparable OT contexts. Aquinas handles the problem of the sins of the psalmist in Ps. 22 (how can a "figure" mean this and more, in respect of Christ?) differently than Augustine, though they both have Christ speaking on behalf of his church. Antiochene exegesis does not refuse a subsequent christological usage, but it tends to overstate or overdetermine a hypothetical historical context, at times disputing with relish even the

able to move to the subject matter to which it refers, using "history" as the indispensable staging point for that. Aquinas keeps in fine balance inquiry into the referentiality of the psalms in Israel's own carnal history, but finds the literal sense at work here (through word studies, comparisons with other OT passages, Hebrew lexicography) as well as immediately in reference to Christ. The NT need not be useful here in terms of showing this instinct through any specific exegetical example it itself develops. One moves from the New's reference to Psalm 22 and back into a full analysis of the psalm's literal, verse-by-verse, sense. It is useful to consider Aquinas's remarks about history and literal sense given modern preoccupation with historical reference. To conclude, then, if we bring Aquinas's concern for literal sense, figure, and history into the modern debates, what might we learn?

Watson's defence that he is interpreting the historical context of Paul is not just confusing measured against his insistence that we must not do likewise across the canon. So, for example, he insists that we must read Habakkuk not in the historical context of a reconstructed author in Israel's history, but in the canonical context of the XII (in point of fact, he means not "canonical context" in the sense of B. S. Childs, but rather "context of subsequent historical reception"). This leads to an ironic outcome, but one anticipated by Aquinas in his discussion of literal and historical sense in Theodore of Mopsuestia. In our view, Watson's insistence on a "historical sense" in the Second Testament and a different one in the Old,[28] measured

---

ones provided by superscriptions. See the commentary edited by Robert C. Hill, *Diodore of Tarsus: Commentary on Psalms 1–51* (Atlanta: SBL, 2005). Hill's introduction is a careful evaluation of this matter, and he has a similar analysis of Theodore and Chrysostom. Cf. John O'Keefe, "'A Letter that Killeth': Toward a Reassessment of Antiochene Exegesis, or Diodore, Theodore and Theodoret on the Psalms," *JECS* 8, no. 1 (2000): 83–104. My sense of the matter is that Antiochene exegesis can tend to overstipulate a historical context in the OT period, and it may also bristle at prophetical interpretations of Psalms—unless these are to be located within the OT's own historical period. There is a potential for a history-of-religions approach, but the matter must be handled carefully and the "Antiochene" approach is not monochrome. Theodore can allow David to prophesy Christ, but that is because a single sense calls for this reading, in three psalms. He does not like the idea of multiple sense reference and objects when a psalm is applied to Christ if it is theologically inappropriate.

28. This is because the significance of the OT is revealed by how the Second Testament hears it, in contrast to how other voices at the same historical period hear it. So either the "mental state" (authorial intent, mind of the prophet, etc.) or now the canonical sense is

against the concerns of Aquinas, offends against the literal sense—
but now of the NT.

That is, for Aquinas the literal sense of the psalms must be able
to attach to the subject matter Jesus Christ, which referent is revealed in a Second Testament, but which exists—really, materially
and not retrospectively only—under a sign (*figura Christi*) in the
First. Watson's giving priority to the historical context of Paul over
the canonical Paul or the NT as a whole, and his privileging of the
historical context of Paul over the canonical context of the Old (not
in Childs's sense, but in his own special sense of this), shows that
the Old's subject matter is not the Triune God (working in Israel,
in Christ, and in the church) but is instead *Paul's sense of it for his
purposes at one historical moment.* The subject matter of the OT
is Paul's use of it for a Second Testament's local theological claim,
viewed from the standpoint of a putative historical context (Paul's
dialogue with contemporaneous Jewish voices).

For Watson, the *res* or subject matter of "OT stories" is what, after
historical investigation (according to Watson) Paul makes of them;
the *res* is not, as for Aquinas, Calvin, or Luther, God himself: in his
work as Creator, Redeemer, Sanctifier, witnessed to from the OT's
plain sense. At the end of the day, the reason Watson's reading of the
OT is flawed is not simply due to a method inconsistently deployed
across two Testaments ("canonical" in the Old and "historical" in
the New), but rather, because with this he has obscured or evacuated
the subject matter of the OT proper to it as Christian Scripture. The
offense Aquinas saw in Theodore in the Old (restricting the literal
sense to Israel's own self-contained history), Watson manifests in the
New. For in his hands the New's "historical sense" becomes a local
sense and disallows the Old to sound its own Christian notes—and
these do entail the historical dimension of the literal sense as per
Aquinas.[29] This amounts to a Second Testament imitation by Watson
of Theodore's error in the First Testament. The local sense uncovered
by Theodore disallowed extension into the New, while Watson's
historical sense in the New says what needs to be said of the Old's

significant only insofar as it gives up its sense to the reception of it in the Second Testament.
This reception is procured by using historical tools.

29. See Childs, *Church's Guide*, 128–31.

literal sense. The Old makes its sense and having done that, it is handed over to the New's determinative historical appropriation. As we shall see, it is necessary to put modernity's species of history in scare quotes, because it is possible to conceive of history on altogether different terms.

The NT's literal sense—as these three premodern interpreters all assume—is not a kind of restricted historical snapshot in which the Old appears in the photo. It is a sense appropriate to its own testament's medium of witness. When that is properly grasped, it is not surprising to see these interpreters operating in a consistent fashion with the witness of the Old as well.

Conclusions: What Is History?

A final word is in order about history and historical analysis. It is often claimed that a canonical interpreter is opposed to history and just likes theology, abstraction, churchly or dogmatic claims, pious reading, and so forth.[30] The canonical reader is charged with being a kind of docetist, though the matter is usually stated imprecisely. The canonical sense, however, is in no way a sense to be contrasted with the historical sense. What is at issue here is what is meant by history.[31] The canonical sense is a historical sense, just as Aquinas is vitally concerned with the man David and the people Israel and not just appropriations of them seen from a later perspective. Watson works with a species of history in his NT analysis of the Old that now goes its own way, measured against what earlier interpreters saw as history, that is, as ingredient in the literal sense and incapable of divorce from it without doing violence to the subject matter.[32] Any

---

30. Ironically, these are the kind of charges Philip Davies laid at Watson's feet. See the exchange in Philip R. Davies, *Whose Bible Is It Anyway?* JSOTSup 204 (Sheffield: Sheffield Academic Press, 1995) and Francis Watson, "Bible, Theology and the University: A Response to Philip Davies," *JSOT* 71 (1996): 3–16.

31. See my essay, "What Lesson Will History Teach? The Book of the Twelve as History," in *"Behind" the Text: History and Biblical Interpretation*, Scripture and Hermeneutics Series 4, ed. Craig Bartholomew et al. (Grand Rapids: Zondervan, 2003), 443–67.

32. See, for example, his account of Moses and the veil. According to Watson, the historical facts are that Moses wore a veil to conceal the fading glory, so that the people would draw an erroneous conclusion about its permanence and not know the true state of

account of history must be able to understand the providential working of the Triune God within the people of Israel as well as the way
that working is substantive, figural, promising—not just for Israel
but for the church on the other side of a two-testament canonical
stabilization. This working is not collapsed into or circumscribed by
the NT's account of the gospel, but is seen for what it is—now even
by those outside the first covenants and promise—from the perspective of God's good time.[33]

It might be useful to have a feel for the way Paul or Jesus read
or received the OT in their frame of reference. The question is how
this kind of inquiry reattaches itself to theology proper, of a kind
grounded in history and the literal sense of Scripture. If this reattachment were to take place, it may be that one result would be conceiving
of the OT as Christian Scripture, proper to its own testament and

affairs (*Paul and the Hermeneutics of Faith*, 292–94). Paul's reading, as Watson has it, "is
firmly grounded in the Exodus text" (294). By maximizing the relationship between Paul's
interpretation and the OT's own historical sense, the historical events of Israel are only
revealed for what they are by means of this maximalization. "In keeping his transfigured
face concealed behind a veil, Moses prevents the Israelites from beholding the gradual
fading of the glory" (292) and this is what we can know to have been the "history" related
by the book of Exodus.

33. See the handling of this issue in Hans Frei, *The Eclipse of Biblical Narrative* (New
Haven: Yale University Press, 1972). In a careful formulation in respect of Calvin, concerning
the relationship between the enjoyment of the promised land as a reality by the old fathers
(the literal-historical dimension), but also of its figural character, he writes:

> The point is not really that the land of Canaan was a figure of the future inheritance
> at the time if, and only if, "the Israelites" knew it to be such. More important is the
> fact that they enjoyed the land as a figure of the eternal city, and thus it was a figure
> at that time. It is not a figure solely in later retrospective interpretive stance. Calvin is
> clearly contending that figural reading is a reading forward of the sequence. The mean-
> ing pattern of reality is inseparable from its forward motion; it is not the product of
> the wedding of that forward motion with a separate backward perspective on it, i.e.,
> of history and interpretation joined as two logically independent factors. Rather, the
> meaning of the full sequence emerges in the narration of the sequence, and therefore
> interpretation for Calvin must be, as Auerbach suggests it is for the tradition at large,
> part of the flowing stream which is historical life. (35–36)

Watson makes the later interpretation (as he sees it; one can of course contest his
reading of Paul and the veil) not only determine the meaning of the former episode,
but also its actual historical truthfulness, behind, as it were, the book of Exodus, which
never actually speaks in its literal sense of a clear act of concealment. The historical
and the figural have been collapsed into a retrospective divulging of what the actual
state of affairs was.

witness, and not just en route to that by virtue of its utilization in
the New. The turn to the history of interpretation does not show us
how to read the OT in our day any more than the NT does. Rather,
it helps us observe how interpreters allowed each respective testament to sound its theological notes, each as Christian Scripture,
each equidistant and at once proximate to the subject matter they
individually share.

5

OLD AND NEW IN CANONICAL INTERPRETATION

The Old Testament Example for New Testament Canonical Interpretation

In part as a function of its much longer tradition-history,[1] the OT frequently gives prominence in its final-form presentation to the question of how the relationship between original proclamation/setting and subsequent reception is to be understood. Deuteronomy is almost a textbook case of the challenge—and it is both a theological and historical challenge—of fitting a message once delivered into the providential design of its subsequent reception. "Not with our fathers . . . but with us, here, today, all of us" (Deut. 5:3) captures something of this concern: the first and constitutive revelation is appropriated in a second episode of review, so as to make that account permanently constitutive. And in many other places in the OT where the hermeneutical issue is not foregrounded in such an explicit way, we have been taught by observing the special character of OT literature, in its diachronic depth, to be sensitive to the way it has evolved over a long period according to a wide range of concerns. Concern for proper identification with an

---

1. K. Kertelge, "Biblische Exegese im Kontext katholischer Theologie," in Walter Kasper, Eberhard Schockenhoff, and Peter Walter, eds., *Dogma und Glaube: Bausteine für eine theologische Erkenntnislehre: Festschrift für Bischof Walter Kasper* (Mainz: Matthias-Grünewald-Verlag, 1993), 92.

ancient revelation, as an original message encounters generation after generation, is a hallmark of OT literature and may indeed mark it for what it is, whether in narrative, prophetic, or wisdom texts.

For this and other reasons, the OT frequently works with an understanding of "original authorial intention," which is much harder to understand conceptually and to appreciate hermeneutically. One need only consider a construct like "Moses wrote the Pentateuch" to realize at once how unconventional, measured against what is usually meant by authorship, such an understanding is.[2] Isaiah has recently been a virtual proving-ground for changing understandings of what we can say we mean by authorship and inspiration, and also what we can understand of a book in its complicated entirety, seeking to achieve a coherent total statement, even as it bridges innumerable settings and historical contexts en route to its final literary shape and rhetorical form.

At one level, then, this dimension of protraction has the potential to upset any easy act of hermeneutical identification with an author—though it has not prevented interpreters from trying. Though OT authors and editors may not comment on a scriptural legacy in the manner of the NT authors and a stable scriptural witness, OT interpretation has sharpened to a very high degree our capacity for appreciating a wide range of what might be called intratextual associations, whereby later traditions are shown to know and comment upon earlier traditions, and these frequently not just in oral and hypothetical reconstruction, but also in written and more easily attested form.[3] Still one can see right away that, in terms of canonical realities, there is no direct analogy between the use of the OT in the NT and what characterizes the OT's own internal development.[4] The factor of protraction could easily

2. This is stock in trade in OT discussion. See Christopher R. Seitz, *Word without End: The Old Testament as Abiding Theological Witness* (Grand Rapids: Eerdmans, 1998), or Jon D. Levenson, "The Eight Principles of Judaism and the Literary Simultaneity of Scripture," *JR* 68, no. 2 (1988), reprinted in *The Hebrew Bible, the Old Testament, and Historical Criticism* (Louisville: Westminster John Knox, 1993), 62–81.

3. Michael A. Fishbane, *Biblical Interpretation in Ancient Israel* (New York: Oxford University Press, 1985). Also, H. G. M. Williamson, *The Book Called Isaiah* (Oxford: Clarendon, 1994); B. Sommer, *A Prophet Reads Scripture: Allusion in Isaiah 40–66* (Stanford: Stanford University Press, 1998).

4. See my "Two Testaments and One Tradition History," in *Figured Out: Typology and Providence in Christian Scripture* (Louisville: Westminster John Knox, 2001).

have resulted in something like this, but the OT did not evolve to final form, accounting even for its major internal divisions, in anything like the subsequent development of a separate NT canonical division and a twofold canon of Christian Scripture.[5]

I want to call attention to three different places where the canonical shaping of OT books offers us a glimpse at methods of editing and affiliation that might be useful for understanding the canonical shape of the NT canon, especially in the area of hermeneutics and identification. As noted, the hermeneutical instincts of romantic theories of authorial intention have had their way in OT studies for some time, as the quest for the original and the secondary has worked its magic for over two centuries of interpretation. That the books appear to handle matters like authorship very differently has not prevented interpreters from using tools for such analysis even when it looked like they were ill-suited to the specific hermeneutical challenge of the OT. My discussion here must be very brief.[6]

Jeremiah does not have anything like the period of gestation and development that characterizes the book of Isaiah, even though, along with Ezekiel, it forms one of the three large-scale collections of the prophetic division of the canon.[7] The influence of deuteronomistic traditions is everywhere acknowledged, even as what that might mean is nowhere near consensus. We have noted the concern for bridging the generations that features prominently, including teaching the next generations, in deuteronomistic discourse, and this is often a means of identifying the influence of such traditions in books like Jeremiah. In several essays I have sought to show how this concern features differently in canonically shaped and roughly distinguished sections of Jeremiah.[8] In chapters 1–6, for example, the distance between the

---

5. See Childs's perceptive comments in *Biblical Theology of the Old and New Testaments* (Minneapolis: Fortress, 1994), 74–77.

6. See my discussion of nineteenth-century romantic theory in the prophetic literature in Christopher R. Seitz, "On Letting a Text 'Act Like a Man'—The Book of the Twelve: New Horizons for Canonical Reading, with Hermeneutical Reflections," *SBET* 22 (2004): 151–72.

7. On the Book of the Twelve, see Christopher R. Seitz, *Prophecy and Hermeneutics: Towards a New Introduction to the Prophets*, Studies in Theological Interpretation (Grand Rapids: Baker Academic, 2007).

8. Most recently, "The Place of the Reader in Jeremiah," in *Reading the Book of Jeremiah: A Search for Coherence*, ed. M. Kessler (Winona Lake, IN: Eisenbrauns, 2004), 67–75;

authorial situation of Jeremiah, addressing the northern kingdom and using this as an object lesson for the southern kingdom (a move already in line with the phenomenon we are describing), and a subsequent period is made patent at several points. The southern kingdom is not just to be warned by the fate of the northern kingdom, but both serve as object lessons for a generation outside of and after the great judgment of Babylonian defeat and exile. Seeing the lack of repentance in previous generations and the awful trail of judgment this occasioned, they now speak into the past setting a word of penitence and confession. The historical reality is not subsumed by later reflection; it remains for all to see and with penetrating historical force and character. But the editors have allowed the word of Jeremiah to overtake subsequent generations and have done this in such a way as allows all subsequent generations, and not those we might date and locate at some period of editorial work in Babylonian exile, made precise by OT comparisons and sharpened tradition-historical lenses,[9] to join them. Remaining sections of Jeremiah offer similar lessons from history, with different characters and different purposes, themselves based upon the historical particularities that gave them rise in the last days of the Prophet Jeremiah and the kingdom of Judah.

Jeremiah is one of the Three, as distinguished from the Twelve (the matter of Daniel does not effect the evaluation at this point). There is no evidence that the three major prophetic collections have been shaped with an eye toward one another; and the order in which they appear, while well-attested, is not fixed in all lists.[10] Jeremiah appears to be related to Deuteronomy (a book in another canonical division) in some way, but this requires a critical judgment; such influence is by

---

also, "The Prophet Moses and the Canonical Shape of Jeremiah," *ZAW* 101 (1989): 1–15; *Theology in Conflict: Reactions to the Exile in the Book of Jeremiah* (Berlin: de Gruyter, 1989).

9. Ernest W. Nicholson, *Preaching to the Exiles: A Study of the Prose Tradition in the Book of Jeremiah* (Oxford: Blackwell, 1970).

10. *B. Bat.* 14b has an order the rabbis explain as all judgment (Jeremiah), half judgment and half salvation (Ezekiel), and all salvation (Isaiah). See also Julio Trebolle-Barrera, "Qumran Evidence for a Biblical Standard Text and for Non-Standard and Parabiblical Texts," in *The Dead Sea Scrolls in Their Historical Context*, ed. Timothy H. Lim (Edinburgh: T&T Clark, 2000), 89–106, esp. 94–95, 98; and Edgar W. Conrad, *Reading the Latter Prophets: Towards a New Canonical Criticism* (New York: T&T Clark, 2003). Both Trebolle-Barrera and Conrad, though for different reasons, see the significance of the proximity of Isaiah to the XII.

no means restricted to Jeremiah, and the scale of determination of such influence is not an exact science—indeed some dispute it. Deuteronomistic influences have been seen in the Book of the Twelve, but without any urgent need of correlation with Jeremiah. Jeremiah is its own book, canonically speaking, even as signs of affiliation remain in the final form of its presentation with the major, concluding work of the Pentateuch. That book, Deuteronomy, also seeks to take a historical setting—in its case, a constructive and life-giving one—and assure that it remains active and living for generations who were not with Moses but for whom the original address is incapable of historicizing (except as an act of disobedience). Its final location is crucial. Even as it has been viewed as part of the "Deuteronomistic History" that follows it, for which it serves as introduction, its relationship to the pentateuchal books, for the reasons noted above, is hermeneutically decisive. So it belongs properly at the close of the first canonical division (Torah). The function of John in the fourfold Gospel collection might fruitfully be compared here.[11]

Isaiah has had an extremely long and complicated history of development. It shows us far less of its author, and the sharpness of its original historical setting is only occasionally brokered and with nothing like the same set of interests (biography; lament) or in the same manner (historical chronicle; sermons) as we see in Jeremiah. It is its own book. Rarely is much made of deuteronomistic influence in Isaiah. But the key distinguishing feature is the ambition of its historical range, which makes Ezekiel and Jeremiah, even with allowance for subsequent editorial work in them both, appear compressed by comparison. The way in which it accommodates, hermeneutically, this historical range and ambition looks nothing like what we see in Jeremiah, and perhaps that only confirms the prior point. It prefers to work with typology and analogy (Assyria and Babylon; Ahaz and Hezekiah; closing and opening ears; sealed book and disclosed word; daughter Zion and daughter Babylon; servant and servants). In fairness, there is really no other book in the entire canon like it, and not for nothing was it considered from early times in the history of its reception in Christian circles, a "fifth Gospel." It gathers to itself

11. See Seitz, "Booked Up," in *Figured Out*, 91–102.

all the grand themes that could be said typologically to adumbrate the Bible in its two-testament entirety, while its theological ambition marks it as a book worthy of analogy with something like the similarly unique form of a Gospel. But it clearly goes its own way.[12]

What can be said about Isaiah, and is now increasingly emphasized, is that in many ways its closest partner is the Book of the Twelve. They begin with similar historical superscriptions (Hosea 1:1 and Isa. 1:1), exhibit the same historical range, contain almost identical texts (Isa. 2:1–5; Mic. 4:1–5), speak of reversals in the nations' comprehension, and end with similar words of admonition and warning. Both use psalm material to assist the reader in appropriation and reflection.[13] Steck in particular has sought painstakingly to show the mutual influencing in their respective editorial histories. Unlike Isaiah, however, reconstruction of the editorial history of the Twelve is, in theory, aided by the fact that its individual parts are there for examination on terms of the canon's own delivery. Historical-critical study has been persuasive, in large measure, in showing that individual books in the Twelve have found their locations not simply for reasons of chronological sequencing; other factors are at work, and chief among these are hermeneutical ones, involving the application of an ancient word to subsequent generations.[14]

Joel, for example, takes up the challenge posed and unfulfilled, at the end of Hosea ("return, O Israel, to the LORD your God" at 14:1). It depicts an occasion of repentance and illustrates the character of the

12. For fuller treatment and bibliography, see the essays on Isaiah in Seitz, *Word without End.*

13. On this feature in the Twelve, see Seitz, *Prophecy.* On this feature in Isaiah see Rolf Rendtorff, "Isaiah 6 in the Framework of the Composition of the Book," in *Canon and Theology: Overtures to an Old Testament Theology, Overtures to Biblical Theology* (Minneapolis: Fortress, 1993), 170–80; James W. Watts, *Psalm and Hymns in Hebrew Narrative,* JSOTSup 139 (Sheffield: JSOT, 1992); and others. Hezekiah and Habakkuk are types in their respective collections, as both utter psalms of penitence and trust inside periods of judgment.

14. Compare the otherwise intriguing analysis of Francis Watson in *Paul and the Hermeneutics of Faith* (London: T&T Clark, 2004). It seems that his adoption of a sequencing/ historicizing editorial concern stems from a need for Habakkuk to stand out as commenting on divine action (or lack of it) in history. Very few modern interpreters of the redaction history of the XII would follow him at this point. One would have to assume both a high degree of independence of individual books and also an unawareness of their actual setting, such as they could then be fitted into a different historical grid (especially later books like Joel, Obadiah, Jonah).

desisting and forbearing God known by Hosea himself (especially in the marriage-tableau of chaps. 1–3), and now shares that fundamental character for a new generation as a whole (Joel 1:2–3), on precisely the terms of YHWH's constitutive revelation at Sinai (Joel 2:13).[15] Joel gives content to the "Day of the LORD" in a way that both enriches and clarifies the appearance of that same reality in Amos.[16] The hermeneutical contribution of this later book moves both backward in time, to attach on the one hand to Hosea and on the other to Amos;[17] but also forward, by a prophet determined to hear and obey an ancient word and then to make that obedience and new life a genuine reality in a later day, at a time of ecological hardship greater than what Hosea had warned would constitute YHWH's judgment in his own day. The function of Obadiah and Jonah in their respective locations in the XII, and the positioning of Habakkuk before Zephaniah, also serve to illustrate similarly penetrating hermeneutical insights, which inhere with OT prophecy at its most basic level. God speaks words that accomplish things (Isa. 55:11).

A search for authorial intention and identification, if carried out in a narrowly historical-descriptive manner, would rush right past this maturation process and misconstrue the effort of the literature itself, in terms of historical shaping, to build a bridge to subsequent generations and indeed to us. "We are not prophets" but are none the less for it, in view of the canonical process. As with their apostolic counterparts, the prophets see what they see in their day, according to the lavish workings of God's providential insight, but then are taken up into that same providential design and placed down within a mighty cloud of witnesses. The Book of the Twelve shows us this in a kind

15. See among others Raymond C. Van Leeuwen, "Scribal Wisdom and Theodicy in the Book of the Twelve," in *In Search of Wisdom: Essays in Memory of John G. Gammie*, ed. Leo G. Perdue, Bernard B. Scott, and William J. Wiseman (Louisville: Westminster John Knox, 1993).

16. Rolf Rendtorff, "How to Read the Book of the Twelve as a Theological Unity," in *Reading and Hearing the Book of the Twelve*, ed. James D. Nogalski and Marvin A. Sweeney (Atlanta: SBL, 2000), 75–87.

17. On the way in which this process of association begins with Amos and Hosea, see the essay of Jörg Jeremias, "The Interrelationship between Amos and Hosea," in *Forming Prophetic Literature: Essays on Isaiah and the Twelve in Honor of John D. W. Watts*, JSOTSup 235, ed. James W. Watts and Paul R. House (Sheffield: Sheffield Academic Press, 1996), 171–86.

of detail (when historical evaluation is properly tuned to its task) that allows us to see where and how a comparison with canonical shaping in the NT is possible and potentially illuminating.

Recent studies of the final editorial form of the XII, precisely when they acknowledge the diachronic complexity of the arrangement, begin to highlight a process of communication that shifts the locus of interpretation away from "authorial intention" toward "an implied audience." The historical dimension uncovered by attention to the original proclamation and reception is not undercut, but is placed within a far more comprehensive depiction. This comprehensive depiction requires historical-critical labor, but it asks more of it. For the entire movement from original prophetic word to final arrangement must be handled with sensitivity if one is going to be able to assess the effect of the final canonical "book" as it has now been handed over to us. The individuality of the witnesses, and their respective editorial histories, must be respected. But this happens at the service of the final canonical presentation, allowing us to make an identification with the prophets of the most particular sort, *precisely as we understand the difference between themselves and us, in accordance with God's providential ordering.* The literature itself trains us to appreciate this distinction.

> A canonical reading of the Twelve, far from shutting off the experiential world of Amos and his colleagues, situates us properly, and him, and them, so that we might gaze on the history of God's word with Israel, and nations, and creation, and finally with his own Son. Such a reading teaches us where to stand and where to identify our proper place in that history, which providentially reaches out to enclose us even now in God's judgment and mercy. [George Adam] Smith could move from the world of the prophets to the pulpit, and bring alive the man Amos for his audience. A canonical reading of Amos among the Twelve gives us a world of reference and identification no less bold and no less enclosing of us and our world than that; *and it does it on the terms of its own deliverance.* We are made to stand before the Twelve and see the word go forth, address generations, enclose the prophets in a history larger than themselves, and then reach out and locate us in its grand sweep—in judgment and in mercy—before that same holy God.[18]

18. "Prophecy and Hermeneutics: Canonical Reading and Hermeneutical Reflections," in Seitz, *Prophecy*, 244–45.

"Scripture and Tradition" in the Light of Biblical Tradition-History

Recent studies of the Pauline Letter collection are beginning to ask questions like the ones posed above in the Book of the Twelve.[19] The difference between the two canonical realities (Paul and the XII) is obvious enough, and in the context of modern historical-critical study of the Bible, where work on the different Testaments rarely overlaps, this has served to annex entirely any interest in understanding shared features of canonical shaping, not to mention the possibility that *at a formal level, the OT has had a decisive influence on the final shaping of the NT canon.* We can ask about the way NT figures like Paul use the OT and even seek to imitate them in practices historical study has taught us to appreciate; the hermeneutical limitations of this are the subject of the present discussion. Yet further, how often does NT scholarship consider the influence of the OT in guiding, controlling, or constraining the formal, canonical character of the NT? The imbalance in assessment of the two-testament canon of Scripture is a function of specific historical, developmental preoccupations in biblical studies, but it also has to do with the way in which Christian readers have understood the Testaments to function canonically in respect of identification and appropriation in the church. The use of the OT in the NT is a classic example of the danger of confusing historical-critical and canonical-historical categories. The result is a diminishment of the effect of the NT canonical form on the interpretation of individual witnesses in the NT, not limited to their use of the OT, as well as a misunderstanding of how the OT functions canonically as Christian Scripture.

Proper appreciation of the formal differences between the canonical divisions of the OT and NT will be best secured when we ask similar questions about the nature of affiliation and relationship that the canonical process has effected in each respective division. What does

19. Stanley E. Porter, ed., *The Pauline Canon* (Leiden: Brill, 2004); Robert W. Wall, "Reading the New Testament in Canonical Context," in *Hearing the New Testament*, ed. Joel B. Green (Grand Rapids: Eerdmans, 1995), 370–93; David Trobisch, *Paul's Letter Collection: Tracing the Origins* (Minneapolis: Fortress, 1994); Brevard S. Childs, *The Church's Guide for Reading Paul* (Grand Rapids: Eerdmans, 2008).

it mean that NT letters have been attributed to one author, even given the now-agreed dimension of editing and redaction history operative in individual books? What does it mean that Paul's letters do not appear, strictly speaking, in a chronological order that historical criticism has taught us to appreciate? What does it mean that letters that may not be written by Paul have been brought within his orbit? And where are there signs that the material has been presented in such a way as to highlight the intentionality of Paul—even his appropriation of the Scriptures of Israel for his argument—without confusing the distinction between his apostolic office and those to whom he speaks? Can we see signs of editorial arrangement in the final shaping of the material, including a concern for the application of Paul's message to an implied audience, and not just the one we have been sensitized into conceiving on primarily historical/original setting terms?

Investigation of canonical shaping in the Book of the Twelve is one place where an appreciation of the Pauline Letter collection (a "book of thirteen") might benefit, especially in the area of hermeneutics, identification, and appropriation. The nature of the difference between these two collections is obvious when one considers the ingredient parts and the genre differences. But there is less clear a distinction when one asks about the effect of placing individual works in a certain sequence, with signs of editorial affiliation, even of a different sort to what we see in the XII; here the possibility of fruitful comparison should be followed up. Whatever can be said on this score, our point in this treatment involves the way in which the canon properly constrains our interpretation of individual writings and identification with authorial intention. We have focused on the phenomenon of the use by NT authors of OT writings, because the potential for understanding this as a major category for biblical theology and hermeneutical application has proven high in recent NT scholarship.

Childs has rightly cautioned about the problems of biblicism inherent in such a NT appeal and has offered the caution, "we are not prophets or apostles." The phrase, however, requires explanation and elaboration. We have sought to provide this. The canon is the best guide to identification with biblical authors, and theological appropriation of the OT and NT would best proceed by asking whether and how the canonical shaping has sought to anticipate questions of identification and has provided an answer at the formal level of the canon. Naturally, if one disregards the canon as an empty container or considers it a pernicious factor whose shape and limits must be eliminated, such a conclusion would not follow. But then, as mentioned in the first section of this chapter, we would at least go some way toward distinguishing what kind of biblical project is being undertaken in the area of theology and hermeneutics.

The church "is not prophet or apostle," but what an Isaiah or a Paul delivers to the church is not for this reason in a historical archive, a holy shrine, or a classroom for studied imitation. The hermeneutical and theological challenge is greater than this. Historical criticism has sharpened our eye in enormously productive ways in terms of appreciating the historically situated character of OT and NT, including now great sensitivity toward the exegesis of the OT in the NT as an empirical reality. But it will have stopped short if it does not ask about the effect of canonical shaping in the final form of the canon as a historical reality as well. Too often the attention to the stability of a reconstructed historical setting has been properly augmented by attention to the dynamic of tradition-history, in both OT and NT, without an assessment of the stability achieved at the end of the process, as a form of historical, theological, and hermeneutical maturation, worthy of our careful attention. We conclude with a final example that illustrates this point.

Roman Catholic Considerations in the Light of "Scripture and Tradition"

In a recent essay, Kertelge describes the extraordinary challenges for Roman Catholic scholarship occasioned by acceptance of historical-critical methods and the changes these methods have made in how one properly understands the relationship between NT studies, systematic theology, and the life of the church.[20] He rightly sees that any movement to embrace such methods will entail concomitantly a revisiting of the question of the Roman Catholic Church's investment in "tradition" as a "source" of authority. Here then the question of

---

20. Kertelge, "Biblische Exegese," 88–99.

churchly identification with the canon is raised from a different direction of concern. In Roman Catholic circles, unlike those in which Hays or Lincoln move, the question of identification with Scripture has been tied up with ecclesial realities in a fairly immediate sense. "Scripture and Tradition" can be said to circumscribe the question of identification within the context of ecclesial authority. If the relationship of tradition to Scripture is differently conceived, and if the former ceases to be an authority alongside Scripture, or a warrant for ecclesially determined identifications by the faithful, and instead is Scripture as it lives its life in the challenges and decisions faced through time by the church, the matter of identification and canon are reopened from a different direction than what we have seen in the discussion thus far.

Kertelge's account of NT scholarship focuses on the dynamic of tradition-history said to be characteristic of the gospel's proclamation, from inception through to final canonical form. This tradition-history NT scholarship has painstakingly and comprehensively charted. There is therefore only a relative priority to the idea of canonical stability and temporal priority, over against tradition. For "tradition" formerly conceived is now understood as the organic extension of the same tradition-historical process, uncovered by NT scholarship, as it moves into the lived life of the church. It is not that "tradition" is an independent source of authority, as in former articulations, to be set alongside Scripture. Rather, Scripture itself contains a tradition-history said to be virtually identical in character to what transpires in the church—on the basis of Scripture's living application—even as it is temporally posterior to the NT's own declarations.

With this adjustment in place, Kertelge does not prioritize identification with authorial intention as historical scholarship might reconstruct this, highlighting this feature at the center of the NT canon. Indeed he cautions about this kind of single focus on a biblical figure, presumably because it could wrongly highlight the moment of inception in the tradition-historical process he has otherwise chosen to emphasize. Overemphasis on Paul as the great Protestant hero and the central, model interpreter of Christ in the NT (as well as interpreter of the OT) may also lie behind his concern, though this is not stated. Kertelge speaks of attention to the implied audience of Paul and the effective history of his message. The situating of the church, not so much with Paul, but with the church to whom he speaks, and the emphasis on generations beyond the historical Paul, resonates in some measure with the canonical concerns of our present discussion. But for Kertelge the canon is not a decisive feature, beyond being that "container" that gives us access to the dynamic tradition-historical process said to lie within it, and behind it, which will in time spill out beyond it.

It is for this reason that the church may not identify with prophet or apostle in the manner of Hays or Lincoln, but in a far broader sense it identifies with a process of tradition-history taking place within the NT and giving rise to a church that without complication is continuous through time, in a newly defined "tradition," enclosing the present Roman Catholic Church without obvious seam or disjunction. The effect on the OT as a specific canonical witness to Christ in its *per se* voice is not a topic under discussion in the essay, but Kertelge contrasts its own long tradition-history with that of the NT in such a way as to suggest that the work it does is *in initiating a tradition-history process leading into the NT*. Its contribution as canonical witness to God in Christ would then be seen chiefly in these tradition-historical, developmentally significant terms.

The appeal to tradition-historical process, even in a highly theological form, as a governing category for biblical theology is problematical on a number of levels. On both sides of the canonical division, it substitutes an organic process lying below the final form for an assessment of the dynamic of the canonical character of the Scriptures in their present, received shape. Second, it tends to blur the distinction between the Testaments as constitutive of their character as Christian Scripture for the church; two Testaments become instead one tradition history. Third, it will represent the ongoing revelatory and inspired character of Christian Scripture in largely developmental terms, and whatever may be true about that apart from an appeal to tradition-history, it ignores the theological insight at work in the appeal in antiquity to the "rule of faith." This rule sought to ground the authority of the OT in theological terms, having to do with the revelation of the One God under two distinct orders of disclosure, one latent, and one patent, the second (NT) in accordance with the first (OT); a tradition-historical account will have difficulty retaining this fundamental insight, grounded at the level of God's eternal self and will. As we have seen in the case of Hebrews, Psalm 8 does not deliver its meaning chiefly as Hebrews hears it, but rather as, in the light of the fuller claims of the NT as a canonical totality, the psalm can be seen to bear witness to God's work in Israel and in Jesus Christ, for the world of God's redeeming care.

To return to the discussion with which this chapter began: The church is not somehow in a more natural place of identification with apostle than with prophet. Neither does the apostolic witness, as it makes material use of the prophetic, give us an exhaustive account of the OT's work as Christian Scripture, and this not least because it has taken up so little of its final form in its own material witnessing. It was precisely for this reason, and others, that the early church deployed a rule of faith, not as a Geiger counter, which could demonstrate which parts of the OT were theologically useful and which ones not, or which ones could do their work because the NT said so, or which portions of the OT could now be safely set aside and a new tradition-historical OT canon constructed in its place.[21] Rather, the rule of faith made maximal claims about the way the OT was available for Christian interpretation, precisely because of the insistence that the God made known in Jesus Christ was fully at work in the revelation of the Scriptures that promised his appearing. One could now read the OT Scriptures according to their own idiom, and yet in that idiom as bearing witness to the work of God in Christ. The OT would teach the church about its historical past to be sure, but also primarily about its moral life; the figural adumbration of its liturgical practices; basic doctrinal insights due to the expanse of its theophanic range and the theological density of talk about God (see Hab. 3 in discussions about creation, providence, and incarnation in precritical exegesis); and about the Christian's final eschatological purpose and hope. But the main contribution of the OT was seen

---

21. See my recent discussion of modern appeals to a rule of faith in Christopher Seitz, *The Goodly Fellowship of the Prophets: The Achievement of Association in Canon Formation* (Grand Rapids: Baker Academic, 2009), as well as the final chapter below.

to be in its articulation of God's identity, pressuring the trinitarian claims as basic to its own literal sense.[22]

The church confuses its place as neither prophet nor apostle, but because of its specific providential location, is able to hear both OT and NT canonical witness as Christian Scripture, each according to the purpose God has ordained. This was the point made in the previous chapter. *The turn to the history of interpretation does not show us how to read the OT in our day, any more than the NT does. Rather, it helps us observe how earlier interpreters allowed each respective Testament to sound its theological notes, each as Christian Scripture, each equidistant and at once proximate to the subject matter they both share.*

In the next chapter we will examine, with the aid of a practical example, how the "rule of faith" serves to open the Scriptures of Israel for the early church, and for the church in our day, and so assure that basic theological claims are not sacrificed due to a faulty appraisal of the nature of the two-testament witness to Jesus Christ. We seek to give a practical example of the "rule of faith" by attention to the role of worship and liturgy as a lens on hermeneutics and theological appropriation of the canon, especially the OT as Christian Scripture. The final chapter will look more closely at the appeal to the rule of faith in the ante-Nicene period, in order to determine the theological and exegetical claims to which the rule points. These function in relationship to the sole scriptural witness (OT) and stipulate, in a wide variety of ways, its (incipiently) "trinitarian" character. The rule, then, is not a general statement of catholic faith, or a "gist" of the Scriptures' economic account, en route to the declaratory creeds of the church. Rather, it focuses on the ontological realities of God in Christ through the various economies of the OT. These open up the dimension of "accordance" as this finds articulation collaterally in the apostolic writings of the period, en route to a "New Testament."

---

22. Kavin Rowe's fine essay joins the work of Yeago and Bauckham on this topic. See my essay on "The Trinity in the Old Testament" (Oxford University Press, forthcoming).

6

"Be Ye Sure That the Lord He Is God"—Crisis in Interpretation and the Two-Testament Voice of Christian Scripture

This chapter looks at the two-testament character of Christian Scripture from the standpoint of a contemporary crisis in the church. As such it does not represent an extension of the argument of the book, strictly speaking, but is instead a sort of laboratory in which to evaluate the claims being made about the character of Christian Scripture and especially the way the OT functions theologically. The tone will therefore be different. It is hoped that by providing a concrete example of the breakdown of the rule of faith, as reinforced practically in the worship tradition of one segment of the church, it will be easier to understand the methodological and conceptual argument being pursued in the preceding chapters. The final chapter will return to the main argument and give a grounding for the rule of faith by attention to more formal matters of church history, scriptural interpretation, and theology.

The following points will emerge in the course of the chapter:

1. The same-sex crisis in the American Episcopal Church (TEC) and in other churches is a symptom of a deeper disagreement over the interpretation of Scripture.

2. Particularly challenging—though not often stated clearly—is the formal character of Scripture, that is, as consisting of two Testaments.

3. In the early church the rule of faith functioned to assure that certain minimal theological claims were not being obscured or compromised: chief among these was that the OT functioned as Christian Scripture, because the risen and worshiped Lord was one with the named LORD of Israel's revealed witness. Negatively ruled out were understandings of the OT as primarily a *phase of religious development*.

4. Anglicans and others can see the "rule of faith" most obviously at work in the canticles of Morning Prayer worship, when OT psalms (e.g., Ps. 100, the "Jubilate Deo") are concluded with, "Glory be to the Father, and to the Son, and to the Holy Ghost, as it was in the beginning, etc."

5. This Book of Common Prayer practice, which goes well back into the tradition, represents a doxological reinforcement of the rule of faith, allowing the two-testament voice of Scripture to be properly heard.

6. If the intention of the doxology is not being grasped in respect to a rule of faith, we have a breakdown at a level I will call "tacit knowledge."

Such a breakdown has occurred. Resolution will not therefore be forthcoming until basic assumptions about Scripture find their conviction again, at the level of tacit knowledge. This points more to a spiritual problem than to the need for new exegetical techniques or the provision of practical schemes for accommodation.

Introduction: Crisis in Interpretation

Like a great many American churches, the Episcopal Church (TEC) is in crisis. One can say that now and not be considered an alarmist. Newspaper headlines regularly announce the crisis, which manifests itself in a wide variety of ways, from membership decline, to lawsuits over property, to public brawls between churches and bishops, to conflicted detachments from TEC and realignments elsewhere. The larger communion and its identity, and ECUSA's place in it, are the subject of serious reflection, evaluation, trial proposals, action, and counteraction. The scope of the problem entails the life of the Episcopal Church in a global communion, so the public accounting tracks along the same global lines.

The crisis has also resurfaced older issues, and anyone following the new "blog" environment will know these matters are discussed with varying degrees of energy and intelligence—whether women's ordination, or Catholic and Protestant emphases in Anglicanism, or basic matters like the authority of Scripture, the desirability of a confessional identity, the nature of global accountability, and so forth. It is fair to say that the same-sex issue, whatever else it may be in its own right, has shaken the foundations not just of the Episcopal Church as an institution, but the very identity, logic, and historical claim of Anglicanism to be what it has said it is. Other churches in the West experience the crisis in ways that mirror their own history, polity, and demography. That the epicenter of much of the Anglican turmoil is in the United States, where freedom of choice is a basic right and a supermarket of churches exists to choose from or start up, only exacerbates the issue, as people flee to this or that purer or better church, in their mind's eye or in reality.

Just exactly why we are in crisis is not easy to pinpoint. The blessing of same-sex relationships is what it is, but it is probably as much a symptom as a cause.

All along it has been reasonably clear that the Bible and the character of its authority are where the disagreements, broadly speaking, locate themselves—however much one might have preferred to talk about human rights, church authority, the role of human experience in theological argument, differing understandings of communion and autonomy, and so forth. Recently various parties in the struggle appear to be willing to acknowledge that a chief, maybe the chief, disagreement is over the interpretation of Scripture and the question of whether the Bible has something like a plain sense, in the case of same-sex behavior and in other areas.

But we need to pause and consider how we have come to this point. I have been involved in the discussion over exegesis of Scripture and homosexuality long enough to know that the ground has shifted over the past two decades. That we may now agree about the centrality of the interpretation of Scripture in this crisis is not something that has come about straightforwardly, and because of this the potential for confusion, ongoing conflict, and final irresolution is very high.

Because my concern is not with the same-sex issue as such, but with the crisis over the interpretation of Scripture more generally, let me move briskly through three phases.

Phase One. Initially it was argued that biblical texts could be reevaluated and now were thought to be saying something that no one had heard them say quite rightly before. Sodom was about inhospitality, not homosexuality; chapter 1 of Romans was about specific, exotic *kinds* of homosexual misconduct in late antiquity; and so forth. This approach was bolstered by a general confidence in historical-critical methods and how they promised to show us original contexts that would then override a manifest consensus in the prior history of interpretation.[1]

Phase Two. Then it was conceded—often by *proponents* of a change in sexual teaching—that the texts did in fact say what they had previously been heard to say, in a great many cases and in spite of a robust application of historical-critical acids.[2] And so it was conceded that the Bible really was consistently negative about same-sex behavior. Now it would need to be argued that what the Bible gave us was a kind of rough guide on how to make decisions.[3] Biblical

---

1. Note here the probably unexpected transformation of the principle of *sola Scriptura* in Enlightenment hands.

2. David Balch, *Homosexuality, Science, and the "Plain Sense" of Scripture* (Grand Rapids: Eerdmans, 2000).

3. George A. Lindbeck refers to this mode of reading Scripture as experiential-expressive (*The Nature of Doctrine: Religion and Theology in a Postliberal Age* [Philadelphia: Westminster, 1984]), and the early title of Luke T. Johnson's work points in this direction: *Decision Making in the Church: A Biblical Model* (Philadelphia: Fortress, 1983).

people had to exercise judgment, and they went about this with certain flexible systems that allowed them to negotiate religious principles with changing times. Usually the Council of Jerusalem (in Acts 15) was used as the NT example of such flexibility,[4] but more ambitious minds thought they could track this kind of religious process-thinking across both Old and New Testaments.[5] Still, I stay with this phase of interpretation for a moment to note a trend: when one begins to think that the Bible offers examples of how people go about making decisions, generally speaking, one will probably already have decided that it does this better at later moments than earlier ones. Things progress and get better (presumably because of trial and error over time). This phase of interpretation is actually only a staging point for where we now find ourselves.

Phase Three. The present view seems to be that the Bible does not help us with same-sex behavior in our day, because what we have in our day was unknown in biblical times. The notion of developmental change and wisdom appropriate to assess it requires some kind of religious justification, and what we usually find here is an appeal to the Holy Spirit's ongoing work and enlightenment in our special day. This is what one hears when reading the general remarks of two presiding bishops of TEC, and other religious leaders, on the issue. What has happened through these three overlapping phases is that the Bible has been turned into a book of religious development, from one Testament to the next. Once this happens, it is easy, and I would say necessary, for the arguments to end where they now do. Let me try to describe the impasse.

On the one side, people argue that the Bible cannot speak a word directly into our day on the issue of same-sex behavior, because it cannot be expected to know something that lies developmentally outside its own two-testament range of religious progressing. This also allows those with such an interpretive (hermeneutical) view to

4. See my discussion in "Dispirited: Scripture as Rule of Faith and Recent Misuse of the Council of Jerusalem," in *Figured Out: Typology and Providence in Christian Scripture* (Louisville: Westminster John Knox, 2001).

5. Stephen Fowl's work (*Engaging Scripture*) is relevant here, as is Ellen Davis's chapter in *Reading Scripture*. See Stephen E. Fowl, *Engaging Scripture: A Model for Theological Interpretation* (Malden, MA: Blackwell, 1998); Ellen F. Davis and Richard Hays, eds., *The Art of Reading Scripture* (Grand Rapids: Eerdmans, 2003).

maintain a residual hunch that the biblical texts in question have multiple meanings, or that their meaning is contested and cannot be delivered plainly, because serial deployments of historical-critical readings, with varying results, have confused the issue and made the very notion of a "plain sense" nostalgic or illusory. That is, the idea of developing religious wisdom goes hand in hand with an acceptance that texts from past contexts *can only with real difficulty have any kind of meaning for the present full-stop*. The Bible becomes "stories" or "resources," at best, and its language is evocative or imaginative; it has no legislative (halakhic), exhortative, constraining, or strictly referential sense; it has "themes," which resonate with intuitions or convictions already in place, and so forth. This is why proponents for change in a teaching that runs against the entire history of the Bible's reception, in church and synagogue, have still said, even if reluctantly, that what is at issue is the interpretation of Scripture. What they mean is that there is sufficient confusion about what any text means, that the only thing we can be sure of is what people report to be true in their present experience. Progressivism has thrived for its own sake and because the Bible no longer has anything like a plain sense to which appeal can be made. It is instead an example of the very same internal progressivism and disagreement said to be true of our own age. The Bible looks like us. That is our interpretive conclusion.

On the other side, people want to say that the Bible has authority, and a plain sense, and that what others see as homophobia or traditionalism, is for them a crisis having to do with the Bible becoming a kind of "wax nose" capable of any interpretation. It is not so much that same-sex behavior is a particularly loathsome sin or that those claiming a gay lifestyle are special sinners—one could conclude that we in the West have been culturally desensitized to all manner of sexual conduct to such an extent that the very notion of sexual sin is almost antique and irrelevant. No, what the other side feels threatened by is the Bible's possible inability to speak in any clear or straightforward way at all. What for one side is freedom of the spirit or attention to a "cultural injustice" is for the other an example of a "plain sense" hearing of Scripture being taken away altogether. It is crucial to catch the concern here: If the Bible's consistently negative word about homosexual conduct is wrong, or outdated, *who will then decide in what other ways the Bible is or is not to be trusted or cannot comprehend our day and its struggles, under God?* Appeal to Scripture's plain sense is born of the conviction that the Bible *can have something to say without other forces needing to regulate that or introduce a special hermeneutics from outside the text so we can know when and where it can speak.*[6] The other side feels that the Bible is being forfeited in the specific area of sufficiency and trustworthiness, and that no cause, however well intentioned, can have that as an acceptable fallout.

But having said all this, have we really got our finger on the nature of the disagreement? To say that the Bible has a plain sense is not to say that, as with the Koran, it delivers this like a dispensing machine, one verse after another, until all the verses run out.

Here we are forced to return to a fact noted by progressives, and that is that the Bible has internal movement. Put simply, unlike the Koran, Christian Scripture has two Testaments. How it speaks the Word of God must contend with a difference built into its formal character, as God speaks to Israel (and through them to the nations) and then to the world in Christ Jesus. It is my conviction that our present crisis has to do with *the way Scripture makes its specifically two-testament voice heard.* This crisis is as much theological as exegetical or hermeneutical. We ought not to be surprised that once the Bible was understood to be developing internally, and once that progression was a kind of "religious universal" transferable to our own time and place, it would be very difficult to understand how a two-testament voice from God himself might properly be apprehended. For at the heart of the internal movement of a two-testament Scripture is a collateral conviction: that God is One, and unchanging. Or, to use the language of Prayer Book worship: "As it was in the beginning, is now, and ever shall be, world without end." This summary insists that the two Testaments speak of the same God in Christ, though in different dispensations and in different figural directions.

Every serious interpreter in the history of the Bible's reception has kept this mystery at the very center of every act of interpreta-

---

6. See my brief discussion of the "virtuous reader" in *Figured Out*, 28–29.

tion. If the pressure for each text to speak particularly and eternally is released, or compromised, the consequences for our use of the Bible more generally are enormous. Under the acids of historicism and Western progressivism, a two-testament delivery of God's Word and character has been replaced with a different kind of economic account of God, in which (1) the work of the Holy Spirit is now said to be going on in a way fully detachable (and unsurprisingly and energetically so) from Scripture's prior testimony; and in which (2) the OT cannot be said to speak of God as he is or of God in Christ, but only of a developmental phase of religion en route to a NT religion and then a more enlightened Holy Spirit religion.

It is beyond the scope of this chapter, but when Calvin or Luther or Aquinas read the third chapter of Habakkuk, they take the "plain sense" descriptions of God found there as fully normative accounts of all manner of theological truth concerning God's power, hiddenness, and ways in creation, in Israel, in Christ, and in the world of their present living and moving; and in this they follow along lines of interpretation in which such normative use of the OT to speak about God is self-evident (the debates they are aware of have to do with whether Hab. 3 is about God's actions in Christ, prophetically announced, or God's acts in Israel; even here this "God of Habakkuk" is incomprehensible except as the Triune God). Indeed, what the OT does in this explicitly doctrinal area is seen by them as a far more detailed and expansive account of God and his ways than anything that can be found in the NT; and this is so, so far as they are concerned, because the NT assumes exactly the same perspective on this as they do. It has no fresh doctrines of God but sees the fulfillment of what has been revealed to Israel in the Son, and all space between Israel's LORD and the Lord is collapsed into God's eternity.[7]

What is at stake in these self-evidences are two basic creedal confessions: (1) that the Holy Spirit "spake by the prophets," that is, reliably and sufficiently from Israel's particular prophetic vocation

---

7. See Gerald Bray's account of ontology in the church fathers in "The Church Fathers and Biblical Theology," in *Out of Egypt: Biblical Theology and Biblical Interpretation*, Scripture and Hermeneutics Series 5, ed. C. Bartholomew et al. (Grand Rapids: Zondervan, 2004), 23–40.

among the nations,[8] and (2) that Christ died and rose again "in accordance with the Scriptures," that is, congruent with the OT's own plain delivery of God and his ways, in reality and in promise.[9]

"Be Ye Sure That the Lord He Is God"

It is now time to turn to (1) how these creedal statements existed at the earliest moments in the life of the church, prior to the formation of the NT canon, in the rule of faith; and (2) how something like a "rule of faith" must again be recovered if we are to have any hope of letting Scripture do its fullest two-testament work. A rule of faith has been reinforced in worship traditions, though often in unnoticed ways. Yet without a clear reaffirmation of this basic rule in our public praying (*lex orandi*), our public believing (*lex credendi*) will quickly go out of order, as is now happening in the present crisis.

It is appropriate at this juncture to be more specific about where I believe our crisis has its starting point, if in fact we agree that the interpretation of Scripture is where the disagreements are to be located (as some churches seem increasingly willing to do).

My thesis is probably not going to sound popular, and it is not in any way clever or "refined" (as Calvin negatively used the word). Still, I believe my proposal is actually the *radical obverse* of the claim that the Holy Spirit teaches new truths outside the range of Scripture's literal and spiritual sense. *Our crisis has to do with the failure to know how to use the OT theologically and doctrinally. Our crisis has to do with not knowing how to deal in a balanced and appropriate way with the dual voice of Christian Scripture, New and Old Testaments both.* Without an anchor in the doctrinal universe of the OT's declarations about God, we will drift and invariably find ourselves, whether on the right or left of the theological spectrum, in the difficult and progressivist waters of

---

8. See Christine Helmer's penetrating analysis of Luther's appeal to this creedal confession in his disputes with "enthusiasts" and anti-creedal rationalists (Servetus) on the one side, and Roman Catholic insistence that the Spirit works only in the post-Easter declarations of the church, on the other. There is an obvious pertinence to this debate ("Luther's Trinitarian Hermeneutic and the Old Testament," *ModTh* 18 [2002]: 49–73).

9. See my essay "In Accordance with the Scriptures," in *Word without End: The Old Testament as Abiding Theological Witness* (Grand Rapids: Eerdmans, 1998), 51–60.

the kind that "mainstream" churches like the Episcopal Church now find rushing around them. At issue, to repeat, is the specific formal character of Christian Scripture as having two Testaments, each declaring Christ, but also modeling his church, in different figural directions.

There is a correlate of this thesis, and it is that basic convictions about the way the Bible—and especially the OT—speaks of the Triune God are not sophisticated or theologically complicated ones. Rather, they emerge in the rhythms of worship: in baptismal confession and catechetical incorporation; in the specific selection and ordering of Scripture in lectionary presentation; and especially in the ordered statements of Prayer Book praying. You do not need to attend seminary to know them or experience them. These form the worshiping equivalent of what Polanyi has in recent days called "tacit knowledge." It is this kind of tacit, deep, and integral knowing that has fallen out in our present situation. The rhythms of worshiping confession will make threshold claims, and unless one passes through the right kind of threshold, one will end up in rooms that cannot finally all exist in the same structure of knowing and living and praying and hoping. To adopt another metaphor: One can sail brilliantly, with fine speed and enormous skill, and keep as close to the bearings on the GPS as humanly possible, but when the waypoints are wrongly entered, one will get lost—and energetically so.

I can illustrate my point with reference to a doctoral exam I examined recently on Adolf Schlatter. Schlatter lived at the turn of the twentieth century and taught New Testament and Theology, Church History, and Metaphysics; he was a keen churchperson and much loved pastor. The shadow cast by Harnack was long enough to keep him on his mettle, and the young Bultmann had not yet made his mark, though the challenges he threw down would soon occupy formal theology. Schlatter was known for his work on God's action in the world. He was a NT scholar who worked closely in the OT and especially Genesis 1–3. Nowhere does Schlatter work to establish the philosophical warrant for his using the OT doctrinally to account for how God might be said to act in time and space. There is a natural movement between Old and New Testaments and into the doctrines of Christian believing and living. Schlatter takes it as a given—at the level of metaphysics—that in order to know who God is and how he acts, in "creation, preservation, and in all the blessings of this life" (*BCP* 58) one reads as closely as possible the sentences about this activity as the OT sets them forth. One feels nothing of the later environment of the history-of-religions; or of theories of development in authorship of the Pentateuch or in comparative Near Eastern studies of creation accounts. And yet there is nothing of the air of creationism or defensive apologetics either, and in this he is rightly regarded as a sophisticated forerunner of Karl Barth. There is just the exhilarating task of letting Scripture—OT and NT—have its theological say, tracking as closely as possible the way in which it says that according to its own idiom.

I found myself asking: how can Schlatter do this? And why has it been an instinct of my own, as a teacher of the OT, to believe it has the capacity to speak of God as God is, and not as a God en route to some subsequent recalibration or development? Why has it become almost impossible for one to speak of the "immanent" or "ontological trinity" in the OT? Or, of the eternal Word, Jesus Christ, bound up within the words and sentences and paragraphs of the OT (so Irenaeus, from beginning to end, in *Demonstration of the Apostolic Preaching*)? And why would I sense the absence of this as a great loss and so read a Barth or a Schlatter and discover in them something of the same tacit knowledge, of God's Word and self, which animated the earlier history of biblical interpretation, in figures as diverse as Origen, Augustine, Aquinas, Calvin, and Luther?

I believe the answer lies in the field of tacit knowledge: the way a form of Prayer Book worship (as I was exposed to in my upbringing as an Episcopalian) functioned to reinforce what was in the early church called the rule of faith. This same kind of exposure could account for why Schlatter was able to use the Bible the way he did and also remain committed to preaching, pastoral care, and the no doubt messy counsels of German Protestant Church life and mission before the onslaught of two world wars.

The rule of faith made certain threshold claims about the character of God in that time before the formation of a Second Testament of Scripture, one whose name and authoritative character as a "New Testament" drew for its inspiration the sole scriptural witness handed to disciples of Jesus Christ from the bosom of Israel, what would in time be called the OT. The rule of faith, whatever else it may have been and however we understand its actual usage, insisted that the risen Lord of Christian worship, Jesus Christ, was one with the named LORD of the Scriptures. This Lord and Creator had given his name, the name above every name, to Jesus, so that at his name, every knee would bow, to the glory of the Father.[10] The Triune God was the LORD of Israel in reality and in promise both. In turn, this confession assured that one now knew how to open and read these Scriptures, as setting forth Christ in a wide variety of ways: not just in prophetic promise pointing beyond itself, but primarily inside its world, as a type and a figure, alongside the new covenant church itself, prefigured, in judgment and in blessing, in Israel herself.[11] For no other reason than this would it have been apt to speak of Christian ministers as new covenant priests with a high priest Jesus Christ, or of promises related to the name of Israel's God among the nations now having to do with naming in Christian baptism, and so forth.[12]

It would be possible to enlarge on this theme, but the basic point should be secure. My own conviction is that precisely these threshold assumptions about God, established by the rule of faith, have their liturgical reinforcement in the Prayer-Book worship of Anglicanism and have governed my own theological instincts at levels as difficult to detect as what I sensed in Schlatter. When in the worship of Morning Prayer one says or sings a canticle, as the Jubilate Deo or the Venite, these traditional Latin names never disguised the fact that we were citing specific words from an OT psalm and by so doing were introducing ourselves at the very start of worship, at the threshold of our attending to our lives before God, to the only God with whom we had to do in Jesus Christ. *The rule of faith was never anything more or less*

---

10. David S. Yeago, "The New Testament and Nicene Dogma: A Contribution to the Recovery of Theological Exegesis," *ProEccl* 3 (1994): 152–64; C. Seitz, "Handing Over the Name: Christian Reflection on the Divine Name YHWH," and "Our Help Is in the Name of the LORD, the Maker of Heaven and Earth," in *Figured Out*, 131–44; 177–90; Bauckham, *God Crucified: Monotheism and Christology in the New Testament* (Carlisle: Paternoster, 1998).

11. Ephraim Radner, "The Absence of the Comforter: Scripture and the Divided Church," in *Theological Exegesis: Essays in Honor of Brevard S. Childs*, ed. Christopher R. Seitz and Kathryn Greene-McCreight (Grand Rapids: Eerdmans, 1999), 355–94.

12. Richard Bauckham, "James and the Gentiles (Acts 15.13–21)," in *History, Literature, and Society in the Book of Acts*, ed. B. Witherington (Cambridge: Cambridge University Press, 1996), 154–84; Seitz, *Figured Out*, 127.

than the doxological affirmation with which these OT psalms were concluded: "Glory be to the Father and to the Son and to the Holy Spirit, as it was in the beginning, is now, and ever shall be." Here we encountered, in succinct form, the logic behind prayers of this same ordered worship, addressed to the Father, in the Son, by the power of the Holy Spirit. No one was being called upon here other than the one Lord of the OT's scriptural declaration, understood, from the standpoint of our inclusion in Jesus Christ, as the LORD: the Father, the Son, and Holy Spirit.

Again the logic of this tacit knowing can be unfolded with reference to the Jubilate Deo's command: "Be ye sure that the Lord he is God." Three brief things are being said here in one very compressed sentence. The psalm verse is an exhortation: we are *enjoined* to be sure of something, because its security is not naturally to be assumed and cannot naturally be known through experience (or what some now claim is meant by an independent faculty called "reason").[13] Second, we are enjoined to be sure that God is not just anything, or everything, or several possible things: God is the named LORD of Israel, maker of heaven and earth. If it were naturally so, then we would find instead a tautology, "be sure that God is God" (that is, empty of any referential claim concerning the personal, and named, promising and living God of the old covenant who in a new covenant adopted as sons and daughters those now calling on his name). And finally, the psalm is addressed to us outside the covenants with Israel, yet from the voice of Israel's psalmist, in former days of the church's life understood to be David, Israel, and Christ and his body: "O be joyful in the LORD *all ye lands.*" The knowledge of God is the source of joy and the place where this God can be known is in his ways with Israel, and through them, with "all ye lands" and with all creation itself.

My remarks would be wrongly taken to imply this or that advocacy project in respect of the Book of Common Prayer or Morning Prayer and its place in Anglican Sunday worship. Nevertheless, it is worth asking why this kind of rule-of-faith governing claim appears so hard to detect at work in our theological reflections, as we seek

13. See the discussion of "natural" and "positive" law in Carl E. Braaten and Christopher R. Seitz, eds., *I Am the Lord Your God: Christian Reflections on the Ten Commandments* (Grand Rapids: Eerdmans, 2005), 18–38.

to understand a serious disagreement over Scripture's two-testament word in late modern church life.

Several questions about the secure place of a rule of faith in our present life come to mind.

1. Can Jesus make any kind of independent NT sense, unless we think about his work in relation to the holiness, righteousness, promise, and judgment rooted in the claims about God found in the Scriptures of his promising?

2. Can we understand anything of the claims of the NT about the law given through Moses without correlating Jesus himself with the provision of that law itself, over which he claims an authority grounded in his eternal life with the Father?

3. Can we understand anything about the church's supposed correlate-ability with the triune life of God (as is popular in certain recent accounts of the Trinity), unless we are clearer about how that life is grasped through the whole scriptural witness, and how the church never exists outside the judgments of a sovereign God who is Lord both in election and in adoption in Christ as sons and daughters? And finally,

4. Can our minds recover the ability to hear Israel's Scriptures as an OT lesson in a lectionary schema, without the OT becoming either a booster rocket that falls into the sea (as it delivers a payload unfortunately still dependent upon it for first-order theological claims),[14] or an example of important religious lessons from the history of past efforts to be religious in the best possible sense? These questions are but a sample of what the rule of faith sought to clarify.

Because I teach OT it would easy to conclude that my concerns would be met, if indeed one was so minded, if the Scriptures of Israel were appropriately honored in this second sense, that is, as really important religious lessons of the very best kind—with some significant exceptions that a NT Geiger counter of some sort will help us identity and root out.

---

14. In the spirit of the letters to Timothy and the Petrine epistles.

Yet here we run straight into the kinds of concerns with which my remarks began. For once one begins thinking along these lines, that is, of using the New's allegedly "new religion" to sort out the "religion of a First Testament," instead of seeking to hear God's Word of triune address in both Testaments, appropriate to their character as "prophet and apostle," it is then an almost effortless transition to believing both Old and New Testaments *are themselves only the provisional proving ground for religious virtues said to be en route to a Holy Spirit's fresh declaration of unprecedented "new truth" in our day.* This would seem to me to be the logic of much of the new thinking holding the levers of power today in the ECUSA. This would seem to be the logic of much of the new thinking influencing the direction of TEC and other churches today.

Conclusion

The OT is Christian Scripture, and naming it in this way, instead of as Hebrew Bible or "Great Past Religious Lessons with Exceptions," indicates that God's Word and self declare themselves to the church by formal means of a two-testament record. *How* this happens is where we appropriately speak of the Holy Spirit's fresh and quickening work: in the church's disciplines of prayerful close reading, theological reflection, preaching, and pastoral care. There is no shortcut for this, to be followed by those claiming to be Bible believers, or by those who want the Bible to find some kind of negotiable place alongside varieties of what are imprecisely called Anglican "authorities," or legs on a stool of dubious vintage, unknown in the history of earlier biblical interpretation, Anglican or otherwise.[15]

We now return to the context of crisis with which I began, and specifically to the challenge presented by the decision to consecrate gay and lesbian bishops in the American Anglicanism of TEC and to seriously consider the development of rites for same-sex blessing or

---

15. Richard Hooker spoke originally of a threefold cord and reflexively gave Scripture the preeminence. "Reason" in his usage is a conviction about creation and the capacity for his Word to be received through Scripture and tradition, not an independent authority accessing a discrete mode of revelation.

marriage, within the context of a much wider acceptance of sexual intimacy between members of the same sex.

The regnant position on Scripture, when it touches on this issue specifically, appears to be: Jesus says nothing about it, Paul says something about something else, and the Holy Spirit is leading us into a new truth about a new thing nowhere discussed (on the terms we mean) in the NT. This particular understanding also judges the OT as a kind of partial or outdated word (a lens onto a religion to which it points as its chief function as religious literature), which is in a developmentally immature or even harmful phase, and which will receive a kind of "course correction," impartial though it be, in the NT.

I have written elsewhere on the problem of turning the OT into a book that describes a phase in the history-of-religion and evacuates its status as canon and Scripture, and it is only possible to summarize here.[16] When the NT refers to the OT it does not have in mind a phase in the history-of-religion. When it does do something along these lines, it will seek to distinguish such a thing from the OT as Scripture. So, it speaks of the "traditions of men" or states "you have heard it said" or uses other such religious departures, according to Jesus, distinguishable from the "it is written" or the otherwise direct testimony of the plain sense of Moses and the Prophets, according to which Jesus's death and resurrection, and active earthly teaching and living, are coordinated.[17] Jesus Christ is the OT's true interpreter only because the OT is everywhere, finally, about him (Luke 24:27). Only the eternal Son of God can see the true heart and intention of the OT's abiding word, because the OT is a word delivered by him from all eternity.

It is only partially helpful to point out that the NT can be read in a very different way than just described when it comes to same-sex blessing and approval in the ECUSA, that is, as setting forth a Jesus who is by no means silent on sexual conduct or a Paul who indeed means what he has been traditionally held to mean when it comes to sexual conduct in the new covenant community. This is because the OT is not just a book that finds its logic only by a subsequent religious

16. See "Scripture Becomes Religion," in *Figured Out*, 13–33.
17. See E. Earle Ellis, *The Old Testament in Early Christianity* (Tübingen: Mohr, 1991), 116–18, 125–38.

adoption and modification of it, as the NT is said to comment upon it. In certain key ways its doctrinal word is assumed to be final and is only confirmed and deferred to by the second scriptural witness. The OT sets forth a nest of declarations about sexual life under God, which cannot be reduced to a list of individual biblical verses in some narrow sense or of some religious virtues said to be animating the consciousness of Jesus, in his own alleged religious experience and commendation. The OT does not function as a religious resource for Jesus or the NT, but as a word whose finality is embraced and sharply focused, by the Son of God himself, now before the entirety of creation in an eschatological climax.

The kind of sexual living and thriving Christians have traditionally confessed and taught is explicitly reliant on a network of assumptions available in the OT. These have to do with creation, election, covenant love, Israel as bride, God's forbearance, forgiveness, and blessing inside that covenant. These assumptions are riveted to the character of God as revealed in his life with Israel and as "the maker of heaven and earth." It ought to come as no surprise that once this constitutive role of the Scriptures of the OT is reduced to a phase of religion, or said only to find warrant as the NT itself materially uses it, where the NT is claimed to be silent (and this controversially so) one is left in a state of confusion and crisis, such as is now manifestly and publicly plaguing the church.

It would require serious reflection about whether the kind of tacit knowledge underscored by the doxological affirmation of the plain sense of the OT, "glory be the Father and to the Son and to the Holy Spirit, as it was in the beginning, is now and ever shall be," has now become so reduced in public worship as to demand sustained reinstatement and underscoring. What does it mean to say "Lord have mercy" in eucharistic worship without hearing the Decalogue or an otherwise clear declaration as to just who this LORD is before whom we petition mercy; and also why we might wish to "incline our hearts to keep" his law, and how we might indeed do that, in Christ? And what does it mean to hear in lectionary presentation an OT lesson in figural and constitutive relationship with the Gospel lesson, but which is all too often left without even a sentence of comment, or even some brief explanation as to its place in the economy of God's ways with Israel and the church, in Christ?

My point in this chapter is not to urge a long (in our day, probably historicistic) investment in sermons on Joel or Leviticus—though it might bear reflection why the major theologians in the catholic tradition would not have thought sustained Christian commentary on OT books so odd and personally provided their own excellent resources in commentary, song, and meditation. I have only sought to understand why TEC is in a crisis and just how that crisis indeed turns on the interpretation of Scripture.

It is my conviction that at the heart of the problem is a model of approaching the Bible in which the two Testaments of Christian Scripture have been reduced to phases in the history-of-religion, one improving upon the other, and then finally, a new religious phase improving on them both and giving us a new word to guide our sexual lives under God. When this model also finds no course correction at the level of our worshiping life, the fallout will be, and indeed is now, significant. That is why we have a crisis and why simply listening to one another restate arguments is not likely to bring about resolution. For, tragically, it appears basic agreement is missing over how God makes his voice heard and his identity and person known, through the two-testament voice of Christian Scripture. Such a fundamental disagreement about the source of authority, from "prophets and apostles," OT and NT, offers little hope of any final and lasting resolution.

And it may be that this recognition is now dawning on all sides in the present struggle. Perhaps it would be good if we came to terms with where it begins, and that is not with ill will or lack of charity (only), but with fundamentally divergent understandings of the character and authority of Christian Scripture. If such disagreements were clarified, we would at least better understand why we are in such a crisis, and why it has not to do with sexual conduct as such—that is but a symptom—but with basic theological convictions about Scripture functioning often at the level of tacit knowledge. Something tacit has gone missing.

7

THE RULE OF FAITH, HERMENEUTICS, AND THE CHARACTER OF CHRISTIAN SCRIPTURE

A proper understanding of the significance of a critical period of early church history is necessary, hermeneutically, if we are to appreciate the character of Christian Scripture and its relationship to a host of other decisive matters.[1] At stake are

1. "We must remember that by 'Scripture' the Fathers, up to Irenaeus, Hippolytus, and Theophilus of Antioch, usually meant the Old Testament. At first this was the only approved and recommended collection of writings. But the *paradosis* of the Church, faithful to that of the apostles, was precisely this transmission of the Christ-event, as based documentarily on the Old Testament writings and, at the same time, explaining the meaning of these writings" (Yves Congar, *Tradition and Traditions* [London: Burns and Oates, 1966], 31). "In the Christian faith from the very first both elements, Jesus and the Scripture, were mutually and inseparably related" (Hans von Campenhausen, *The Formation of the Christian Bible* [Philadelphia: Fortress, 1972], 21).

1. the nature of the OT as Christian Scripture,
2. the so-called rule of faith, as a historical reality with exegetical significance, and as a point of reference in popular modern treatments of the authority of Scripture,
3. a proper estimate of the material reality that the OT is used in the New, and the theological consequences following from this, and
4. a proper understanding of the authority of the NT as canon, within a larger two-testament witness.

If this critical period, and the hermeneutical significance it has for our estimation of Scripture, is not grasped, a wide range of misapprehensions follow. These ramify and extend into how one assesses

1. the relationship between Scripture and tradition,
2. what the nature of the canonical process is, in the OT, and especially the relationship between what is called "closure" and scriptural authority,
3. an understanding of the rule of faith and its relationship to later creedal statements (interrogatory and declaratory), and any coherent appeal to the rule in the present period, and especially
4. a proper understanding of the "serial" as well as interrelated movements from Scripture (OT), to rule of faith, to emergent NT canon, to two-testament biblical canon, to creeds.

On this latter score, all too often in the recent period one encounters an assessment of the canon of Christian Scripture that emphasizes a development from OT to NT to rule to creeds and then seeks to understand the authority of Scripture as related to an underlying "rule," which in its way is said to provide a kind of creedal summary derived from Scripture, or operating independently and crucially from it, so as to provide the rationale or lens or delimiting evaluation of what the significance of Scripture might be said, perennially, to be.[2]

---

2. "What the Church *believed* was canonical prior to that belief taking written, codified forms. In effect, the earliest 'canons' or norms of the preaching and defending of the early tradition served as the standard for the canonization of texts" (Daniel H. Williams, ed., *Tradition, Scripture, and Interpretation* [Grand Rapids: Baker Academic, 2006], 23).

Several mistakes follow from this. First, the exegetical and herme-neutical character of the rule is insufficiently grasped, as if the rule were a "gist" (an economic retelling in compressed form) derived from Scriptures' total witness (by this is meant the OT and the NT together).[3] Second, and related to this, is a misunderstanding of the role of the NT as part of what just now was termed a "total witness." The NT (apostolic writings of various sorts) is only in emerging form when the rule is operating in the period in question, and its yet-to-be status is not seen as a deficiency (insofar as the matter is even con-ceived of in this way) or as some kind of crucial correlate of a wit-ness in need of amplification or supplementation.[4] The Scriptures of

---

Missing here is any sense of the anterior scriptural (canonical and textual) role of the OT. This is even more acute in Allert, who tends to speak reflexively as though Scripture can only mean Bible, and Bible means New Testament, and all this happened at a date later than the fathers, so "before there was even Scripture, there was the faith" (Craig D. Allert, *A High View of Scripture? The Authority of the Bible and the Formation of the New Testament Canon* [Grand Rapids: Baker Academic, 2007], 82) and kindred comments. "Technically, when we talk of the fathers and the Bible, we are speaking anachronistically because the fathers of the first four centuries did not have a common Bible to which they appealed" (74)—which is open to wide misunderstanding, presumably because Allert is most concerned to disabuse evangelical friends from taking this as a warrant for "plenary inspiration" and other modernist convictions. So, Allert accepts Sundberg's view of an open OT group of writings and then simply subsumes the OT's authority into decisions about the wider Bible in the later period. This leads him to claim that Irenaeus "had no need of a New Testament" and then to mean by that no Scripture at all—a claim he credits to von Campenhausen. But the point is completely different: Irenaeus had no need of a NT (if that is a correct way to summarize the view he believes he is citing) because he had a Scripture (Law and the Prophets). See also the discussion of Lee M. McDonald, "Identifying Scripture and Canon in the Early Church: The Criteria Question," in *The Canon Debate*, eds. Lee M. McDonald and James A. Sanders (Peabody, MA: Hendrickson, 2002), 416–39. By contrast, consider the remarks of Flesseman-Van Leer regarding the canon of the Scriptures of Israel in the appeal to the rule of faith: "There is, of course, no need to argue the authority or the extent of the Old Testament, for the Old Testament canon was in practice an already long established fact. For the New Testament books it is different" (Ellen Flesseman-Van Leer, *Tradition and Scripture in the Early Church* [Assen: Van Gorcum, 1954], 131).

3. Or, a "gist" that precedes Scripture, as in Williams's statement, quoted by Allert, whereby the rule of faith is "an elastic summary of the fundamental doctrines of Chris-tianity" (*Evangelicals and Tradition: The Formative Influence of the Early Church* [Grand Rapids: Baker, 2005], 155).

4. "The Christian Bible is not a completely new formation. Through its 'Old Testament' it is linked with Judaism, whose 'Scriptures' Christianity took over at the moment of its emergence, and has retained ever since. This was something that happened long before it was possible to speak of a 'New Testament'" (Von Campenhausen, *Formation*, 1). Also: "The situation is perfectly clear, and should not be disguised: there is still absolutely no

Israel are viewed as fully sufficient to preach Christ, prophesy Christ, adumbrate Christ, demonstrate Christ and the Holy Spirit both as active and functioning from beginning to end, through the various economies of the Scriptures' long story. Indeed, that is precisely what is at issue in this period.[5]

'New Testament' which might be placed alongside the 'Old Testament' as a collection of documents of similarly binding force. The ancient Jewish Bible is and at first remains the single scriptural norm of the Church, and—even if with varying emphasis—is everywhere recognized as such" (63). And: "It is quite wrong to say that the Old Testament had no authority in its own right for the first Christians, and that it was taken over purely because people saw that it 'treated of Christ' or pointed toward him. The critical problem, to which Luther's well-known but much misused formula supplies an answer, had not yet been posed. The situation was in fact quite the reverse. Christ is certainly vindicated to unbelievers out of the Scripture; but the converse necessity, to justify the Scriptures on the authority of Christ, is as yet nowhere even envisaged" (63–64).

5. "The message of the Old Testament is fundamentally the same as that of the New Testament. This could not be well otherwise, considering that the Law of Moses and the grace of the New Covenant were given by one and the same God, adapted to their respective times; that the Logos who speaks in the New Testament has also spoken to Moses; that what Moses and the other prophets proclaim are really the words of Christ" (Flesseman-Van Leer, *Tradition*, 133). On the centrality of the older Scriptures for demonstrating Christ, John Behr notes:

Although Irenaeus clearly knows the apostolic writings [en route to a New Testament canon], the substance of his exposition is drawn exclusively from Scripture: that Jesus was born of a virgin and worked miracles is shown from Isaiah and others; while the names of Pilate and Herod are known from the evangelists, that Christ was bound and brought before them is shown by Hosea; that he was crucified, raised and exalted is again shown by the prophets. In the first part of the work ([*Demonstration*] 3b–42a), Irenaeus recounts the scriptural history of God's salvific work which culminates in the apostolic proclamation of Christ. In the second part of the work (4b–97), Irenaeus demonstrates how all the things which have come to pass in Jesus Christ, were spoken by the prophets, both so that we might believe in God, as what he previously proclaimed has come to pass, and also to demonstrate that Scripture throughout does in fact speak of Jesus Christ, the Word of God, as preached by the apostles. (John Behr, *The Formation of Christian Theology*, vol. 1, *The Way to Nicaea* [Crestwood, NY: St. Vladimir's Seminary Press, 2001], 30)

See also my "In Accordance with the Scriptures," in *Word without End: The Old Testament as Abiding Theological Witness* (Grand Rapids: Eerdmans, 1998), 51–60. Note the emphasis in Irenaeus on a strictly theological grounding ("what did God do") as inseparable from any christological statements, and also the necessity to see Christ as embedded in the scriptural story because of convictions about his ontological relationship to the God of Israel. In our view, this is the chief concern of an appeal to a rule of faith, that is, demonstrating that the God of the Scriptures and Jesus Christ are one, and active together in the selfsame witness. Prior to the existence of a second canonical witness, the first is doing primary theological work of an incipiently trinitarian sort, and the cruciality of that is undiminished by the existence of apostolic writings.

The various challenges to catholic Christian "ruled reading" we read of in the ante-Nicene Fathers imply that the Scriptures (Law, Prophets, and Writings) are (1) insufficient, (2) misleading or useful only to show a wrong theological way, (3) in need of further testimony privately given to special teachers, (4) positive in range and potential but really only because they can be aligned with all kinds of new revelations (Valentinian maximalism due to a belief that Scripture only accidentally provides revelation more broadly available). On points 3 and 4, the challenges will be such that in time the emergent NT (as canon) will usefully serve to clarify the nature of "apostolic" teaching as public (as against secret or private), as constraining what is meant by "apostolic" (as against claims of further apostolic teaching), as "in accordance with the Scriptures" (as against the idea that "the apostolic" and "the prophetic" writings are subject to what were to be called "antitheses" and this at a number of points), and as confirming both the scope and anterior authority of the Scriptures and thereby laying claim to a similar status of their own, in effect producing an "Old" Testament where there had been a Scripture, and a correlate, accorded witness, the "New" Testament. The individual apostolic writings are addressing these matters insofar as they represent relevant challenges in the original, precanonical, occasional settings presupposed by them. But as a total witness, an eventual NT *canon* will serve to describe the apostolic limits and public character of Christian claims as a comprehensive matter.

The rule of faith in the period in question *is based upon* a proper identification of what the fathers called the "hypothesis" of Scripture, and an assumption of this, in the area of "order" (*taxis*) and "arrangement" or "connection" (*hiermas*). The rule does not take the same form when we see it articulated, because it is not a fixed formula and it does not point to an incipient creedal declaration or response, or externalized or externalizable statement. It is not an effort at a precise statement of the "hypothesis" of Scripture but rather *is based upon* a proper identification and apprehension of this, as over against alternatives; that is in fact the claim being made. The alternatives operate with a faulty assessment of the order and arrangement of Scripture, which at bottom lies in the area of what we might call in dogmatic terms a failure to grasp the reality of the significance of

the inherited writings, *tota Scriptura*. That is, given the protection of
and concern for the maximal authority of the Scriptures, it follows
that the challenge is how to guard the total literary witness, and this
"guarding" entails understanding, or perceiving, how order and larger
coherence can be grasped across a diverse witness.[6] When this occurs,
as over against the challenges being confronted (and these are exegetical and hermeneutical in character) it is also the case that the subject
of Scripture emerges into clear light. This "subject" is the Creator
God, with whom the Son is eternally related, and the Scriptures allow
the Holy Spirit scope and opportunity for declaring this through the
economies and episodes of God's ways in and with Israel.

That is, Jesus Christ is known not because all that can be said about
him exists in clear apostolic form independently from an account of
what God was doing in the material witness of the OT.[7] This would
presumably make the task something like demonstrating that there
was a "Christian sense" of the OT that existed that was otherwise
not really there (a matter Trypho, for example, would appear to be
willing to grant, but which Justin sees as a wrong concession and a
dangerous trail to follow). It would also assume that a kind of "set

6. This "aggregate" of writings as a total witness is not affected by the assertion of
questions over the number of books as a precise matter. See below.

7. John Behr, in *On the Apostolic Preaching* (Crestwood, NY: St. Vladimir's Seminary
Press, 1997), notes:

Most striking, however, is that in recounting this history, the New Testament writings
are not utilized by Irenaeus as the foundation for his presentation. He clearly knows
these writings, and regards them as Scripture, as is amply demonstrated by his other
work, *Against the Heresies*, and by the fact that, in the *Demonstration*, he cites a verse
from the Old Testament, attributing it in the form used by the New Testament (e.g.,
the passage attributed to Jeremiah in Matt. 27:9–10, cited in chap. 81). However, in
the *Demonstration*, that Jesus was born from the Virgin and worked miracles is shown
from Isaiah and others; while the names of Pontius Pilate and Herod are known from
the Gospels, that Christ was bound and brought before them is shown by Osee; that he
was crucified, raised, and exulted is again shown by other prophets. The whole account
of the apostolic preaching is derived, for Irenaeus, from the Old Testament, which, in
turn, implies a recognition of the scriptural, that is, ultimate authority of the apostolic
preaching. To gain a better understanding of the *Demonstration*, it will be useful to
consider some earlier Christian writings. The earliest post-apostolic Christian writings that we have, the works of the apostolic fathers, clearly indicate that they know,
in varying degrees, some of the writings of the apostles, but with few exceptions, they
do not cite these writings or appeal to them as authoritative sources of revelation, that
is, as Scripture. Scripture for the apostolic fathers, as in the New Testament itself, refers
to the writings of the Old Testament. (7–9; italics original)

of givens" about Christ could be had without reference to who he was in relationship to prior revelation about God in the Scriptures. Armed with these givens, one would then use an external apostolic confession of Christ to show that the OT delivers a meaning not somehow critical to or ingredient in its own *sensus literalis*. Right away, in a strict sense one can see that any such effort would have to assume that who Christ is—who he is apprehended to be in his life, death, resurrection, and ascension—is capable of articulation and delimitation without reference to the one who sent him, with whom he is in eternity as unbegotten (as the later language will declare, based upon, it is to be emphasized, Scripture's deliverances in Prov. 8), to whom he speaks, whose law he fulfilled, whose power he claimed to exercise, whose Spirit rested on him and gave him strength and purpose, who raised him from the dead, and at whose right hand he sits, returning where he was before, and who will return because appointed by God so to do, for judgment. All of these convictions inhere in what it means to speak of Jesus, and because of them, conversely, the Scriptures of Israel now have a meaning to declare that belongs to all they are and have ever been.[8]

At issue then is not bringing a delimited "given" about Jesus Christ, shown to be what it is in the time and space provided by his earthly mission and the apostolic testimony to it, and using it to "claim" a Scripture from outside. If this were the case, we might also see the decision to sort out what parts of the *tota Scriptura* best served this purpose and retain these only; instead, the canon exists as a given and in this material form it speaks of Christ (hence the language of Luke 24:27). No formal adjustments of the inherited witness were seen to be first-order affairs, requiring a testing and examination of the canonical totality. Where this does occur, the thread being pulled threatens to unravel the idea of canonical testimony in written form

---

8. Behr in introducing part 2 of the Demonstration writes: "That all of those things would thus come to pass was foretold by the Spirit of God through the prophets, that the faith of those who truly worship God might be certain in these things, for whatever was impossible for our nature, and because of this would bring disbelief to mankind, these things God made known beforehand through the prophets, that, by foretelling them a long time beforehand, when they were fully accomplished in this way, just as they were foretold, we might know that it was God who previously proclaimed to us our salvation" (Behr, trans., *On the Apostolic Preaching*, 68).

altogether, as when Marcion decides very little of the apostolic writings can be retained to speak of the true Christ or of his true God.

The rule of faith is the scripturally grounded articulation, based upon a proper perception of the hypothesis of Scripture, that Jesus Christ is one with the God who sent him and who is active in the Scriptures inherited, the Holy Spirit being the means of testifying to his active, if hidden, life in the "Old Testament" and our apprehension of that. Testimony to who Jesus is, in the period of his earthly life and the apostolic testimony to that, "accorded testimony" is in the very nature of the claim to speak rightly of him. It is this claim that the rule seeks to guard, ruling out alternatives that have failed to see the order and coherence of the Scriptures, in their totality, as speaking of Christ. This is why the rule takes the form, not chiefly of a kind of economic retelling, where the *magnalia dei* in the OT serve chiefly to describe crucial or merely preliminary episodes prior to Christ's advent. The rule stipulates that the work of Christ is in the various economies before his earthly descent, alongside the Scriptures' speaking both of Christ's first and also his second advent.[9] Irenaeus and Tertullian can both confidently assume, consistent with the logic and conceptuality of a rule of faith, that where the invisible God, YHWH, is said to be seen by those who so testify, they have seen the Son or Word of God. When on the Mount of Transfiguration Jesus is speaking face-to-face with Moses and Elijah, this is a kind of reprise of what had happened

---

9. Irenaeus provides innumerable examples of this ontological identification, as he sees it, illuminating the Scriptures of Israel. Speaking of Christ as Logos, he writes,

This is He who, in the bush, spoke with Moses and said, "I have surely seen the afflictions of my people who are in Egypt, and I have come down to deliver them." This is He who ascended and descended for the salvation of the afflicted, delivering us from the dominion of the Egyptians, that is, from all idolatry and ungodliness, and saving us from the Red Sea, that is, from the deadly turbulence of the heathen and from the bitter current of their blasphemy—for in these [things] our [affairs] were pre-formed (*promeletaō*), the Word of God at that time demonstrating in advance, by types, things to come, but now, truly removing us out of the cruel slavery of the heathen, He caused a stream of water to gush forth abundantly from a rock in the desert, and the rock is Himself, and [also] gave [us] twelve springs, that is, the teaching of the twelve apostles; and killing the unbelievers in the desert, while leading those who believed in Him and were infants in malice into the inheritance of the patriarchs, which, not Moses, but Jesus <gave us an inheritance>, who saves us from Amalek by stretching out His hands and leading us into the Father's Kingdom. (Behr, *On the Apostolic Preaching*, 70, in his translation of *Demonstration*, 46).

before, now in its eternal form as the apostles are brought into that circle of recognition. What Moses and Elijah got before, Jesus wants to be sure they, his chosen ones, get now. "Before Abraham was, I am" is the way John describes this "ontological" reality. The rule of faith or truth is the statement in the ante-Nicene fathers that articulates this fundamental correlative truth, based upon a proper apprehension of how the Scriptures of Israel "deliver" this ontological claim about Christ, YHWH ("the name above every name"), and the Holy Spirit ("who spake by the prophets").

On this understanding, then, the canon of faith is not a pre-creedal (post-NT) digest that helps ground the authority of a two-testament canon, thus providing as it were the warrant for our recourse to Scripture as authoritative.[10] This view of the matter would appear to assume that the rule of faith is the means by which the actual formal decisions regarding the canon of Scripture were made, and this, it would appear, would be the reason we understand its cruciality and insist upon it on those terms today.[11] This is not the place to take up the matter of the formation of the NT canon and the question of whether the rule of faith could be said to be functional in helping determine its limits or stipulate its authority. At issue is a failure to grasp that matters of canonicity in respect of the NT do not simply pull within their orbit the status of the Scriptures, that is, what in time will be called the OT, in the unfolding of its own canonical (NT) stabilization. This seems to be a major misunderstanding operating in various reconstructions.

This needs to be said quite emphatically. The canonization of the NT is a matter that must be assessed on its own terms. As for the Scriptures of Israel (the Law and Prophets) it must likewise be

10. "The point of the canon of truth is not so much to give fixed, and abstract, statements of Christian doctrine. Nor does it provide a narrative description of Christian belief, the literary hypothesis of Scripture [*pace* Blowers]. Rather, the canon of truth expresses the correct hypothesis of Scripture itself, that by which one can see in Scripture the picture of a king, Christ, rather than a dog or a fox. It is ultimately the presupposition of the apostolic Christ himself, the one who is 'according to the Scripture' and, in reverse, the subject of Scripture throughout, being spoken of by the Spirit through prophets, and so revealing the One God and Father" (Behr, *Formation of Christian Theology*, 1:35–36).

11. Allert, *High View of Scripture?* For further discussion, see Christopher Seitz, *The Goodly Fellowship of the Prophets: The Achievement of Association in Canon Formation* (Grand Rapids: Baker Academic, 2009).

underscored that even technical discussions that claim "canon" is a decisive concept and must only apply to a completely set and ordered collection of books, and is illegitimate otherwise, usually do so in order to leave the question of the authority of the Scriptures (OT) an open matter at the time of the apostolic writings and in the period of the life of the earthly Jesus. This gives a false proportion to the issue, as I have argued elsewhere. In fact, it prioritizes a set of issues nowhere identified as particularly significant when one reads the references to the rule of faith at the period in question. The challenges being opposed by recourse to the rule are not ones having to do with an "open collection" of writings and the deficiencies that might be said to characterize them because of this. This is nowhere identified as a particularly important issue. Whether Chronicles or Ezra-Nehemiah concludes the sacred writings, or whether the existence of a variety of different orders could be called on for this or that reason to argue for an attenuation in the claims of the Scriptures to speak of Christ, is not a factor.

The rule/canon of faith is not a "prescriptural" canon or heurism that helps ground the authority of the canon of Scripture, but it arises on the basis of a stable, anterior witness (the OT), no matter its precise limits and internal form. Here one must simply observe that discussions of canon that make the limits of the OT as a literary witness the chief affair also tend to do so in order to suggest that the formation of the NT canon was somehow the occasion for stipulating its authority and canonicity as well. A subset of this kind of thinking may also then argue that Scripture is a creation of the church and mean that in strong terms, or alternatively, that all writings at this time are in fact best described as "tradition," thus reconstruing an older Reformation debate and changing the terms under discussion.[12] It cannot be emphasized enough that the role of the Scriptures (OT) in the period under discussion is crucial to a proper apprehension of this older discussion, else terms like "rule of faith" will cease to illumine the present discussion and will begin

---

12. Compare the statement of Yves Congar: "The doctrinal content of Tradition, insofar as it is distinct from Scripture, is the meaning of Scripture. When St. Irenaeus defines the rather vague word *paradosis*, he calls it 'the exposition of Scripture'" (*Tradition and Traditions*, 32).

to sound like appeals to the authority of the church, the authority of creedal delimitations and lenses, or a kind of oral formulation of "core" beliefs said to give rise to Scripture or help provide warrant for its authority and scope. This is true neither of the NT nor especially of the "Law and the Prophets." On such an account, it is easy to see why objections to a rule of faith might well arise in the present period as assisting with the matter of interpretation, canon, and a proper assessment of the OT.[13]

The desire to claim that there is no authority to the OT unless the literary limits are closed in some straightforward way leads to the necessity to claim that this (now quite crucial aspect) happens later, when the NT is achieving its canonical status. This makes "closure" more significant than it is; it tends then to misrepresent stability and authority in an "open" canon; and it leaves vacated any sense that the Scriptures address the church and provide the very canon of truth operative in the period in question, which is crucial to an account of the OT as Christian Scripture. The rule of faith is then turned into a subsequent, criteriological statement, assisting with claims about canon and Scripture, instead of deriving from these. Not only does the church determine Scripture; the rule of faith helps with this. This statement is in inverse proportion to the truth of the matter, as the evidence of the early church has it.

Statements about the work and mission of Jesus Christ (the gospel) are of course circulating as the NT begins to take form and as it takes form as a mature canonical witness. The individual apostolic writings begin to preserve a formal account of this. In the lived life of the church and especially in its worship, these statements and this confession find articulation. In this latter context we know that the practice of reading Scripture is central, so in this instance the correlative and accorded character of what is said about Jesus Christ is underscored in the nature of the case. It is hard to imagine in apostolic preaching and in the memory of Jesus (eyewitness testimony of the sort Bauckham has sought to emphasize) just how central the wit-

---

13. So John Goldingay. See the discussion of Goldingay's views, in response to his essay, in Christopher R. Seitz, "Canon, Narrative, and the Old Testament's Literal Sense," *TynBul* 59 (2008): 27–34.

ness of the Scriptures was to the original proclamation; the Gospels and other apostolic writings give every indication of this centrality.[14]

Mentioned in the opening section was a concern with the proper theological appraisal of the use of the OT in the NT, and chapters in the present work have focused on this challenge. Proper assessment of the rule of faith and the centrality of the OT at this period further shows that material use of the OT in the NT does not provide the warrant or the guideline for theological use of the OT, but is derived from, or to be ranged alongside of, this prior Christian reading of the Scriptures as such. Strictly speaking, the NT's use of the OT does not occur prior to this theological and exegetical appeal to the Scriptures, but exists alongside of and after it. The eventual canonization of the NT and the appearance of a two-testament witness runs the danger in the modern period, absent proper appreciation of the status of the Scriptures at the time of Christ and in the earliest apostolic period, of improper historicization and developmentalism. It opens the possibility that the older witness will function at best as crucial background for the second witness and at worst as a phase in the history-of-religion. Because the second witness speaks of the first and relies upon it for general intelligibility, this possibility is increased and not decreased. And in the area of our general concern in this book, it makes the material use of the Old appear to be a normative species of theological appropriation, a major exemplar for how the church is to use the OT as Christian Scripture today, and a phenomenon that turns more on reference and displacement than deference and accordance.

What the period in question reveals is the way in which the ontological claims of the OT are decisive to what it will eventually mean to read this witness as part of a two-testament Bible. In that sense, the use of the OT in the NT is not a normative claim about how the OT is to function Christianly, but a species of this within the strict framework of its own providential time and space. This use opens the door onto an enterprise of exegesis of the OT, now in conjunction with a larger canonical witness, each witness sounding the notes appropriate to its theological register; it does not restrict but points

---

14. See Christopher Seitz, "The Scriptures of Israel as Eyewitness," *Nova et Vetera* 6 (2008): 513–22.

beyond itself. The danger of letting use of the OT in the NT become a normative and functional *discrimens* for Christian interpretation is further that, in the modern period, this project is dominated by ever more refined reconstructions of the techniques and intentions of the NT author in question, and this comes with the correlate of greater specificity and individualization.[15] Missing is an effort to reflect on the use of the OT in the NT as a canonical reality, that is, as tracking across the length and breadth of the NT as canon. Even should this be undertaken with a kind of ideal comprehensiveness, it would still only point beyond itself to the need to let the OT speak in its own idiom as Christian Scripture.

In sum, the use of the rule of faith, with its assumptions about the character of the Scriptures that would in time become an older Testament, should serve a limiting function, guarding against an account of the two Testaments of Scripture that views them as one-after-the-other and not as mutually informing, mutually influencing witnesses, and turning the OT as Christian Scripture into a species of *Vetus Testamentum in Novo receptum*. Rightly understood, the early appeal to the rule of faith is a guard against this precisely because the Scriptures of Israel make their Christian notes sound within the literal sense of their own stable deliverances and are seen to be decisive just for this reason.

---

15. We leave aside here the very significant potential for misunderstanding the status of the OT in translation, which is the form in which it exists (or forms) in the very nature of the case.

EPILOGUE

In researching a commentary on Colossians for the Brazos Theological Commentary Series, several issues raised in this book find specific relevance and application. Unlike Romans, which cites the Scriptures of Israel ("the oracles of God entrusted to the Jews") fifty-nine times, Colossians has no formula citations whatsoever. There have been several important studies of Paul's use of the OT in Romans.[1] What does one do with a letter like Colossians? One could reach the conclusion that here is confirmation of the non-Pauline character of the book and so be released from the obligation of answering the question. Or, one could defend the Pauline authorship and seek explanations for why Colossians has no direct citations. This would be a study of allusions of various description, and a project like that could be married with other such studies where allusions stand alongside citations proper, warranting study and evaluation as such.[2]

1. So, for example, J. Ross Wagner, *Heralds of the Good News: Isaiah and Paul in Concert in the Letter to the Romans* (Boston: Brill, 2003). See also the useful volume edited by G. K. Beale and D. A. Carson, *Commentary on the New Testament Use of the Old Testament* (Grand Rapids: Baker Academic, 2007), and specifically Mark A. Seifrid's entry on "Romans," 607–94.
2. See the fine recent study by Christopher R. Beetham, *Echoes of Scripture in the Letter of Paul to the Colossians* (Leiden: Brill, 2008) and Beale and Carson, eds., *Commentary*, 841–70.

In both cases, as well, the question has been raised as to what the actual recipients of the letter would have been able to make of allusions, especially if there is no clear evidence they were Jews or Jewish Christians.[3] So, many argue for the gentile Christian audience predominating in Rome—this may include God-fearers who "know the law" (Rom. 7:1)—and then wrestle with the implications of their knowledge, or lack thereof, of Paul's Bible. In Colossians, such a reconstruction is more complicated, and here in addition we have a church Paul only knows about second-hand. He has never visited the church there or in Laodicea (and he can even direct that the letters both churches possess be exchanged; Col. 4:16). Some feel that a focus on the audience in this manner (a so-called mirror-reading), misjudges what Paul's communicative intention is.[4] Or, it is held that Paul will expect those in his audience to learn the Scriptures as he has learned them and so to be persuaded by his arguments if not also in time appreciate his allusions—even ones he may not be aware he is making, so thoroughly marked is his mental map by the Scriptures he has himself internalized through his education (Phil. 3:5). To speak of the church growing and the gospel spreading, with the language of "be fruitful and multiply" ("bearing fruit and growing," so Col. 1:6), and to speak of Christ as "image" of the invisible God (Col. 1:15), is to work within the logic of Genesis's opening chapters, with a new Adam accomplishing in the mystery of the church (Col. 1:26) a growth once described in creation, in a creation now new.

At the close of the letter Paul speaks of the worship life of the church at Colossae, and he mentions the place of the psalms (Col. 3:16). We know that the Scriptures of Israel formed "the Law and the Prophets lectionary" of the synagogue where Paul argued and made his case, and that these Scriptures and "the memoirs of the apostles" were read side by side in the early church.[5] At other places in the NT,

---

3. Christopher D. Stanley, *Arguing with Scripture: The Rhetoric of Quotations in the Letters of Paul* (New York: T&T Clark, 2004); "'Pearls Before Swine': Did Paul's Audiences Understand His Biblical Quotations?" *NovT* (1999): 124–44. On Colossians in the light of this, see Beetham, *Echoes*, 255–57.

4. See the compact discussion of Leander Keck in *Romans*, Abingdon New Testament Commentaries (Nashville: Abingdon, 2005), 19–23.

5. See the remarks of Justin Martyr in *Dialogue with Trypho*, chaps. 100–107 (*ANF* 1:249–52).

the Scriptures are referred to as bringing up the Christian to maturity in Christ (2 Tim. 3:14–17), and of their being now read afresh and of their disclosing a reality that is deep within their literal sense, but not releasing the riches of God's intention until the time of the church (1 Pet. 1:10–12), the Israel of God. In Colossians, Proverbs 8, and Genesis 1 are examples of such texts.[6]

An account of the use of the OT in the New that operates with a thick view of authorial intentionality (within the compass of a single letter), or alternatively, of audience competence, will wrestle with the intentionality claimed as crucial in the earliest reception history of the Scriptures of Israel (now an OT). That reception history reads the NT canonically, in the sense that it does not prioritize an intentionality that is focused on single authorial consciousness, within the scope of an individual letter, or a concern for understanding how an individual letter handles the Scriptures of Israel, in terms of methods or patterns for replication. These may help focus the specifics of interpretation in an initial sense—though without the kind of historical specification now seen as essential—but the associations between and across Paul's letters, and the ongoing opening of the literal sense of the Scriptures to which they all refer, are more crucial finally. Ironically, our knowledge of the Greco-Roman milieu may be greater than Paul's, or the early church's, when it comes to understanding something like the religious life on the ground in Colossae and in turn using that as crucial for the letter's proper interpretation—or so it is thought.

At issue in many ways is the status of the NT as canon and what it means for Paul's letters now to circulate in a thirteen-letter collection. This makes the use of the OT in letters as diverse as Romans (which heads the collection and arguably functions as a lens through which to read the other witnesses) and Colossians (which shares the central theme of the mystery disclosed, concerning Jew and Greek as fellow heirs, and which contains no formula citations) still stand before a single scriptural horizon that continues to function creatively for the church. In time those who read Romans and those who read Colossians will also read them both in the light of Scripture, now

---

6. Essential reading is the older essay by C. F. Burney, "Christ as the APXH of Creation (Prov. viii 22, Col. i 15-18, Rev. iii 14)," *JTS* 27 (1925–26): 160–77.

become a First Testamental witness. The significance of Proverbs 8 will not be due to the prevalence of its citation in the NT, but will have to do with the way it considers agency in respect of the one Lord God of Israel.[7] So too Genesis 1:1–3. It will have been clear to the earliest readers that Paul was hearing in the one literal sense of the Scriptures a depth that was truly there, but which required the according work of Christ for proper apprehension. That Colossians speaks of this in one way in 1:15–20 and that Romans and other letters use the Scriptures for other ends and in other ways actually commends the one selfsame scriptural horizon and asks the church to read the "oracles entrusted to the Jews" in fresh ways. In time, Paul's own letters will find association with these Scriptures (2 Pet. 3:15–16), and the church will commend them both—not in terms of imitating Paul's own exegesis so much as asking a rule of faith to penetrate through the one literal sense to a triune account of God in Christ, enabled by the Holy Spirit—the same Spirit at work in Israel and now enlivening the church's reception of prophet and apostle, OT and NT.

The Pauline Letter collection is shaped in such a way that development in Paul's thought or explicit and restrictive occasionality are not the primary registers. The letters are not organized in this way and with this priority formally reinforced. Some letters retain a high degree of occasionality and some arguably very little. Indeed, once one speaks of exchanging letters, or once one considers the possibility that Paul knows a shadow is falling on his own apostleship and that in time the letters will "surrogate" him (as they are doing in Colossians, and for different reasons, in Romans), it may be possible to speak of a letter collection as itself within the intentionality of Paul. The fact that these letters use the OT differently is not an invitation to read them individually in order to gain a closer look at their deployment of the Scriptures, but an invitation, in light of the letter collection as a whole, *to consider the horizon Paul assumes the OT will continue to extend, beyond his lifetime and his own conscious intentions as an author.* The Pauline Letter collection is its own factor in the interpre-

7. See the numerous essays by Francis Young that indicate the centrality of Prov. 8 in the church's early exegesis, a sample of which can be found in *Biblical Exegesis and the Formation of Christian Culture* (Cambridge: Cambridge University Press, 1997).

tation of individual letters as well as in conjunction with Acts with which it circulated, the Gospels, General Epistles, and Revelation.

Here the example of the Minor Prophets comes to mind, for there as well it is necessary to consider the hermeneutical effect of the final form and how the individual witnesses are maintained (some with a high degree of occasionality and some with very little), on the one hand, but also exist within a larger total framework of interpretation, on the other. The reference to the "Torah of Moses" and the prophet Elijah at the end of the collection gives indication of the horizon the older canonical witness is intended to extend, as one reads the prophetic witness of the Twelve. The notes that frame Zechariah 1–8 reckon with the influence of the "former prophets" and their ongoing word. In something of the same way we can consider the role of the "former Scriptures" in relationship to Paul's letters, though here with the added reality that they are quoted formally and alluded to in a way only possible because of their authoritative place in Paul's world and thought.

Luther captured something of the sense of this in one of his more memorable quotes, where he likened the church to surprised guests at the reading of a will, discovering that we had been given a share of an inheritance we did not know was there in earnest, ready to be passed on to us:

> For the New Testament is nothing more than a revelation of the Old. Just as one receives a sealed letter which is not to be opened until after the writer's death. So the Old Testament is the will and testament of Christ, which he has opened after his death and read and everywhere proclaimed through the Gospel.[8]

A proper understanding of the character of Christian Scripture will read the NT's use of the Old with a sense of proportion and with attention to the role the OT will continue to play in interpreting the work of Christ and sounding its own prophetic notes as an abiding witness,

---

8. Luther's Sermon on John 1.1–14, "Third Christmas Day (Or the Principal Christmas Service)," in *Sermons of Martin Luther*, ed. and trans. J. N. Lenker et al. (Grand Rapids: Baker, 1983). Originally published in *The Precious and Sacred Writings of Martin Luther*, vols. 7–14 (Minneapolis: Lutherans in All Lands, 1904–9).

a "word without end."[9] The rule of faith attends to the ontological potential of the OT for clarifying the relationship between the Father and the Son, as already expressed within an account of the work of YHWH in the literal sense of Scripture, by inspiration of the Holy Spirit ("who spake by the prophets"). In this way the character of the two-testament Christian Bible is kept in proper alignment, as the rule allows the image of a King to appear (as in Irenaeus's metaphor), and not the fox of disfiguration, economic eclipse, or obliging but bygone resourcefulness. To read the OT canonically is to do likewise with the NT. The challenge is ever before the church to open its Scriptures and hear the living voice of God, true to its character as one Bible in two Testaments. It is hoped that this book has made a contribution to an understanding of the character of Christian Scripture as a two-testament witness.

9. Seitz, *Word without End: The Old Testament as Abiding Theological Witness* (Grand Rapids: Eerdmans, 1998).

Subject Index

211

Author Index

SCRIPTURE INDEX